HITLER
Came for
NIEMOELLER

D1528527

A rare picture showing Pastor Niemoeller leaving his church at Dahlem from his last confirmation service, prior to his arrest and imprisonment

HITLER
Came for
NIEMOELLER
The Nazi War
Against Religion

By Leo Stein

Foreword by Norman Vincent Peale

PELICAN PUBLISHING COMPANY

Gretna 2003

Copyright © 1942
By Fleming H. Revell Company

Copyright © 2003
By Pelican Publishing Company, Inc.
All rights reserved

First edition, 1942
First Pelican edition, 2003

*The word "Pelican" and the depiction of a pelican are trademarks
of Pelican Publishing Company, Inc., and are registered
in the U.S. Patent and Trademark Office.*

Library of Congress Cataloging-in-Publication Data

Stein, Leo.
    Hitler came for Niemoeller : the Nazi War against religion /
by Leo Stein ; foreword by Norman Vincent Peale.— 1st
Pelican ed.
        p. cm.
    Originally published: New York : F. H. Revell, 1942.
    Includes bibliographical references.
    ISBN 1-58980-063-X (pbk.)
    1. Niemoeller, Martin, 1892- 2. Lutheran Church—Germany—
Clergy—Biography. I. Title.

BX8080.N48S74 2003
284.1'092—dc21
[B]

                         2002193016

Printed in the United States of America
Published by Pelican Publishing Company, Inc.
1000 Burmaster Street, Gretna, Louisiana 70053

CONTENTS

5

FOREWORD

TO SAY that this is a *good* book is to say nothing. To advise one to read it for entertainment is a sacrilege. To urge its reading for information, or even for inspiration, is to reveal a lack of insight. This book is a revelation of hell on earth, of the existence of a malignant wickedness and evil in this world. If any man can read it and not be stirred to his depths, it is because he has no depths.

The author passed through the most degrading and awful experiences imaginable, but emerged unscathed to write his story with the coolness of a reporter staring facts—facts so terrible that they need no interpretation or embellishment. Their mere statement is their own ghastly condemnation.

I read the book at one sitting. I could not put it down, save occasionally to recover myself. Stories are related of such sublime faith and Christlikeness of spirit that one is awed, as one's eyes fill with tears. We Christians who occasionally suffer a little difficulty will be ashamed, on reading this book, of complaining of our "light afflictions." This man Niemoeller is drawn by Stein as a man touched by the splendor of God. One is convinced that Niemoeller will rank among the great martyrs of the faith. He will give new life to religion, for he actually has demonstrated what we preach, that one can through prayer and faith overcome anything in this world. When the war is over and history records this period of time, it is not impossible that the greatest name, a name to inspire men for years to come, will be that of the magnificent Christian, Martin Niemoeller.

Occasionally we hear people say that the Church should have nothing to do with this war. We all hate war. As Christians, how could we do otherwise? After reading this book, however, if we have not previously realized it, we will be convinced that there is an evil more virulent even than war, and against that evil we must set our face. We must do more than admire Niemoeller and pay tribute to his greatness. The evil thing against which he fights must be destroyed. This demon must be exorcised from human society. We frequently talk about loving our Christian brothers in all lands, and we do love them; but how can we love them and not do all in our power to set them free?

Personally, I would give almost anything if I could have the privilege some happy day of walking into that German concentration camp, straight up to Niemoeller, and saying, "My brother in Christ, the Nazi evil is no more. With God's help, we destroyed it. Come back, Martin Niemoeller, to your old pulpit, and preach with no let or hindrance."

To behold that saint, white of hair, emaciated of body, as a result of his suffering, as he would climb the pulpit stair in a great free Germany, and to think that I in even a small way had helped to make it possible, would give me the deepest joy I can imagine. Never forget, also, that there are many others like Niemoeller, Catholic, Protestant and Jew, and thousands of fine German people who undramatically feel in their hearts as he does.

If in giving my support to war, which is the means for making this great freedom possible, I am guilty of sin, then I believe that the same understanding Heavenly Father (who can unravel all dilemmas), who has often forgiven me of other sins, will absolve me of this one, also. As a Christian I must fight against wickedness. I can do so without hate. On the contrary, I can do so with a great sense of love, because I am struggling for something that is of the best in men, the death of which would mean tragedy indescribable. I believe that God sees me in this dilemma and understands.

It must also be stated that only a great soul could have written this book. Dr. Stein also suffered, but he says little of his own sufferings. He writes with no hate. He writes simply, calmly; and perhaps for that reason as well as because of the subject matter the book has dramatic power. Dr. Stein suffered, but I believe he would say it was worth it to have lived with one of the world's immortal figures in a supreme event of history.

This book should go throughout the world, like the bugle call which it is, summoning men to stand for their faith—the faith which sets men free.

NORMAN VINCENT PEALE

New York

PUBLISHER'S NOTE

Only once before now have I thought it important to write a note for a publication of Pelican's. The first was "An Open Letter to a Soviet Citizen," published in *Best Editorial Cartoons of the Year: 1980 Edition*. This was in response to the banning of previous issues of that book at the Moscow Book Fair of 1979, after we were invited to exhibit by Brezhnev. The letter was a description of the utter failure of their system and its trajectory toward ultimate doom. I didn't anticipate Ronald Reagan becoming president, nor that the doom would come in nine short years.

IN 1950 Whittaker Chambers published *Witness*, probably the most important book of the twentieth century. A letter to his children served as its introduction. In this letter, he laid out the two visions of man: the religious vision of freedom under the law of God and the socialist vision of man without God. He describes the two great belief systems of mankind. One has a vision of God as the creative intelligence of the world, with man's greatest achievement being to know and follow the mind of God. The other vision is of man's mind, with its rational intelligence, replacing God, even becoming God.

When Chambers wrote in 1950, he thought he was joining the losing side. The growth of Communism (the most aggressive form of Socialism after World War II) was spreading inexorably over the face of the globe.

11

Socialism as an idea sprang up in the French Revolution. Joshua Muravchik says, in *Heaven on Earth: The Rise and Fall of Socialism*, that Socialism was man's most ambitious attempt to supplant religion with a doctrine claiming to be rational and scientific.

A predominant characteristic of Socialism, in its political aspect, has always been antireligiosity. The twentieth century saw it evolve into its most virulent forms. It took the form of National Socialism under Hitler in Germany. Under Mussolini in Italy, its form was Fascism. The earliest of the twentieth-century forms in Russia was Communism, first under Lenin and then perfected by Stalin. Lenin found it spread better by the sword. In this form, it metastasized to Eastern Europe, China, Cuba, North Korea, North Vietnam, and other lesser states. With the exception of Italy, all were mercilessly antireligious, and persecution of religious citizens was routine policy.

In the twentieth century, there were many admirers and supporters of these Socialist tyrannies. Their support was particularly strong among so-called intellectuals—those who made a living by speaking, thinking, and writing. Paul Johnson contemptuously called them the "chattering classes." With no responsibility to anyone but themselves, they could praise the most outrageous behavior of those they admired. George Orwell wrote that they were slavishly devoted to Stalin, even after his excesses were known. Lillian Hellman's defense (until her death in 1984) of Stalin's terror and the show trials of the 1930s is a good example. Walter Duranty's eyewitness account of Stalin's starvation of the Ukrainians (whom he described as "the happy peasants on the plantation"[my characterization]) in the 1920s won him a Pulitzer Prize when his work was published in the *New York Times* in 1932. It was not until the publication of Robert Conquest's book *The Great Terror: A Reassessment* that the truth was known. The Pulitzer has not been renounced by any of the parties concerned.

It was not until Ronald Reagan freed Granada in 1982 that any communist advance, once established in a country, had ever been rolled back. Within the decade, Reagan's diplomacy had destroyed the old Soviet Union without firing a shot, and Russia took its first tentative steps as a free country.

Much is generally known about Hitler's treatment of the Jews. Less is known about his treatment of Christians and other religious groups. He was building a pagan society and only old pagan gods would suffice. SS officers had to renounce Christianity. To be a high civilian leader was to embrace these gods. There was no place in Hitler's new order for any other religion. With the approval of the university leaders and thinkers, the killing of deformed babies began the Holocaust. This was followed by the killing of the hopelessly insane. As the killings became accepted, the killings of gypsies, the enemies of the state, and Jews and Christians followed. The state seized control of the schools and then of the youth organizations. The youth organizations were turned into paramilitary organizations and told that their loyalty was to the state and not their parents. The churches were forbidden to operate such organizations. Finally, religious expression could be made only within the church walls. The story of Niemoeller is the struggle of Hitler to coopt the church. Because of a heroic performance by Niemoeller, it failed. The Germans in 1933 were basically a religious people. The journey to avoid the stamping out of this group's religious influence is the theme of this book. Niemoeller refused to sell his soul to Hitler.

Subsequent to the account of Niemoeller's fight against Hitler's assault on religion, we have added two chapters from Hermann Rauschning's book *The Voice of Destruction.*

(Rauschning was the president of the Danzig senate and an intimate of Hitler even before he came to power. He was a frequent guest at the Eagle's Nest.) From it readers will hear Hitler's own words on the subject of religion. Finally, we have added, as an appendix, the essay by William J. Donovan, written in 1945, outlining specifics of this war against religion.

This event in the life of Niemoeller is instructive to us today. It describes the war against religion by the National Socialist Party of Germany (Nazis). The left's war continues today. Similarities of tactics may be recognizable. It is eerily like what was happening in the U.S. with the rise of Margaret Sanger and her eugenics movement. There was birth control and sterilization to decrease the growth of the lesser breeds. Mayhem on a large scale did not begin until the Supreme Court ruling of 1973, which opened the floodgates to abortion. It is again mainly the intellectuals and Sanger's successors who have pushed this agenda. Supporters of this agenda have pushed the attack on the family, on the Boy Scouts, and on the flag of the country. Some elements have embraced euthanasia.

The war between the two visions of man continues in the twenty-first century. The cockpit of the battle is the United States of America. Did Chambers join the winning or losing side? It is still not perfectly clear. We shall see.

INTRODUCTION

IT IS a far cry from the mad inferno of a Nazi prison camp in Eastern Germany to the comfortable office in America where I have just completed dictating my first work in English.

Previous stories about Pastor Niemoeller and our experiences together in prison and concentration camp that have been appearing in American magazines were translated from my German text and errors and discrepancies may have crept in, because of my unfamiliarity with American customs and the English language at the time of their preparation for publication.

It is with a real sense of triumph that I am able to send forth this complete story, written by me in English, of the daily hardship, torture and peril inflicted on the devoted pastor and former U-boat commander by the Nazi regime for his steady refusal to betray the Cause for which he stands. Whether it will result in further hardships for him or not, I know that it is his wish that the world at large, and especially the people of America, should be enlightened as to the part he has played against the Nazi attempt to destroy Christianity throughout the world.

I make no apology for, or claim of verbal inerrancy in, the use of the direct quotations. Since the conversations were all held in the German tongue and oft-repeated, I have sought to reproduce the substance of the talks in the form most easily remembered and most easily understood by my readers.

My first meeting with Martin Niemoeller was in connection with my professional duties. My title covers Doctor of Jurisprudence and Church Laws, and my visit to his church at Dahlem was to secure necessary information. At the time of my visit I was impressed not only by his devotion to his Cause, but by the efficient way in which his church was being maintained.

Pastor Niemoeller, therefore, was not an utter stranger to me when we were first thrown together at Moabit Prison, and the many conversations we had, often under difficult circumstances, impressed me strongly with the fact that the Nazi Government could never succeed in changing his convictions, and that he desired, above all else, that the Christian world should always remember him as a defender of the Faith.

In conclusion, I wish to add that original German documents establishing my identity have been submitted to my publishers.

LEO STEIN

New York, N.Y.

I

MY MEETING WITH NIEMOELLER

"I HEARD some one scream, 'You murderer! You murderer! I don't want to die.'

"It was my first night in Ploetzensee prison. This blood-curdling screaming had been going on for hours, it seemed to me. When the dawn came, I heard the terrible, monotonous tolling of a bell. Noise coming from the prison yard caused me to look out of my cell window. A number of men were crossing the yard to the opposite wall. A prisoner in brown uniform, with his hands tied behind him, was being dragged along bodily by two giant guards. He struggled feebly, and his body was crumpled like a half-empty sack. Behind them walked a man whom I knew to be the executioner. He was short, but strongly built. He was dressed in formal clothes—frock coat and top hat. At his side walked an assistant carrying an ax that glistened in the weak light of dawn. And then came a priest, and the judge and the prosecutor, both in formal black. I thought of them as being the bodyguards of death.

"At the opposite wall the procession halted, and I could see a block being released from the wall. It came down slowly, until it rested on the ground. Now the condemned man, resisting violently, was thrown to his knees by the guards. Then his head was thrust on the block. A moment later I saw the ax flashing down, and I heard the sound of a blow. A stream of blood gushed out, and the severed head fell into the sand. The execution was finished."

Pastor Niemoeller's face was gray, like dank moss one sees in the woods. He paused, as if gathering strength to go on. We were in the yard of Moabit prison, taking our exercise, with the watchful eyes of the guard upon us. The dead sound of shuffling feet walking round and round in a small circle mocked the lone bird singing in a linden tree in the middle of the yard. Presently it took wing and soared out of sight. Pastor Niemoeller was whispering again. He, too, had heard the bird, and had stopped to catch the song. His voice came audibly, for in prison whispering becomes an art, and one's ears become attuned to catch even the faintest sigh.

"I cannot describe my feelings when I saw all this," he said, "especially as I knew that I was charged with high treason, for which death is the punishment. It became clear to me that I had been brought to this particular cell [in Ploetzensee prison] with deliberate intent. They wanted me to see the execution—to break my will. I must confess that for a moment I nearly gave way. I—I dreaded the ax—dying like that. But it was only for a moment. Strength is given to us at such times. I prayed, prayed for a long time, and the strength came to me. After a week I was transferred here."

Then he fell silent, and I could hear again the dull sound of shuffling feet. I think I shall always hear that sound. It comes to me above the shrill noises of the street, above the roar of the subway. And the pasty-faced, broken men, marching round and round, I shall see always in my dreams as long as I am alive to dream.

The Nazi racial doctrine had stopped at the prison door, at the gate to the concentration camp—a bit of irony that had not then made the tiniest cut on Hitler's thick veneer. Martin Niemoeller, whose ancestry is of the purest origin according to the Nazi creed, and I, a member of an outcast people, had been brought together in the same prison by that same decree. I little realized at our first meeting that it was to be the beginning of a close intimacy that would extend over a period of nearly two years and enable me to give to the world this inside story of the persecution and suffering of this beloved pastor. Outside, the Jew was being walled in from the rest of the world, or being systematically exterminated. Here there was no distinction between Aryan and Jewish victims of Nazi hate and fear. But one could not reflect then. Life was reduced to its starkest realities. Blood was on every street, on the thresholds of thousands of homes in every city in Germany, and there was no one to dam the flow. Law had been thrown to the dungheap. Rule was by personal fiat. Whether the headsman's ax was to be sharpened for me I could not tell. Pain gnawed at my stomach, and there were moments when I could hear the thumping of my heart.

But let us go back to the beginning.

It was on a bright morning in midsummer that Pastor Niemoeller and I were first brought together. A few rays penetrating the gloom of my cell brought me news that the sun was shining. On the Wilhelmstrasse, I knew, the grass would be green, and the birds would be singing in the lindens. They still would be free, happily unaware of the terror and anguish beneath them. A guard opened my cell and informed me that I would not go into the prison yard for recreation. I knew at once what this meant. I was to go before an inquisitorial court, before a judge who was also a prosecutor. Shortly after 9 o'clock the guard came to take me down to the great hall of the prison, from where an assistant guard took me to the anteroom of the court of the political department. A number of prisoners were already in the antechamber. Among them was a former Nazi, who, according to his loudly-voiced story, had been the chief of the Gestapo in Berlin. He had been arrested because of his connection with Captain Ernst Roehm, victim of the bloody purge of 1934, and was still awaiting trial. He had lost none of his arrogance. Perhaps he was trying to bolster himself for the coming ordeal. Now he was telling the other prisoners of his importance, of what he had done to further the Nazi power.

"You," he said to the white-faced group near him, "are mere criminals, vermin to be trodden under foot. But I am a personage. For me there will be only a life term or death, for I am dangerous. I know too much. But that does not matter. I am still a fervent Nazi. The worst thing that can happen to me is happening now, when I am compelled to be sitting among Jews, all staring at me. I will complain of this to the judge, you swine."

Perhaps he was mad, for the grave knows no difference between Aryan and Jew, and in the end their dust is mingled together. And I, a Jew, could have reminded him of the teachings of another Jew.

A few feet away sat a man whom I had not noticed before. He must be a new prisoner, I thought, and I was ready to avert my eyes. But suddenly it came to me that I had seen him somewhere before. I looked at him more closely, trying at the same time not to attract his attention. His body slouched forward, he was resting his arms on a windowsill, holding his head in his hands. He looked haggard. His eyes half closed, he seemed to be suffering from exhaustion. I strained my memory in vain. I could not recognize him.

The room and prisoners faded away like an illusion while I continued to gaze at the haunting face. It had a spiritual quality that touched off a spark in my own soul. From the outer blackness came again the voice of the Nazi: "Jews . . . parasites . . . bloodsuckers . . . Now, Goebbels said to me . . ." There was a nervous shuffling of feet. A prisoner near me sighed heavily. But my eyes were held by the man at the window. He had half turned at the noise. I saw the aspect painters have given the Christian martyrs.

Then, suddenly, I knew. The man was Martin Niemoeller. Now I remembered where I had seen him—in the pulpit of a church in Dahlem. He was the leading force of the German Evangelical Church. He had dared challenge Hitler.

The tragic lines around his sensitive mouth and the dark depth of his eyes touched me, drew me into some sort of fellowship with him, into a vague understanding that I could not quite fathom then. The lines in his face had not been engraved by physical suffering alone. They were more the telltale marks of spiritual anguish. I remembered his fighting sermons, that he had remained steadfast to his faith in spite of the growing menace of Nazi might and the appeals of former friends who would have saved his body at the expense of his soul. Many of them had sought shelter in the refuge provided by Alfred Rosenberg, doctrinaire of the new church, the church which would make full obeisance to the new lord. I recalled something of all this, but as I had been arrested a year before, I had not been able to keep up with the development of the battle between the revived paganism and the old faith. The only newspapers I had been allowed to read after my arrest were the *Voelkischer Beobachter* and the *Angriff*, neither of which, of course, mentioned the struggle between Pastor Niemoeller and Hitler. Before my arrest I had kept pace with the news. Now we could read only the Nazi propaganda. My interest had been partly because of my profession. I was a lecturer on law, and as in Germany churches are public institutions and subject to government regulations, my lectures included also church law.

It was because of my interest in church law and in the tremendous spiritual struggle between the Rosenberg fabrication and the German Evangelical Church that I had gone, in company with a friend, to hear Pastor Niemoeller preach. Dahlem is a fashionable suburb of Berlin, and Niemoeller's congregation consisted largely of retired army and navy officers and government officials, who belonged to the conservative school. Listening to him, I had been struck with Niemoeller's religious consistency, the stem purity of his faith, and his spiritual approach to the tragic problems then confronting Church arid State. I had come to look upon him as not only a great Protestant pastor, but as a living symbol of Christianity and humanity. Jews in general looked upon him as a representative of all that was best in German culture and tradition. Though I was already sunk in misery and despair, seeing him in prison shocked me and brought me a new awareness of my own peril. If the Nazis could deliberately lay a famous U-boat commander on their altar of blood and soil, what would they not do to those who have always been the first victims of savagery and lust?

The prison hall was silent now. All the other prisoners had been taken before the inquiring judge, and Niemoeller and I were alone. I was very anxious to talk with him, but I felt that the situation was too embarrassing for me to make the first move.

Presently, however, Niemoeller came over to me and laid a gentle hand on my shoulder. "You are a Jew," he said. "Don't mind what that Nazi said. He doesn't know what he's talking about—to utter such nonsense."

He was interrupted by a sharp command. The guard had come to take him before the judge. His unexpected kindness had left me speechless, and I sat groping in mental darkness, wondering what the end would be. I could only wait, with four blank walls closing down on me.

Then came my summons, and the guard escorted me into the judge's chamber.

By now I was mentally alert again, and as I entered the

chamber I immediately fastened my eyes on the judge, seated at a desk before me, trying to catch in his face something of what had transpired between him and Pastor Niemoeller and of what was in store for me. It was Judge Walter, whom I had encountered in an earlier inquisition. As always, he was elegantly dressed and sartorially correct to the last detail. In his lapel was an unusually large swastika, such as generally worn by Nazi officials. Perhaps it is a measure of their self-importance.

I advanced to within a few paces of the desk, bowed, and said, "Good day, *Herr Amtsgerichtsrat* (Mr. Counselor of the District Court)." How many times before I had given him that friendly greeting!

"Heil Hitler," he replied importantly, at the same time making the Nazi salute. "You are addressing Judge Walter," which I already knew. Then, icily suave, "*Herr Doktor*, be seated."

I proceeded to a chair, and sat down, and the guard who had escorted me in left the room. On one side of the desk sat a male secretary, pencil poised to take stenographic notes of the hearing.

Judge Walter ruffled through some papers on his desk, and then cleared his throat. "*Herr Doktor* " he began pompously, "it is my duty to inform you that the attorney for the Reich at the People's Court has investigated the charge of high treason brought against you, and has decided to drop it for lack of evidence. Of the many witnesses who were questioned, only one made such statements as would tend to convict you. But there are impelling reasons to doubt his veracity. I congratulate you. You are lucky. You see, there is still justice in the Third Reich, even for the Jews!"

My heart leaped. I was to be freed. I would see again what was beyond those windows—return to the arms of my wife.

"But," the icy voice went on, "there remains a charge

against you of failing to live up to the commands of our Fuehrer and other members of the government. About this I will question you some other day. You will now read and sign the stenographic report."

Then I was led away, stunned and hopeless.

As I was to learn later, the man who had testified falsely against me, whose testimony would have sent me to the executioner's block if there had been sufficient perjury to support it, was a man whom the Gestapo had sent as a spy to my lectures. He had been confronted with some of my students, evidently still friendly to me, who had directly contradicted his statements. The investigation which followed showed him to have been a thief and embezzler, so that no word of his could have carried weight. That was why the attorney for the Reich had dropped the more serious charge against me. It was not because the Third Reich was interested in justice towards the Jews, as Judge Walter had boasted.

The new charge against me concerned implied criticisms of the Nazi regime in my lectures on law, which had been based on the general law of the land before Hitler came to power. If convicted of this new "crime" I could be sentenced to one to five years in prison.

I was returned to my cell. In a cell near by, as I was soon to learn, was the man who was to be my stay and comfort through many harrowing experiences, Pastor Niemoeller.

II

ARRESTED BY THE GESTAPO

A T THE time I met Pastor Niemoeller I had been in prison a year. The Hitlerian venom had begun penetrating to all the roots of Germany's social structure, and the Gestapo, that foul-begotten offspring of servility and corruption, was busily and happily engaged in its campaign of spying and terrorization. It had improved even on the Ogpu. Men had been brought to fear their neighbors and to suspect even their closest friends. There are innumerable examples of betrayals even within the family.

But because of my profession and my connections—for I had many friends among "Aryan" Germans and a few relatives by marriage—I had let myself believe that I would go unscathed and that in time the Terror would subside and Germany come out of her hideous nightmare. So far as I knew, no stealthy agent was shadowing me and trying to trap me in order to cover himself with tinsel glory. I was mistaken!

In addition to being a law lecturer, I had been an associate justice of the Landgericht, a state court for the trial of cases involving minor infractions of the law. This experience helped me in my lectures. I gave courses for students of the University of Berlin and other universities to prepare them for their doctor's degree and the bar examination. The German universities give only abstract lectures on law, and private tutoring is peculiar to the German system. I had been very successful, and numbered hundreds of students in my classes, some of them officers of the SS and SA. They ranged from sons of working men to sons of the nobility. With many of them I was on very friendly terms, and I had often entertained them in my home at lunch or dinner. One day, while we were discussing the situation in Germany, one of these young men said to me that he wished that the French or British would invade Germany and police the country until the last vestige of Nazism was destroyed. I was rather surprised at the outburst, and replied that even if he were opposed to Hitler and all that Hitler stood for, he should never wish to see a foreign army on German soil.

Suddenly, one summer morning, while I was in the midst of a lecture, six agents of the Gestapo stormed into my classroom, brushed me aside, and began taking the addresses of all the students. When they had finished, they ordered the students to leave the room. Considerably perturbed, I remonstrated and asked the agents the reason for their abrupt action. With the impetuous air of newly bestowed authority, they refused to give me any information, save to tell me that I would soon learn the nature of their business and what I might expect to follow. Then they conducted a systematic search of the room, which resulted in the confiscation of my books, among them what they thought was a telltale volume. It was a book dealing with the Russian revolution. One of them shook it in my face and gave me a look of triumph. No doubt I was a Communist.

Resistance was useless. With one man on each side of me and a third behind me to give me a shove in case I proved laggard, I was bundled out of the room, placed in a car, and driven to the Gestapo headquarters. There I learned that the Gestapo had information that I had been advising my students not to obey Nazi laws and regulations. In short, I had committed treason. When I demanded proof, the Gestapo official yelled shrilly, "What do you think? Don't you realize where you are? You are talking now to the Gestapo."

But I was naive enough to tell him that even the Gestapo had to present proof in support of an accusation. This so infuriated him that he yelled, "I never saw such an impertinent Jew. You seem still not to know where you are." With the words he drew a pistol and aimed it at me. But, to his astonishment—and my own now—I remained cool. Being a lawyer, I knew he wouldn't shoot me there. Besides, it had been agreed among some of my influential friends that they would intervene for me if ever I fell into the clutches of the Gestapo.

Caught off his guard by my attitude and evidently not knowing how to deal with such semblance of defiance, the official said, "Well, I'll give you the proof." He dispatched an underling from the room with a whispered order. In a few minutes the latter returned, bringing with him a young man in whom I recognized a student who had enrolled in my course a few weeks before. He was a Gestapo agent, and it developed that I had been under surveillance for several months and that the Gestapo had posted men before the door of the building to observe who attended my lectures. My interlocutor pretended to great fury that Aryans and members of the SA and SS had attended my classes, and remarked loudly, "I cannot understand how Germans could come to you. You must have blackmailed them. No true German would willingly listen to a Jew. In any event, you are dangerous to the German people; you have been giving your students a wrong conception of the law."

I was perturbed, not so much by the man's threats and menacing gestures as by his childishness. Couple infantilism with authority, and you have a most dangerous combination.

Fortunately for me, the man who had spied on me was an incompetent who somehow had attached himself to the service of the Gestapo. In my various lectures on the basic laws of the land I had, of course, criticized the Nazi inventions and distortions by implication, but the ambitious spy was unable to give a coherent account of what he alleged I had said, and I was able to make him contradict himself. This was made the easier because the Gestapo official was almost as ignorant of the law as his stooge. The Nazi official became inarticulate with rage and sputtered venomously. He had been thwarted, temporarily at least, of his intended victim. The knife had been whetted for the slaughter, but the victim was still at bay. When he had regained his composure, the official attempted an air of meticulous sternness, and told me sharply that I would have to stay at the Gestapo headquarters nevertheless and submit to further questioning the next morning.

With unceremonious haste, I was conducted down into the cellar of the building, where the prison cells are located. But every cell was full. After much marching back and forth, shouting of orders, and other juvenile show of authority, it was decided that I should be taken to the Columbia house at Tempelhof, where the late Kaiser Wilhelm II used to give his pompous displays of military might. One of the buildings there was a military prison, which was now used by the Gestapo to accommodate prisoners waiting to be questioned. I was taken inside a long corridor, where the guards ordered me to stand at attention, with my face pressed to the wall. In this rigid attitude I remained until a cell had been found for me. A few minutes later a heavy iron door clanged behind me, a key turned in the lock, and I was alone—a prisoner of the Gestapo. Meanwhile, no word had gone to my wife. What had happened to me was left to her imagination.

Now I was nervous. Stories and rumors of strange disappearances flooded my memory—stories of midnight rappings on doors and little packages being handed in to those who answered. Would an agent of the Gestapo rap some night on my door and hand in to my wife all that was left of me—a little package of dust? I paced back and forth in my cell, terror striking at my vitals. Presently I heard a mocking laugh. The guard who had searched me before locking me up was peering through the iron grill. "The Jew is still walking back and forth," he jeered. It was like a sadistic boy jeering at an animal he had wounded.

The cell was furnished with a small table and chair, and an iron cot, on which was a straw mattress. I had not been allowed to bring any clothing with me, and finally, in desperation, I lay down on the cot as I was. Sleep was impossible; I could only stare into the darkness, an impenetrable pall. Sounds came to me from the other cells—men groaning and moaning in their sleep, long sighs like those that sweep through hospital wards as wounded men struggle against pain. Amongst the groans I soon caught my own.

Early the next morning a guard came to escort me to Gestapo headquarters. There I was confronted with a few of my students, who had been summoned by telephone. All had been Nazis before Hitler had assumed the chancellorship. One was a *standarten Fuehrer* and another was a member of the Supreme Council of the Nazi party *(Oberste Fuehrung der National Sozialistischen Partei)*. This fact was conveyed to me when the same official who had examined me the day before began asking them what I had said against the government during my lectures. I became terribly uneasy, for I knew I had said some things which the Gestapo could interpret as treasonable and it would be easy to misquote me or to misinterpret anything I had said and make it appear that I had committed high treason. (The law covering high treason had been so expanded as to make it virtually optional what the Nazis should constitute a violation. For instance, persons could be charged with treasonable conduct if they were heard to criticize the Hitler regime, or if they found an illegal newspaper and read it before turning it over to the next policeman or SS guard). To my surprise and relief, all the witnesses brought against me testified that they had not heard me say anything that could be construed as a violation of the law. The examiner flushed angrily, and appeared nonplused. Probably because of the position of the witnesses' families, he did not question their integrity, and after a few moments' hesitation ordered that I be returned to my cell in Tempelhof. Me he gave a baleful glare. It was enough. Though not a single word of incriminating evidence had been uttered against me during either of the examinations, I was as completely in the toils as if I had been caught in the act of shouting from the roof tops that Hitler had been convicted out of his own mouth of being a liar, a murderer and an assassin of whole peoples.

I was hustled back into my cell, where I remained a few days more to ponder on my "crime." Then, because of the intervention of friends, as I learned later, I was ordered transferred to Moabit prison, in custody of the Department of Justice, with the same charge still hanging over me. My friends hoped that I would be tried before a regular judge by whom I would be released because of lack of evidence. I was taken in a Gestapo car to the headquarters of the regular police at the Alexanderplatz, which is the routine method, for the Gestapo is under the Ministry of the Interior and uses the regular police as the intermediary between itself and the Department of Justice.

At Alexanderplatz I was received by an affable old police officer of the pre-Nazi regime. He looked at me curiously, and asked why I had been brought there. When I had told him my story, he pondered a moment, and said, "Yes, I know, everybody here is a political prisoner. It is a long time since I have seen a common criminal." I felt a sense of comfort in the presence of this grizzled veteran. He was the sort of German I knew, punctilious, and heedful of the law he represented. He asked me whether I would like to have a cell to myself, and when I expressed a desire to be alone, he assented. Another lonely, nightlong vigil over my thoughts, tracking down the memories of my happy yesterdays, and I was taken before a police judge for what I thought was to be my final hearing.

With the coming of the dawn my spirits had risen. There was every reason to believe that a police judge would be bound by the rules of evidence and that the charge against me would be dismissed. But he merely took my name, and before I could collect myself I had been returned to my cell. That evening I was taken to Moabit, where I was informed that I would first have to be confined in the Ploetzensee prison until the attorney general had formally ordered my transfer to Moabit. Hope waned in the shadow that enveloped me, and the full realization of my plight struck into my consciousness.

III

MY ARRIVAL AT MOABIT PRISON

IT SHOULD be understood that at the time I was taken by the Gestapo there had been no mass arrests of Jews. The Nazis were proceeding against them individually, and there was then no baiting of Jews to whet the Nazi appetite for greater game. But my historical sense warned me now that we were probably entering upon a program such as other governments in other times had instituted to conceal a larger purpose. The strained look I had met occasionally in the eyes of some of my Aryan friends had now a definite meaning. They were being whipped into shape to overcome their moral scruples against the great blood bath in which Hitler was to purge the German conscience. Slowly the faucets were being turned on, not only in Germany, but all over Europe, and I was soon to know that the Star of David was to become the symbol of shame, the mark of the great adultress who had robbed Germany of her manhood. All this in spite of the former German attitude, which had welcomed the Jews as citizens of a common country, to which the Jews, in turn, had given their fealty and devotion. My concern was the deeper because, as I looked back, the events which had occurred since the dark day when Hitler's forelock appeared over the political horizon began to unroll themselves in a pattern whose ultimate purpose could not be mistaken. In all this the arrest of the former U-boat commander. Pastor Martin Niemoeller, had a profound significance.

After a few days that seemed an eternity of doubt and misgiving, I was informed that the attorney general of the District of Berlin had ordered that I be transferred to the Moabit prison. On the morning following this announcement a guard unlocked my cell and led me outside. The bright light made my eyes blink, but no time was given me to look around. I was hustled into a police car, much like the police cars one sees in New York. It was already so crowded that I had to be squeezed in. Both seats, which ran lengthwise of the car, were filled, so that there was hardly room for me to sit down, and presently the aisle between was filled with prisoners standing. The morning was very hot, and as it was a closed car we nearly suffocated. Most of the prisoners were very pale and looked anemic. In their faces I could read what was in store for me. Some of the prisoners, I learned from whispered conversation, were being taken to the People's Court, which was in the heart of Berlin, on one of the fashionable streets leading to the Tiergarten. These prisoners were charged with violating the new laws governing the transfer of money. Among them were two Roman Catholic priests, one of whom appeared old enough to be the other's father. Both had the appearance of highly cultivated men, and both manifested that ascetic calm which so often distinguishes the priests of the Catholic faith. They were standing, and presently the older man exhibited signs of suffering, probably from the effort to keep his equilibrium as well as from the suffocating condition of the car. I would have offered him my seat, but dared not make a move. However, the younger man placed an assisting hand under the other's elbow, and it was touching to observe the answering smile of gratitude and affection. Strange it was to see this devotion flowering in that air stinking with inhuman brutality.

The prisoners continued conversing in whispers, and I was able to catch that some of them had been before the People's Court many times, for the trials would last for several days, or even for weeks. But there was a measure of satisfaction in it for them, for they would have a better lunch than they would have had in prison. They would have frankfurters and potato salad.

One thing that surprised me was the general air of submissiveness, as if there was no question in the prisoners' minds concerning the justness of their arrest. I was not able to determine then whether this attitude was a consequence of their long stay in prison or due to the impression sedulously cultivated in the German mind that any action is correct which is based on a formal law. Whatever the cause, I could not discern any trace of a rebellious spirit among those about me. Both Jews and Gentiles were in the group, and all, apparently, had been accustomed to financial comfort, as I judged by their clothes and general appearance, and were evidently people of culture and refinement. This made their air of resignation all the more surprising to me. In me indignation at the injustice of it all was seething up through my doubts and fears.

At length we passed through the gates of Moabit prison. I had hardly descended from the car before I found myself in a room occupied by the prison administration. There I had to submit to a formal inquisition, and then had to undress myself so that my weight and height could be recorded. Then I was finger-printed and photographed, like any common criminal. Finally, I was taken to a bathroom to make myself clean for a loathsome cell. This was the formal routine for first arrivals at Moabit.

When I was dressed again, I was taken into the large central hall, where I was ordered to stand, with my back to the wall. I was deeply dejected, because the transfer to Moabit, I knew, confirmed the seriousness of the Gestapo's charge against me. In Moabit were confined those who were likely to be condemned to death or to imprisonment for life.

The hall, or room, was circular, and its ceiling was the ceiling for the whole building—a one-story affair. From this room stairways led to four galleries, one above the other. The corridors in front of the cell blocks were protected by iron balustrades. Each cell block had a guard. In the middle of the floor of the room was a large desk for the use of the chief of the guards. It was provided with a telephone, which rang almost incessantly. When the chief of guards answered, he would call out a prisoner's name to one of his assistants, who would look up his cell number, and then yell name and number to the guard on duty on the proper gallery and tell him to bring the prisoner down. It would be to see visitors or an attorney. The place seemed to be in constant turmoil.

Other prisoners were ranged along the wall on either side of me, eyes downcast, almost motionless, and as dejected as I. They were unshaven, and their clothes showed signs of long neglect. The guards, on the other hand, looked clean and healthy. They were a noisy lot, laughing loudly, gesticulating, and affecting a spirit of gaiety. The contrast between them and the silent prisoners affected my nerves, and every minute I felt as if I must break under the strain.

Finally, one of the guards led me up to a gallery, and locked me in a cell. The cell was slightly larger and somewhat brighter than the one I had occupied in Ploetzensee. It was newly painted, and the guard remarked on the fact facetiously as he turned the key. In Ploetzensee I had shared a cell with another prisoner, and I had resented the forced intimacy. Here, for some reason I did not know, I was alone, although Moabit prison was overcrowded. I wondered whether the solitary confinement was meant to be a privilege or a punishment. But the question did not bother me;

I was only too glad to be alone. I sat down on the only chair before a little wooden table, and buried my head in my hands. But I was too exhausted, too worn down by apprehension, to compose my thoughts. Two refrains hammered alternately on my brain: How will it end? What will become of my wife? Hitler's iron heel was making its impression in my soul. Perhaps to those who have been justly charged there is some consolation in the knowledge that their punishment is merited. But what consolation can come to the victims of injustice?

After a long time there was the noise of keys, and the cell door was opened. A guard handed me a bowl filled with watery soup and a tiny piece of bread. It was my supper. I placed the food on the table, and left it untouched. By and by darkness shut me in, and I knew that the sun was setting. A hush fell over the prison, and from the far outside I could hear the subdued song of a nightingale. The notes aroused me. Birds still could sing! I listened until the song was done. Then I lay down on the straw mattress, through which I could feel the hardness of the iron cot. Sleep! Who could sleep after his whole world had disintegrated about him?

Yesterday was years away, and it would be years before the dawn. But, finally, day did peep into my cell. Soon afterwards a bell rang, and then came a guard bearing my breakfast of dry bread and muddy coffee. He informed me that prison routine required that I be taken again before the inquiring judge. I put the bread and coffee on the table, untouched, and waited. A burly guard came, unlocked the cell and ordered me out. But I knew the way. A long tunnel connects the prison with the criminal court of the District of Berlin, and I had often passed through it when I worked in the office of the District Attorney and had to visit prisoners in the course of my duties. Then I had looked upon prisoners as merely objects of the law, who could have no rights until the law had been requited. Then law had been identified in my mind with justice. Now I was learning that law is too often the refuge of injustice.

I was horribly nervous, and found it difficult to keep up with the guard. He cuffed me on the ear, and I tried to hurry. Presently we were out of the tunnel, entering a corridor, from which we passed through several halls on our way to the anteroom of the criminal court. Judges and clerks were constantly passing and repassing, and I felt as if all eyes were on me—a former judge. Some I recognized, but they gave me only a fleeting glance of amused contempt. None addressed me, nor did the guard speak.

We entered the antechamber, a long, narrow room, with one barred window, which looked out on a small yard. Opposite the door I entered was the door leading to the court room. A number of hard-wood chairs were ranged against the walls, and most of them were occupied by prisoners also awaiting inquisition. Among them was a professor of the famous Catholic seminary at Breslau. He had been arrested on a charge of high treason because of his support of the Catholic opposition to Nazism under the leadership of Cardinal Faulhaber of Munich.

Finally, my turn came, and the guard ushered me into the judge's chamber. I bowed to the man at the desk, and said, "Good day." It was the usual perfunctory greeting, for Jews are not permitted to use the Nazi salutation, even if they wish to abase themselves.

The judge rose from his chair, and I immediately recognized a former acquaintance. It was Judge Walter. "Heil Hitler," he said, and then, "*Amtsgerichtsrat* Walter is my name. Please be seated, *Herr Doktor.*" He bowed slightly towards a chair in front of his desk, and I sat down. The courteous manner in which I was addressed surprised me, and I felt new hope swelling in my breast that here, at last, the case against me would be gone into thoroughly and I would be immediately released. The National Socialist propaganda had always proclaimed that the Third Reich had not abandoned the principle of justice, and the tremendous swastika which Judge Walter wore did not seem to contradict my hope. While he searched for my papers on his desk, I had time to glance around the chamber.

It was a large square room, with three large windows on one side overlooking the street. The windows were barred. There were two doors, one leading to the waiting room from which I had just come, the other to a corridor, through which prisoners were taken out after the ordeal. At one side of the judge's desk was a small table, at which sat a stenographer. I knew that I would have to be careful in my replies, for I had heard that sometimes poorly educated prisoners were trapped into making false admissions when they failed to follow the rapid reading of the stenographic report of the hearing, which always followed the inquisition. This procedure was a violation of the old law, which expressly prescribed that prisoners should have the opportunity to read their statements before signing them.

With the papers in front of him, Judge Walter took my personal history, apologizing that it was only a matter of routine. Then his manner changed abruptly. He stiffened himself in his chair, and said sharply, "And now, *Herr Doktor*, let us come to the business which brings you here. You have committed an attempt at high treason by declaring in your lectures before an audience of students that our Fuehrer and our Reich should be destroyed."

"But, Herr *Amtsgerichtsrat*" I exclaimed in surprise, "there is not the slightest evidence that I am guilty of attempted high treason. I am only charged with it."

"Yes," Judge Walter replied, an evil smile on his lips, "there is no so-called evidence against you yet. But we do not stumble over such threads. Besides, I find that the Gestapo has not gone into your case as methodically as usual. Why didn't they make you confess your crime?"

Why hadn't they made me confess? Why hadn't they tortured me? The full implication of what Judge Walter meant struck me like a sledge hammer. It knocked out my last vestige of faith in the justice of Prussian law and Prussian judges.

I must have looked my utter astonishment at his callousness.

But he merely tapped the desk with his long fingers, and said, "The Gestapo has handled your case with unbelievable carelessness. We will have to start from the beginning again. I cannot understand why only one of your students testified against you. But we will see. This is enough for one day. You will hear from us again."

He continued drumming the desk with his fingers while the clerk transposed his notes. I sat silent and bewildered for a while, and then summoned courage to ask Judge Walter how long it would take him to find out the truth of the charge against me.

"God knows," he answered, "God knows. I am afraid you will have to be patient, unless, of course, you wish to make a confession. But you wouldn't do that, I suppose. However, don't worry. We will take good care of you."

The clerk read the report of the hearing to me, and I signed it. Then Judge Walter pressed a button, and a guard came in. As I was led away, Judge Walter turned his back. Through the tunnel I was escorted back to my cell. The day was already far gone, and I resigned myself to another long night of contemplation of the circumstances which had brought me from the bench to a criminal's lodging.

My cell was approximately seven steps in length and four steps in width, so that there was little room to pace up and down when I was restless, which was the case most of the time. Each cell was provided with an iron cot, fitted to the wall, from which it was let down when in use; a little wood table, and a wood chair. On the wall was a small shelf, on which the prisoner could place the extra food which he bought with his own money. There was also a toilet, and we had a small bowl in which to wash face and hands. If two prisoners occupied a cell, an extra chair was provided, and one had to sleep on the floor, on a mattress. The mattresses were very hard, and both cot and mattresses were alive with bedbugs. There was one small window, very high, and difficult to reach when it had to be opened and cleaned. It was barred on the outside.

I was still awake when the guard rattled at my cell door the next morning and formally introduced me to prison routine, which I might as well describe now.

In Moabit the day started at 7 o'clock, with the ringing of a bell, which was the signal for the prisoners to get up and dress (which was not a long operation, as there was no change of clothing). Fifteen minutes later the cells were unlocked by the guards on duty, and the prisoners put out their pitchers, which were filled with water by trusties. Then we washed ourselves as best we could, and a quarter of an hour later breakfast was handed in. This consisted of a bitter black liquid, without sugar or milk, which was called "coffee," and a piece of "rye" bread, which was so badly prepared that frequently it made the prisoners ill. This bread was baked in the prison kitchen. It is doubtful that it contained any flour at all. When it was fresh it was too soggy to be eaten. But prisoners were sometimes so hungry that they would wolf it down and then become sick. It took me a long time to become accustomed to it, and often it gave me a stomach ache.

After breakfast we had to make up our "beds" and clean our cells. The "beds" had to be made in military fashion, which I always found difficult to do. Often it got me into trouble with the guards, and I would have to make the "bed" over again. After the "beds" were done, we swept the floor. On Saturdays, after the recreation, or exercise, hour, we had to clean our cells very thoroughly. Guards brought in brooms, pails and buckets, and we had to go to the gallery to fill the pails. We scrubbed the floors and washed the windows. As the windows are very high and I am short, washing my window was very difficult for me, and I was frequently harshly scolded for not doing it properly. Later on, I often met Pastor Niemoeller when we went to the gallery to fill our pails, and we would greet each other in passing.

About eight-thirty the bell rang for the recreation hour. A few minutes later the guards would arrive and unlock our cells. Then each prisoner stepped out and waited in front of his cell door. Another bell rang, and we stepped forward and turned to the right, and then marched in military formation down to the yard. The recreation continued an hour or sometimes longer. I shall tell about that later. After we had been exercised, we were marched back to our cells. Lunch was brought to us at noon. It consisted of watery soup and a piece of the same sort of awful bread we had for breakfast. On Sundays, however, we received two ounces of pork and a small dish of potatoes in addition. At 5 o'clock the guards brought us our supper—another piece of bread, a little soup, thinner than that we had for lunch, and sometimes tea, which we all thought was made from the leaves of the linden tree in the yard. We always had to hurry through supper (not that it would have taken long to eat it) because the guards would return in a few minutes to take away our plates and other utensils. Then we were locked up for the night. Under the old law, which the Nazis had not changed at this time, prisoners being held for trial were not made to work. However, under the restraints imposed by the Nazis, this turned out to be a hardship, for, except for the daily hour of exercise, prisoners had nothing to occupy their minds or hands. They could think only of themselves and the plight they were in.

True, there was a library in Moabit, but prisoners were allowed to read only National Socialist literature and newspapers. Relatives were not allowed to bring in books or magazines. I remember that I once asked my wife when she was visiting me to bring me Ranke's *History of the Reformation* from my library at home. But she was not allowed to do so because Ranke's conception of history did not conform with that of the National Socialists. Since, naturally, Nazi literature did not appeal to the prisoners, most of them did not read at all.

Ironically, there was one exception to the general ban. There was a copy of the New Testament in every cell. But the Old Testament was *verboten*. Afterwards, the New Testament, too, was relegated to the ash heap. Religious services also were permitted when I went to Moabit. They were held every second Sunday, each creed being allowed to have its own pastor. Even the Jews could have a rabbi attend them. The Christian services were held in a small chapel and the Jewish services in a room provided for the purpose. Also pastors, priests, and rabbis were allowed to make personal calls on their followers in prison. In Sachsenhausen, however, I learned from prisoners who followed me from Moabit that these services were finally prohibited. I was a regular attendant at the Jewish services, but found the rabbi rutted in a predicament. Because of the possible effect on himself and the Jewish prisoners he feared to preach a sermon directed towards their present needs, and merely repeated sermons he used to preach to criminals when he was employed as a prison chaplain. "You know," he said to me one day, "in Hitler's eyes every Jew is a born criminal."

During my first days in Moabit I gave the other prisoners

little attention, being too engrossed with my own thoughts. But presently some of them began talking with me, asking where I had come from, what I was charged with, how I had been treated, etc. Most of them, I observed, had the same appearance as the prisoners I had met in the police car. They were worn and faded semblances of their former selves. One of the first questions was how had I found the food at Ploetzensee, and some who had been confined in that prison inquired about certain of the guards. I was amazed at the pettiness of the inquiries and the general conversation. Later on, I learned that long confinement narrows the mental horizon and curtains the mind. Except when a prisoner was taken to a hospital, or was removed to be seen no more, there was little to talk about, and petty details assumed a large importance. Having been a judge myself, who had sentenced men to prison, I now had the opportunity to observe the practical consequences of a prison sentence. I found that it means much more than the mere deprivation of liberty for a stated time. It brings a change in the mental state which has serious results. Men become childish, inclined to quarrel over trifles. The Moabit guards were unable to understand this phenomenon, and they treated the prisoners with coarse brutality, laughing contemptuously when, for instance, one quarreled because another had gotten a larger potato or a bigger piece of bread. Fearing that I too might become reduced to this condition, I determined to watch myself carefully. I occupied myself with plans to procure my discharge. I tried to think of a way by which I could bring my protest to the authorities. When he called on me I attempted to induce my attorney to make a formal protest to the attorney general. But he refused, on the ground that he would not dare such an effort in a political case. He reminded me that I had been committed on a charge of attempted high treason. When all recourse had failed and I had come fully to realize that I was helpless, I decided on a hunger strike.

One morning I refused to accept the food given to me, and I remained firm against the appeals of hunger. But every morning I drank a few drops of water. During the first four days hunger gnawed at my stomach, and it felt as if it were being compressed in a vise. On the fourth day I felt very ill, and I had to pull myself together and summon all my latent resources to withstand the desire to eat. To make sure of myself, I did not even accept the food, and the guard took it away. But that evening I could not resist the temptation to accept a piece of bread. But I did not eat it; I merely smelled it. Then I threw it away.

For the first time, I managed to sleep that night. When I awoke the next morning my hunger had abated. From that time on I was without appetite. I felt myself growing weaker and weaker, and fell into a sort of apathy, which was by no means unpleasant, but strangely sweet. I thought it would be pleasant to die like that. It would be like floating away. I was becoming light-headed. Strangely, the remembered scent of linden trees came to me, and I heard again the singing of the nightingale. Several times during my period of self-imposed starvation the prison doctor came to see me and urged me to eat. But I declined, saying that I would not eat until justice had been done me. He shrugged his shoulders, and said, "You fool, don't you know that justice doesn't exist in Germany any more? I must inform you that hunger strikes are forbidden and are considered to be resistance to the State. If I should report you, you would immediately be brought before a special court, which would condemn you to death without further ado. Be reasonable, and don't make unnecessary trouble. I am speaking for your own good."

He did not report me. Instead, on the sixteenth day of my

ordeal he had me brought down to his office, where he took my weight. I had lost sixteen kilograms, almost thirty-six pounds in American weight. The doctor ordered me to the prison hospital. I have often wondered since how it came about that Dr. — was serving in Moabit prison, and why he took an interest in me and was kind to me. Evidently he had not yet been poisoned with the Nazi virus.

The hospital in Moabit is, or was at that time, the largest and best prison hospital in Prussia. Prisoners who were seriously ill and could not receive proper treatment in their own prison hospitals were brought to Moabit for treatment. But even the Moabit hospital did not have the equipment of a normal hospital, and prisoner patients of the older regime who needed a major operation were transferred to private hospitals. This practice was discontinued after Hitler came to power. The result of this was that during the almost eight months I stayed in the Moabit hospital I knew of no major operation that was successful. Patients died either on the operating table or a short time afterward for lack of capable doctors, of necessary instruments, and of proper care. The head doctor was a Roman Catholic, and the only one who behaved like a human being. But even he was restricted by the regulations and the lack of proper equipment and assistance. He confided to me one day that he was not a competent surgeon, but was required to perform operations nevertheless. But most of the operations were performed by a young surgeon, a fervent Nazi, who had had no experience whatever. As he considered the patients beneath him, he was heedless of what happened to them after he had used his knife. For instance, one day a prisoner was brought in who had cut his jugular vein in an attempt at suicide, and the young Nazi surgeon exclaimed, "Why didn't he finish the job while he was about it?"

Most of the people imprisoned after the beginning of

Hitler's regime were political prisoners. I estimate that the total number of prisoners when I was one of them was about one and a half million, of which not more than two hundred thousand had been arrested for non-political reasons. In addition, there were approximately one million men in the concentration camps. The Nazis were bent on destroying the least vestige of opposition. In many cases the charges consisted of reading illicit newspapers, listening to forbidden radio broadcasts, and criticizing the new regime. One case I remember especially. A German working man had visited Switzerland. There he had gone to a reading room and read Swiss papers printed in German. He was observed by a Gestapo agent. He was arrested immediately on re-entering Germany, and was sentenced to serve seven years at hard labor. In the course of time he became ill, and was brought to Moabit hospital for a stomach operation. He died on the operating table. The body was not returned to the family for burial, but cremated. That was the general rule. Bodies were cremated without rite or service of any kind. A little carton of ashes handed to the family was due notice of death.

When I entered the hospital it had become little better than a chamber of horrors. Purification of the racial strain had become one of the cardinal objectives of the Nazi regime, this being in keeping with the new biological theory that the Creator had especially endowed the German people and that crime was a symptom of tainted blood. To put this theory into practice, judges were empowered to sentence people convicted of certain offenses to sterilization or emasculation. Among the offenses for which this drastic penalty could be imposed were violations of the law regulating the transfer of money, of the racial law, and of certain political laws. The racial law covered sex crimes and even innocent relations between Jews and Aryans. It was not long before the list was extended to cover even trivial offenses.

In Moabit I met many victims of this terrible practice. Many of them had been convicted only of some petty offense, which, in a large number of cases, was the first. Nevertheless, the doctors employed by the courts to examine prisoners had declared that they were habitual criminals and that it would be a waste of time merely to imprison or otherwise punish them in accordance with the older laws. Therefore, they were ordered to be sterilized or emasculated to prevent their bringing "criminal" offspring into the world. Crime against sex included any sort of disorderly conduct towards women, so that, for instance, a drunken man who accosted a woman on the street was liable to be subjected to the new punishment. What struck me most was the fact that the majority of men forced to undergo the operation belonged to the underprivileged class. I could not help reflecting sometimes that if there had been such a law in Austria some sixty years ago there might not have been a Hitler. His family tree would not have passed the test he has imposed on others.

There were five or six emasculation or sterilization operations every day, and among all I met who had undergone this cruel punishment were very few of the better social class. These few had been convicted, not of sex crimes, but of violations of the political laws. If Hitler could not completely stifle opposition in one generation, he might, at least, prevent it from germinating in the next. A saddening commentary is that most of the victims had been in perfect physical health, men who might have become good German fathers if they had been able to live under better social conditions. Of course, there were fathers among the unfortunates, whose sons and grandsons may remember this senseless, vindictive sadism when the terrible hour of reckoning comes.

Sometimes prospective victims feared that the operation

would be fatal, and would inquire of the trusties whether there was such danger. But the only reply was some inexpressible vulgarity and that they would not even feel the knife. And, indeed, during the first weeks of my stay in the hospital, the operations were successful. Then, suddenly, came rumors that men were dying on the operating table, that they were unable to withstand the ether. This surprised me as much as it shocked me, and I realized that if there were any truth in the rumors the deaths could not be due to accident, but must be due to design. I did not dare question the head doctor, though he often stopped to talk with me, but I noticed that he looked very disturbed, and this confirmed my suspicion. Even the trusties, who often talked with me frankly, told me to mind my own business when I attempted to question them discreetly.

Finally, a gift of some of the additional food I was able to buy induced one of the trusties to talk. He told me that some of the men who supposedly had been sentenced to emasculation had really been marked for death because doctors had said that they were not fit to live. They were used, therefore, to test new gases, the trusty told me. But the tests had to be carried out in secret, because, at that time at least, there was no law permitting so-called "mercy" killings. So when a man died under one of these tests, it was announced that he had succumbed either to the operation (simple as it is) or to the ether.

Of course, these stories spread among men waiting for the operation, and it was horrible to hear their ravings and struggles when they were being taken into the operating room. Some of them became violently insane while waiting for the ordeal, and these were put in strait-jackets and locked in the cellar of the hospital until the doctors were ready for them. Even many of those who preserved their senses had to be placed in strait-jackets so that the orderlies could get them on the operating table. To dwell longer on this tremendous tragedy would, perhaps, overstrain the emotion of my readers, and further description could not add to what the imagination can conceive.

As for myself during this time, I spent most of the first weeks in bed. I was fed with grape sugar injected in my arm and liquid food through a tube in my nose. Why such care was taken of me I do not know, and I can only hazard the guess that some influence in my behalf was being exercised outside the prison walls. Gradually, I became less nervous, and began to regain my strength.

The long monotony was relieved when the prior of a famous monastery, whom I had met and talked with before being removed to the hospital, was brought into the cell I was occupying. He had been sentenced to ten years at hard labor because his monastery had continued to pay interest on a loan borrowed in Holland. He had come down with a bad case of rheumatism, which made it impossible for him to move without suffering great agony. Day and night he lay almost motionless on his back. But in spite of his condition, he displayed marvelous fortitude and uttered no word of complaint. He took an interest in me, and admonished me to take food in order to keep myself alive. It was not for me to decide whether I should live or die, he said, and he was so convincing that I began accepting food again. My long stay in prison had helped me to adjust myself in some degree, and under the urging of my new friend I decided to hold my head up and not give way to despair. I had made such decision before, but sometimes my powers of resistance gave way.

One day I was permitted to see my wife, the first time since my arrest. Escorted by a guard, she was brought to my bed, and we were allowed fifteen minutes in which to talk, with the guard standing by the whole time. She was wan with fear and worry, and it came to me that she was under greater stress than I, for I knew what each day would bring forth, that existence could hardly hold more terror for me than it held now, while she could put no rein on her imagination. When she was taking her leave, she wanted to kiss me. But it was against the prison rules. She could only give me her hand.

Later on, when I was better, I was transferred to a ward, where there were about twenty other prisoners undergoing various treatments. Some of them had been brought from provincial penitentiaries because their local prison hospitals were not sufficiently equipped to care for them. Among them were men who had spent the last twenty years behind prison walls on convictions varying from robbery to manslaughter. There were Communists, too, who had been arrested for their political activities. So there were occasional discussions about Communism. To my great surprise, the common criminals expressed the utmost sympathy for Communism, although, in private conversations, they had told me that they had resorted to crime because they were dissatisfied with their earnings, which were by no means meager, for they were all artisans of more than average skill. Still, they insisted on being victims of the social order and saw in Communism a remedy for their supposed social ills. "As common criminals we cannot be members of the Communist party," one of them told me, "but we are in full sympathy with it." I often argued that society had given them a very good chance to make a decent living, and one day got such a severe beating for my pains that I had to be transferred back to my bed.

The prior was still there. I told him of my experience in the ward, and complained of having had to live in such close contact with criminals.

"Be patient, my son," he replied. "Not all of those we call

criminals are really criminally inclined. I have learned that some of them have more character and heart than those who now rule our country."

After almost eight months in the hospital, the doctor said I was able to resume prison routine, and I was sent back to the prison and put in the same cell block that I had been in before. This time I had a cell mate. Through the long night I heard his supplicating sighs and nervous shufflings. I wondered again about the future, and fought against the terror that once more clutched at my heart. It is well for me that the veil was not lifted.

IV

NIEMOELLER AT MOABIT

WHEN the cell doors were opened the next morning I recognized the figure of Pastor Niemoeller standing in the door of a cell a few doors from mine. We had been summoned for the recreation hour, and were put in line to march one behind the other down the staircase to the yard. Here we were formed into two circles, one of which, called the great circle, was made up of prisoners deemed to be in good health. In the smaller circle were the prisoners whose health did not permit them to move and walk quickly. Because of my recent release from the hospital and my still weak condition I was placed in the smaller circle. So, under the supervision of the guards, we marched, round and round. Just ahead of me, I noticed, was Pastor Niemoeller, wan and thin. I was glad to see him, because of his kindness and sympathy when I met him in the prison waiting hall. I looked forward to an opportunity to talk with him.

Prisoners were forbidden to talk with each other, as it was feared that the privilege might be used for the transfer of messages from the outside. But the prison routine was such that the rule often was relaxed. Observance depended very much on the guards, some of whom, either through laziness or laxity, were careless in enforcing discipline. Then, too, the prison was so overcrowded (nearly every cell being occupied by two prisoners although the law provided that every prisoner had the right to occupy a cell alone until he was sentenced) that only one guard could be put on duty during the recreation hour. So it was often possible for prisoners to converse with each other, even when the guard was vigilant, especially in the smaller circle, to which the guards devoted less attention than to the great circle, in which the healthier, and therefore more dangerous, prisoners were made to walk. Pastor Niemoeller recognized me when I placed myself behind him, and nodded a friendly greeting. I felt then that I had at least one friend in prison. However, he seemed not inclined to attempt to talk. For a while he was occupied in observing his surroundings, and then became lost in thought, and I did not attempt to break in on his mood.

Moabit is one of the oldest prisons in Germany, having been built soon after the Franco-German War for the detention of prisoners awaiting trial. It consisted of three buildings containing cells, a hospital building, and a building used as a kitchen. A tunnel connected it with the criminal court in Berlin. Two of the cell buildings housed male prisoners, and one was used for female prisoners. The normal capacity was for about twelve hundred, but, as I knew from my experience as a judge, the prison was never filled in normal times. But now there were about three thousand prisoners within its walls, of whom six hundred were women. But arrests had become so numerous that even the overstraining of Moabit's capacity was not enough, and the overflow was taken to penitentiaries, the men to Ploetzensee and the women to the Barnim Strasse in Berlin.

The prisoners in Moabit represented almost every social class and political conviction. Among us were well-known business men, professors, doctors, lawyers, whose offense was that they had not become convinced of Hitler's sagacity as a leader. There were Nazis (fallen from grace), Conservatives,

Socialists, Democrats, and Communists. Then there were real criminals, of the lowest and most brutal sort. For instance, in the cell block which I occupied was a man named Albert Mueller, who had spent most of his life in prison. His specialty had been robbing churches, especially Roman Catholic churches, and cemeteries. It was a peculiar irony of fate, I thought, that the Nazis should bring together in prison a man who had devoted his life to robbing churches, and Pastor Niemoeller, who had given his best to his country and then had devoted his service to God and the Church. History, I think, will prove that one of Hitler's cardinal errors was that he had to depend for support on all the evil instinct in man, that his program of political, economic, and social salvation was the very antithesis of that for which man has striven since he learned that there was something beyond blood and soil.

The treatment of the prisoners in Moabit was correct in so far as it was not permitted to beat them or otherwise maltreat them. On the other hand, the military discipline was severe, and the guards were allowed to insult the prisoners to their hearts' content, and since they were men picked for their sadistic instincts, there were few who did not indulge their appetite. For certain infractions of the rules punishment was regulated by the prison administration. This consisted of putting the prisoners on a diet of bread and water (which was not much worse than the regular diet) or placing them in solitary confinement. Add to this the fact that most of the prisoners were charged only with political offenses and had been given into the hands of unscrupulous judges whose task was not to search for the truth and administer justice, but to prove guilt. The judges were merely the tools of the Gestapo and the Nazi party. Their loyalty was measured by the number of men they sent to prison or to death. Before the advent of Hitler German judges were completely independent of political influence, and they held office for life. Now they were dependent on the good will of the Nazi administration, which could dismiss them for any cause. As Archbishop Soederstrom of Sweden once put it, German justice had been reduced to the status of a prostitute.

The uncertainty of their fate drove many prisoners to desperation. Suicides were frequent, and no effort at prevention was made by the prison administration. In fact, suicide served their purpose. There was little comradeship among the prisoners. Subject to the crudest sort of discipline and realizing that justice was no longer an attribute of German law, they thought only of self-preservation. Each looked only to easing his own situation. This was especially characteristic of former Nazis. They believed that if they spied on their fellow prisoners and were able to show some culpable act, they might be able to regain their freedom and once more be restored to favor. So they would seize any opportunity to denounce their fellow prisoners.

Of course, there were exceptions. After such an experience as this I can well believe that there can be no situation in which there will not be found some leaven of human kindness. When I took my place behind him in the daily routine of exercise in the yard Pastor Niemoeller would always whisper a kind greeting and his sad pale face would light up with understanding. One day we ventured to talk with each other, and he told me the circumstances of his arrest. He had expected it, he said, for Gestapo agents had long been visiting his church on Sundays and taking copious notes of his sermons. Several times he was taken to the Gestapo headquarters and subjected to questioning, but was released after signing a protocol. Each time he would be warned by the Gestapo officials that there would come a day when he wouldn't be released if he continued preaching and working against the Nazi party. "Our Fuehrer has been very patient with you," they would say to him. "If we did what we wanted, we could have locked you up long ago." A short time before his actual arrest friends advised him to leave Germany, and offered to help him get out of the country. But he refused. He said that he felt sometimes that rumors of his coming arrest were given out purposely, either in order to kill him if he attempted to escape, or, more probably, to allow him to flee so that they could say that he had deserted his followers and had not been willing to risk his life for God and the Faith.

So when a number of agents of the Gestapo came for him early one morning, they found him at home. While two of them detained him, the others took his wife and children into another room and searched them. He could hear their excited voices and their crying. Finally, after several hours of this, the Gestapo agents took him to the Gestapo headquarters, saying that he was needed to sign a protocol, after which he would be released. At the Gestapo headquarters he was rushed into the room of a higher Gestapo official, who called himself Rudloff (though it is doubtful that this was his right name, since Gestapo officials rarely gave their correct names, probably for fear of reprisal if the Nazi government should ever be defeated). Rudloff received Pastor Niemoeller very politely, rising and offering him a chair.

Pastor Niemoeller is a gifted and expressive talker, and I shall quote from memory what he told me of the conversation that ensued between him and the man Rudloff.

"We regret very much to have to resort to such methods towards you. Pastor Niemoeller," said Rudloff. "We know that you deserve much at the hands of the Fatherland because of your meritorious service during the World War. And we arc fully aware of your love for the Fatherland. We arc the more astonished, therefore, that you are opposed to the National Socialist movement, which has only the welfare of the Fatherland at heart. What would have become of Germany if it had not been for our Fuehrer? But you need not be afraid."

When Pastor Niemoeller expressed his indignation about the way he had been treated, Rudloff replied, "That is all your own fault. Why do you cause us so much trouble? I assure you that we would rather treat you kindly, but we have to take notice of your attitude towards our Fuehrer." To this Pastor Niemoeller replied, "I am not aware of having attacked the State. I have only defended the Evangelical Church against attack, and it is my duty to defend her against all comers."

Rudloff answered that it was not his intention to discuss the affairs of the Church, and said, "I have been ordered by my Fuehrer to inform you that you will be released immediately if you will fulfill one condition, and that is sign a letter declaring that you have seen your mistake in opposing the National Socialist church policy, and that you are now willing to co-operate with us. In that event you will be allowed to give us your conditions for the form of your co-operation, and I can assure you that your wishes will be carried out. We know how to reward service to the Party."

"I will have to disappoint you, for I cannot fulfill this condition," replied Pastor Niemoeller. "As I have already stated, again and again, I am not looking for any reward for my services. I desire only to keep my conscience clear before my God."

"This all sounds very idealistic, but it is doubtful that it is practical," said Rudloff. "What does God mean nowadays? Today religion is nothing but a chimera. Our Fuehrer has redeemed Germany, and will soon redeem the whole world. Why will you sacrifice yourself for something that doesn't exist? Through positive cooperation with the great aim of National Socialism you can be of the utmost service to the Fatherland. We need men like you."

"Nobody needs to tell me how I must serve the Fatherland," replied Pastor Niemoeller (and he drew himself up very straight when he told me this). "That I have proved throughout my life. I have always done what conformed with my conscience and my honor. What appears to be a chimera to you is to me and innumerable Germans the most sacred thing we know. I will never betray God and my faith."

"Is this your last word?" asked Rudloff.

"Yes," answered Pastor Niemoeller, "this is my last word."

"Then," said Rudloff, "it is my duty to inform you that you cannot be released. You will have to be detained. I regret this action, but I must obey orders." He pressed a button, and a heavily armed SS guard entered the room. "Follow the guard."

The guard, as Pastor Niemoeller told me, took him to the basement of the Gestapo headquarters, and searched him, as was customary. He had to unlace his shoes and give the laces to the guard and also his collar buttons and suspenders. Then he was placed in a cell.

"I was very much wrought up by this time," Pastor Niemoeller told me, "and, of course, I couldn't sleep. And, besides, things went on about me that I shall never forget. I saw them beat priests with whips and curse them as traitors to the Fatherland. I saw Jews dying under the blows of the Storm Troopers. When I heard the screams and blows and curses I fell on my knees and prayed to God to give me strength to endure all this, to let no weakness overcome me."

This was told to me piecemeal, while we were walking, round and round, in the little circle, and while the guard was giving most of his attention to the great circle. It was told to me, not once, but many times, and Pastor Niemoeller's words are indelibly impressed on my memory. I cannot forget, for the very attitude and demeanor of the man impressed me. Besides, I knew full well that at that time, anyway, he need but have said the word to be released from all this horror and agony. One word of regret and penitence, one word to say that he had become converted to the Nazi philosophy, and today Pastor Niemoeller might have been one of Hitler's most favored henchmen. He could have become bishop of the German Christian Church and have been living in splendor like Goering and Goebbels and the rest of them. And yet the Nazis say that the Christian faith weakens the moral fiber and makes men childishly dependent. They say that Christians are always decadent. Well, in some not far-off tomorrow, Goebbels and Rosenberg and Ribbentrop, and even Hitler himself, will remember Pastor Niemoeller, as all Christians today remember their martyrs and Jews remember their ancient prophets.

Bit by bit. Pastor Niemoeller told me more of his story, and I can remember it as a child remembers oft-repeated tales told by his mother.

"Every morning," he told me, "I was brought to Rudloff's room, and he tried, again and again, to make me sign that paper. He put before me every possible argument to convince me that I had wronged the Fuehrer and the National Socialist regime. Those hour-long conversations, in which Rudloff always remained imperturbably polite, were mental torture to me, for I was in a very weak and nervous condition. The small cell in which I was locked was dark almost the whole day, and it contained only a wooden bench, on which I had to sleep, with only a blanket for cover. Besides, I felt physically unclean, because I couldn't shave or change my clothes. When I walked into Rudloff's room, unshaven, unwashed, without a collar, and with my shoes untied, and saw the clean, well-dressed man at the desk, I couldn't suppress a feeling of embarrassment about my appearance. And I realized that Rudloff enjoyed my embarrassment, for, as I entered the room, he would say, 'How are you today, Herr Pastor?' and smile ironically.

"Then, when I was summoned again one day, there sat, instead of Rudloff, the councilor of the Prussian Ministry, Gritzbach, Goering's personal aid, in his capacity as Prussian Prime Minister. I knew Herr Gritzbach very well, for he had lived in Dahlem, and formerly was a member of my congregation. But he had given up his church membership because of his new position. He rose and greeted me cordially, as if we were meeting socially. He asked me how I was, and I said, 'You can see from my appearance how I am.' Then he said, 'It is up to you. Herr Goering is very much worried about your fate, and has sent me to see you. And even the Fuehrer himself feels very badly that he has been compelled to treat a man like you in this way. But the interest of the State is above every personal feeling. You, as a former officer, will be able to understand this. Then he, too, attempted to get me to sign the letter of renunciation. I told him I would not sign it under any circumstance.

"'Think of yourself,' he said to me. 'Do you know what the consequences of your refusal to sign this letter will be? The government is determined to indict you for high treason if I should fail in my efforts to get you to change your mind. And you know what this will mean. Come, be reasonable. You have a wife and children.'

"I told him, 'As an Evangelical pastor I have no right to think of my personal happiness. I am a servant of the Faith, and I cannot see how I have betrayed the State, and my convictions I cannot change.'

"When Gritzbach saw that he could not do anything with me, his manners changed, and he became very cool.

'I will report to Herr Goering, but I am afraid that nothing more can be done for you,' he said. Then he left the room.

"A few mornings later I was taken again before Rudloff. This time the conversation was very short. He asked me only if I would at least cease opposing the government or refrain from preaching at all. When I replied that I could not do even this, he said that I would be charged with high treason. And the following evening I was transferred to the police headquarters prison in Berlin."

From here Pastor Niemoeller was transferred to Ploetzensee prison, where it was that he witnessed the execution, as I have related in the first chapter.

Later he was brought to Moabit prison, and it was here that I met him, in the waiting hall, and became associated with him in the long months that saw us also in the concentration camp at Sachsenhausen, where I was finally freed. I had seen him first in his own church, before the breaking of the storm that was to engulf Germany and reduce all Europe to ruin. So distant seemed those days now, as distant as the first remembered days of childhood, when every morning brings a new adventure into happiness and the only pains are a scratch or an overloaded stomach. Then Pastor Niemoeller was in his vigorous prime, a spirit of gentleness carved in his strong, ascetic face. The lines were deeper now, and there was a brooding air about him, as of a man who turns inward to his soul and sees there things that are beyond the mental horizon of most of us. I always felt calmer after we had talked together.

The little yard in which we had our daily exercise was of bare sand. Its melancholy aspect was lightened by a linden tree and one flower bed, which looked lost in these harsh surroundings. The prisoners were taken out one cell block at a time. A cell block numbered between 120 and 130 men. In our circle there was a strange collection of humanity. One of them was a former judge of the Prussian Supreme Court, who had been installed by the Nazis as successor to a very famous jurist, Leonhard, who had been dismissed because his mother was of Jewish descent, even though he himself had been brought up as a Christian. This man was of especial interest to me because, so far as I knew, he was the only judge in Prussian history ever to be placed on trial. He had been a Nazi long before Hitler attained power, and had been promoted in order to help restore justice in Germany, which the Nazis said had been destroyed under the Jewish (Weimar) Republic.

But he had been convicted of accepting bribes. He was very cynical about the matter in talking with me. "Why do you suppose we put Hitler in power?" he said. "He promised us that we would be above the law, and that we all would get rich. We were supposed to do whatever we pleased, so long as we were good Nazis, and everybody acted accordingly. I didn't do more or less than anyone else who got office under Hitler."

Remembering the high moral standard which formerly had characterized the bench, I was astounded by this man's utter contempt for the law. He said that the real reason he was convicted and imprisoned was not his acceptance of bribes, but a personal difference between him and one of his superiors. It had been rumored long before that money could be used to grease the palms of any Nazi official, yet I could not overcome my surprise at the cynicism of this man Preiser. Another in our circle was the grave robber, Mueller, who was fond of talking about politics and religion. He hated all clergymen, and took an especial pleasure in venting his spite on Catholic priests, of whom there had been several in our cell block before the arrival of Pastor Niemoeller. He called them *verdanmite Pfaffen*, for which there is no proper translation in English. In German it is insulting in the extreme. The word *Pfaffe* was formerly the regular word for priest, but its meaning underwent change, and it is now used in opprobrium.

Another interesting man was a Jew named Lauterbach, who was my cell mate. He was very quiet and retiring. His arrest had come about very strangely. He had had an idea that the Nazis and Jews might come to an understanding, and had talked about it with a neighbor, who was also a Jew. The neighbor apparently approved the idea, and induced Lauterbach to write a memorandum explaining it, which the other would arrange to get into Hitler's hands. Lauterbach followed instructions, and was arrested. His friend, although a Jew, turned out to be a Nazi spy, an agent of the Gestapo. I learned later that the Gestapo frequently employs as agents men who are supposed to be above suspicion, such as Jews, former Communists and Socialists. Often prisoners were released from concentration camps under the promise that they would act as agents for the Gestapo. In my opinion, they could hardly be blamed for accepting their freedom under such conditions. Few would have the strength of character to resist the temptation. Only those who had been imprisoned because of their faith and their conscientious scruples had such capacity.

There was also a Karl Schultze, a skilled laborer, former member of the Social Democratic Party, who had been caught reading a forbidden paper. His wife, too, had been arrested, and she was in the women's department of Moabit prison. Their children had been sent to an orphanage. Another who walked with us was a former captain of the German Imperial Army, Wiesner, who had fought in the World War. He had been arrested for belonging to and promoting a secret organization of Stahlhelm. Such was the environment in which Pastor Niemoeller found himself when he entered our circle.

It was not long before the other prisoners learned the identity of the new man who walked with them. The difference between their attitude towards him and towards the other clerics who had been with us was noticeable. The former Nazis, and the Communists among them especially, had been in the habit of ridiculing the priests and clergymen. But for Pastor Niemoeller they showed some sympathy. "What is the reason for this?" I asked Preiser in a whisper one day.

"He seems to be a different type of man," Preiser answered. "He was an officer, and he is not like the other clergymen, who spend their time close to the churches. He has been out in the world, and he knows people. I am really sorry to see him here."

Before Pastor Niemoeller came to us religion had been a subject of frequent discussion in our circle, most of whom were disbelievers. Their ideas of religion were colored by their political convictions. Both Nazis and Communists were contemptuous of all religious belief, and dismissed with a shrug of the shoulders the idea that there is a God who is concerned in the fate of man. The few clergymen who had been with us were, most of them, worn-out scholars, men tired and enfeebled mentally and physically by the new environment into which they had been violently thrown when the Nazis assumed the reins of government and began dispelling all belief except that in the intellectual and physical might of the German people—a nation set aside by fate to rule the world. In such a creed there could be no room for idealism. So when there was discussion these men usually preferred to keep silent. Perhaps they felt they could avail nothing where God seemed so far removed. This attitude seemed to strengthen the general disbelief and despair. Then, also, some of the prisoners were impudent and vulgar in speaking to the priests. The priests would not answer back, which would convince the prisoners that the priests were intellectually inferior. If evil had triumphed, they reasoned, how could there be a God?

I was, therefore, somewhat curious as to how Pastor Niemoeller would react to this atmosphere. When I had the opportunity, I told him what he had to expect from his fellow prisoners. It did not matter, he said to me. He had always found some good in every one, and he believed that the loudest dissenters had religious convictions that they would not admit. So I said to him, "Pastor Niemoeller, are you still convinced, then, that religion can still have some meaning for man, that the destruction of religion would mean a complete change in our existence?"

"Yes," he said, "I have no doubt of it. The Christian faith has survived all attacks, as it will survive this. Civilization as we know it is based on Christian doctrine and practice. In trying to say that religion is a product of the soil and that there is something peculiar to the German people and not admissible to others the Nazis are attempting the worst fraud in history. It is paganism in the worst form. For where paganism is generally the result of ignorance, the Nazi brand is a deliberate attempt to do away with the idea of God and to substitute for it faith in their own destiny. They ignore the fact that in Germany all progress has come directly or indirectly through the Church. Before we Germans became converted to Christianity we were not much better than animals. And it is to that state that the Nazis would restore us today. We could exist only through perpetual violence, just as the Nazis are living today."

During several days Pastor Niemoeller discussed religion with me, and continually dwelt on the fact that religion had tempered civilization, that belief in God was inescapable, and that even secular history was forced to regard the advent and spread of the Christian Gospel as the greatest single event in the life of mankind, and that it was the only real incentive to human progress and betterment. He was always unfailing in his belief that Nazism could not survive, that, in the end, it would be destroyed by the very thing it seeks itself to destroy. I could not but marvel at the spiritual strength of the man, who, as I have said, could have uttered one word of surrender and gained his freedom and probably a high place in the councils of the Nazi party.

One day Pastor Niemoeller told me of a speech Alfred Rosenberg delivered to a meeting in the Prussian Herrenhaus, an institution in Prussia similar to the British House of Lords. It was in the spring of 1933, when Rosenberg was head of the Foreign Office of the Nazi party.

As nearly as I can remember it, this is what Rosenbcrg said, as Pastor Niemoller told me:

"A conquest of the world, which, as I state here, we consider frankly as our final aim, can be accomplished only by exploiting the decadence of the so-called civilized world. We consider that decadence as a consequence of the sentiments which Christianity has taught mankind.

"Our task, therefore, is to revive the old German spirit by overcoming Christianity and giving our people a new kind of education which shall revive in them the sound instinct and ruthlessness of the beast, which knows only the law of self-preservation. This law must be good, for it is given by nature. Christianity, therefore, at least in its present form, is a natural obstacle to our new ideology. On the other hand, we cannot help acknowledging that Christianity is too deeply fixed in the souls of at least the older generation of our nation. We, therefore, do not think it necessary now to abolish Christianity altogether. But the churches will have to come under the complete control of the Party and the State, and the clergy will have to consider it as their task to use their authority in behalf of our cause, which is the cause of the nation.

"Christian dogma will have to undergo a thorough change to fit it to the needs of the German people and to eliminate un-German ideas, which originated in international Judaism."

This speech was not published in any German newspaper, not even in Nazi organs, because, it appears, the Nazis were not sure of their own followers. The meeting was attended mostly by recreant clergymen and Nazi officials.

"I was dumbfounded when I heard about this blasphemous speech," Pastor Niemoeller told me. "It was unique indeed that a representative of a State should openly deny every law of morality, should blaspheme the Christian faith itself, when every State considers itself as the natural protector of the moral laws, and when no modern State outside of Communistic Russia had dared to hold up the Christian faith to ridicule.

"So, you see, even the Nazis are very well aware that the destruction of Christianity would mean the destruction of our present civilization, which is what they evidently desire, since only by destroying our present civilization could they hope to erect the new order of which they boast. You see, this is a reversion to the law of the jungle, when man depended only on brute strength for his survival.

"But the Nazis cannot hope to eradicate the Christian faith. Proof of the existence of God lies in the souls of men. It was there in the beginning, and you cannot eliminate it any more than you can eliminate any physical law of the universe. If we didn't feel in our innermost thoughts that this life is not the end, but merely a preliminary training, what worth would existence have? The Nazi philosophy is the philosophy of insanity. Religious belief is the all in all of life. And I think that my experience is significant, because I spent a great part of my life in a profession which is in direct contrast with my present status as a pastor of the Evangelical Church. When I was a naval officer in the World War I always had a feeling that we were all fighting for something small and unworthy, something that didn't mean much in the face of eternity. I tried to overcome the feeling, for it seemed at times to be a weakness, a form of cowardice. But, in spite of my efforts to suppress it, that feeling kept growing. After the war ended, when the German navy had to be reorganized, I was one of the few naval officers to be offered a commission in the new navy. But I declined, in spite of the prospect of a splendid career, because I felt in my innermost being that I could no longer be a fighter.

"What should become of me was not clear. I felt only that I must do something that would satisfy my inner clamor, and I decided to become a farmer. I even thought of leaving Germany and starting life again in some other country, in order that I might to some extent forget the ordeal through which the world had passed. My ancestors had been peasants and I thought it best to return to the occupation which seemed natural to me. But when I came into contact with people whom I had never met before, I felt that there was a greater task in front of me—to help in the reconstruction of the morals of our people, which had been so badly shaken by the terrible experience of war. To this call I responded. I could not do otherwise. It was an urge I could not resist. Yes, friend, I felt that I was bidden of God. He was now my Leader. And so I decided to become a servant of the Evangelical Church.

"When I started to study the Word of God I was confirmed in all those feelings that had encompassed my soul. And the more I studied the Bible, the more I became impressed with its majestic truths. And what I have learned has given me strength to withstand all temptations to relieve my physical plight."

Behind the prison pallor glowed an ethereal light in Pastor Niemoeller's face. It warmed my heart as great music stirs the pulse. So I conceive that in the worst and hardest of us a responsive chord can be struck by some one to whom God has given the special touch. I had never given much thought to religion. I had accepted the facts of Judaism and Christianity as one accepts other facts about him. But one could not listen to such a man as Pastor Niemoeller without feeling some agitation in the deeps of his soul.

It was a wonderful morning in July when he unbared all this to me. On a high limb of the lone linden tree in the yard a bird was singing. His song was like a wordless hymn. Pastor Niemoeller looked up and listened as we marched around. Our fellow prisoners, on the other hand, were making the rounds in listless fashion, some of them whispering to each other. The guard was not too attentive. I had the strange feeling of unreality I had experienced before—walking with this man who talked of God and of serene days ahead, when this ordeal should have been finished; who could speak of hope when all hope seemed dead. He was in such contrast to Preiser, for instance, who had sold his soul for a mess of Nazi pottage and then had lost even that. I could not help unburdening myself to Pastor Niemoeller and reflecting on the crass selfishness of men who would escape individual responsibility by merging themselves in a mass form of egoism to fatten on the flesh and blood of others. He smiled a little, and said, "They are only machines of their own desires. They think to build a structure in which they can live apart from reality. But no one can escape reality. No one can long be a fugitive from conscience. No one can alter the concept of life or shape events away from God. Christianity can never submit to the State, and it is for us to show the world that the Christian spirit is alive and that we, as servants of Christ, are ready to suffer and endure for our faith."

It was surprising to me now how much more quickly the days passed. Before Pastor Niemoeller began to walk with us I had suffered from the long monotony of prison life, from the utter sameness of the days and nights. It is difficult to describe this feeling to those who have never experienced it, though returned soldiers have told me that there was such monotony in the trenches during the periods of quiet on the fronts. When dawn broke I would feel my heart nutter, beat nervously, because it would be so long before the fall of night. And when night fell I would be depressed because it would be so long before another day. But now I was all impatience for the morning, because I knew I would be walking with Pastor Niemoeller. And when that hour was over, I could spend the rest of the day recapitulating what he had said and pondering on the burden of his words. Sometimes I would ask myself why I was so fascinated by him. And the answer would come to me—because there was no pretense about him, because of his utter simplicity, because in him one knew that he had found a man. Sometimes he would appear to be lost in contemplation, when his face would have an air of gentleness, as if his thoughts had left this world and were upon matters remote from physical struggle. When one saw him in such a mood, it was difficult to believe that he was the driving force of some of the strongest opposition which Hitler had encountered.

But as soon as he started talking, his face would change completely. It would assume an expression of unbreakable determination and severity. His eyes would light up as if from an inner glow, so that one would feel that he was in the presence of something that was more than a mere human personality.

Before the Nazis had shown themselves in their true colors, Pastor Niemoeller had lent them an attentive ear and had seen in their program some hope of restoring the Fatherland to its former position among the nations. I was curious to learn how he had come to sympathize with such a vicious movement, and one day I broached the question to him.

"I do not understand it myself today," he answered. "For I know now that this was certainly the gravest mistake which I, and, with me, many Evangelical and Catholic clergymen could have made. I know there is no excuse for me, and, therefore, I consider my present sufferings as an expiation for what I have to consider now as a sin. It is true that we all believed that we were acting in the interest of the Church," and when I looked at him in surprise as he said this, he continued, "In order to understand this you will have to become familiar with the situation of the Church in Germany after the World War.

"At the beginning the so-called revolutionary democratic government assumed an attitude towards the Church which by no means could be called hostile, but indifferent. The Weimar constitution proclaimed the separation of Church and State, as had been done by the single states in the German Empire, especially by the Prussian constitution of 1850, when the demand for separation of Church and State was already a postulate of liberalism. But there was one difference which, later on, proved to be deciding.

"In the German Empire the German princes were *summi episcopi* of their respective Evangelical churches. That meant that in spite of formal separation, the churches were closely connected with the State. The crowned heads of the States, who themselves derived the right from God, according to the theory of that time, were interested in the moral authority of the Church, which, on her part, did everything she could to justify and confirm those claims by connecting the worldly power of the crowns with the mysticism of the Faith. So the Faith and the Church were protected by their mutual interests. That meant that the State did not allow any attack on Church or religion and that the Church supported with all her power the Crown and State. Furthermore, the Church received financial support from the State, so that she could fulfill her manifold tasks without having to resort to heavy taxation of her followers. All this was greatly changed under the Weimar constitution. Separation of Church and State now had a practical meaning. The revolutionary Social Democratic government did not depend on the Church to further its program. Rather, because of the conservatisms of the Church and the Marxist characteristic of the new government, the one was a contradiction of the other.

"While it is true that the Weimar government did not permit any propaganda against religion or the Church *ex officio*, it did permit high representatives of the State, and private organizations, as, for instance, the German Labor unions, to indulge in propaganda against the Church. Also, the government ceased all financial support of the Church, which then had to resort to taxation of its followers. This occurred at the time when the sense for morality and respect for authority were at low ebb, a combination of circumstances which could not have been more unfortunate. I know that this was not entirely the fault of the German revolution, but, in great part, attributable to the Versailles Treaty.

"But we had to reckon with facts, and the situation was as bad as it could be. There was a serious decline in religion, and the decline was increasing. The Communistic labor unions fought against the Church savagely. The masses were influenced by fiery speeches against religion, and notary publics were at hand who for a fee of two marks would receipt exemptions from church membership. These receipts were valid under the law, and thus there was almost a daily decrease in church membership. In Berlin alone, at a single meeting, many hundreds availed themselves of this easy opportunity to void their church membership and thus escape contributions to church support. Laxity became general. Marriage under religious auspices became more and more infrequent. People preferred to have the rites performed by civil authorities. Marriage became merely a simple legal contract, easily undertaken and easily dissolved. Many dispensed with even the civil rites, preferring to live in illegal union and to separate whenever it suited their whims. They called it 'companionate marriage.' They thought it nothing to be ashamed of, since there were examples of such marriage among high ranking officials, notably of a high Prussian Cabinet minister, who had worked himself up from a simple laborer to Cabinet rank. He had married a woman who came from the same *milieu*, and had become ashamed of her when she was unable to keep pace with him in his advance. So he separated from her and associated himself with another woman, appearing with her in public. This, of course, had its influence, for what was deemed right and proper for a high official would be right and proper for those of humbler rank.

"Attendance in church declined. Fewer and fewer children were being baptized. The new constitution had abolished compulsory attendance at religious courses in the schools. Children over fourteen could decide for themselves whether they wished to learn anything about religion or not. For children under fourteen the decision rested with the parents. Add to all this the extremely bad financial situation of the Evangelical Church, which did not possess accumulated funds, as did the Catholic Church, and you can see into what a perilous state the religious welfare of the people had fallen. The lack of funds made it impossible for us to fulfill our charitable tasks, and the struggle became one for bare existence. Statistics showed that if these conditions continued, the Church as an organization would be destroyed within thirty years.

"It became clear, then, that the existence of the Evangelical Church depended on her continued connection with the State. What we should have done was to try for reconciliation with the Stare, but we failed to do so. The Catholics, on the other hand, were glad to get rid of their connection with the State, and since they didn't need State support they were able to use their freedom to make Catholic policy. They threw their parliamentary representation to the so-called Center Party, which was able to influence the policy of the country. But the Evangelical Church refused to come to terms with the Social Democratic government, because in doing so it would have lost every vestige of freedom. So we tried to come to agreement with the political parties which aimed at restoring the conditions which had existed before 1918. The most suitable party seemed to be the German National Party, whose leader was Herr Hugenberg.

"But, in the course of time, we became persuaded that the program of this party did not lend itself to our purpose. This was the time when the Nazi Party was gaining more and more in strength, and it attracted our attention. The Nazi leaders then were laying great emphasis on the necessity of reconstructing political conditions as they had existed before the German revolution of 1918. They always declared that the abolishment of the German monarchy was the source of our present misfortune. National Socialism, they said, contemplated the restoration of the Empire based on social justice. They looked upon themselves, they asserted, as mediators between the people and the future German crown.

"All this appealed very much to us because we thought that we had a common aim and that after their success at the polls the Nazis would be able to unite the people and help build a new empire. Although we were aware that the Nazi ideology was, in part, directed against the Jews and that it apparently favored some sort of paganism, we were, as I must admit, little concerned with that. For we took these new shibboleths merely as slogans which would be useful to attract the masses, which would be dropped as soon as the Nazis attained power and assumed political responsibility. Our opinion in this respect was confirmed by Hitler, Rosenberg, Gregor Strasser and others, with whom we had contact before 1933. We were under the impression, therefore, that we would be able to influence the Party and so reduce its radicalism during the period that would elapse before the reconstruction of the Empire. So many of the Evangelical clergy, including myself, did not hesitate to give our support to Hitler, little realizing the full import of our action.

"As soon as we had decided to support the National Socialist Party we got into touch with its leader and informed them of our decision. It was received with great enthusiasm, for the Nazis seemed aware of its importance and to believe that they had made a long step forward in obtaining such support. And so again the Evangelical Church became a strong factor in the life of the nation. At least, that is what we believed. Hitler himself wrote to the Federal Council of the Evangelical Churches, thanking them for their co-operation and promising to further their rights and interests. Alfred Rosenberg, too, declared that religious faith would be necessary for the rebuilding of the morals of our people.

"We were anxious to take practical measures as soon as possible for the fulfillment of the program. The question was whether the political transformation should be effected by a *coup d'etat* or by parliamentary procedure. The decision was not in our hands alone. We had to come to an understanding with the leaders of the Conservative Party, which, in spite of its relatively small membership, still played a very important political role in the person of President von Hindenburg. In the beginning of 1931 the leaders of the Conservative Party held a meeting, at which President

Hindenburg was represented by his son. Colonel von Hindenburg. Through him President Hindenburg let us know that he desired nothing more than the restoration of the Empire. But he was compelled to refuse to consent to a *coup d'etat* because it would be a violation of his sworn pledge to govern according to the Constitution. However, this would not hinder him from supporting a popular movement, provided that it was backed by a majority of the people. Besides, Germany's political relations with foreign Powers would have to be considered, because Germany's situation at that time would make it necessary either to ask for their consent to such an important change in her domestic political structure or to choose a time when the international situation would place Germany in such a strong position that she would be able to proceed without any such consultation.

"This declaration by President von Hindenburg was accepted. Herr von Jannschau-Oldenburg, who was the driving force of the Conservative Party and one of the closest friends and advisers of President von Hindenburg, said that he, too, considered a popular movement as the better means to reconstruct the Empire, because it could be used to revive the military instincts of the people, so that when *der Tag* should arrive a well-trained military force would enable the government to suppress domestic resistance or to take the field against foreign foes.

"Hitler was informed of this decision. At first, he became very excited, because he had expected support for an immediate *coup d'etat,* but was compelled to agree. He was warned that if he attempted violence the army would be used against him.

"A short time later I met Adolf Hitler for the first time in my life."

V

NIEMOELLER MEETS HITLER

THE CONVERSATIONS between Pastor Niemoeller and myself occurred at intervals, and we were never completely without interruption. Sometimes the other prisoners would break in on us with casual whisperings. Under the circumstances the most trivial event would cause remark, if, indeed, any happenings, whether the falling of a leaf or little whirls of dust raised by the wind, could be called trivial when life itself seemed to be at a standstill. And there were occasions, too, when the guard was unusually surly and saw to it that we kept pace in our aimless walking. Round and round we went, until the guard herded us back into our cells to sleep the long night through if we could sleep, or to maintain a lonely vigil till the first streak of dawn broke the gloom.

When again Pastor Niemoeller had a chance to talk, he told me of that first meeting with Hitler. It seemed that the representatives of the Evangelical Church had asked Hitler to present to them in person his plans for the Church. Hitler agreed, and the meeting took place in the Hotel Kaiserhof.

"We were received by Joseph Goebbels, whose manner was very attentive and courteous, a little too much so, I thought," Pastor Niemoeller told me. "Hitler himself arrived late, and we had to wait half an hour for him. When he arrived, he apologized for his tardiness, saying that the airplane from Munich to Berlin had been delayed. He was wearing civilian clothes, and was especially polite and obliging. One of my fellow clergymen took notice of the sumptuous surroundings, and said to me in an aside, 'The splendor of these rooms must surely be beyond Herr Hitler's pocketbook.' But we paid little attention to that. We were eager to hear what Hitler had in store for the Church. Before he began speaking, he bowed deeply."

Pastor Niemoeller recalled for me what Hitler said, and I shall repeat it as best I can. The substance is correct, though the words may not be exactly the same.

"Reverend sirs," Hitler said, "I have gladly accepted your invitation in order to make known to you my program for the churches. I would like to convince you that I am working for the moral recovery of our nation just as you are.

"Since her defeat, Germany needs Christianity more than ever. She needs the churches. We must halt the movement of the godless. We need your support. We need the support of all who have the interests of the Fatherland at heart. I am a Catholic, but I ask for your help in my work. I assure you that it is my aim—and I consider it as part of my mission— to give back to the churches the position they held before the unfortunate revolution. The future State will do everything possible to strengthen the moral authority of religion. For the State we contemplate must be founded on the mysticism which only religion can give it."

Then, Pastor Niemoeller said, Hitler asked for proposals from the churches. He wanted them to present plans for co-operation.

"He promised us," Pastor Niemoeller told me, "financial support, control of the schools, and real collaboration on the part of the State if he should attain power. He promised to restore all the churches' rights, which we could not hope to attain under the Weimar Republic. We were all very favorably impressed with his talk and with his apparent modesty, and I know that from that day on, until our eyes were opened, Hitler had the full support of the Protestant Church in Germany.

"After his address. Hitler had a short talk with Goebbels, and I saw Goebbels point me out to him. Then, suddenly, Hitler came up to me and said, 'I am glad to see you here, *Herr Kapitaenleutnant.*' I replied that I was no longer an officer, but a clergyman. Hitler seemed a little embarrassed by my reply, and said, 'It is people like you that the new Germany will need—you who have gone from a U-boat to the pulpit. The Christian Church in Germany needs today the heroes of the last war.'"

It was in the spring of 1932 that Pastor Niemoeller had his second interview with Hitler, and it was in that interview that Hitler began to unmask himself. At that time the country was anticipating Hitler's seizure of power in the near future. This is what Pastor Niemoeller told me of that interview. It must be remembered, in the meantime, that Pastor Niemoeller went over his reminiscences many times, so that I retain a clear recollection of the substance of all he told me.

"We representatives of the United Protestant Churches of Germany," he said, "wanted to secure from Hitler some very concrete promises and answers to our questions. I found Hitler, Goering, Hess and Rosenberg together. It was one of the most important meetings that the German Protestant Churches ever had with the Nazi heads.

"'I come to you,' I said to Hitler, 'because the Church authorities often read Nazi newspaper attacks on the Church, because the proper Christian spirit is not always evident in the Hitler Youth and in the Storm Troops, and because of the many murders, which are hard for us to explain and excuse.'

"'Murders!' answered Hitler, greatly excited. 'Can you call them murders? The Storm Troopers are ridding Germany of the Communists and the Marxists, of the Jews and the Liberals. That is not murder. That is self-defense. But I shall never permit a hair of the head of a member of the Church to be harmed.'

"Then he became very gentle, and there was a pleading note in his voice. 'Please be sure to understand me,' he said. 'I have ahead of me a great task, my life's work. The masses cannot always be fed with bread and sugar; they need the whip too. I must beat the drum and work like a slave. I must organize and convince in order to put the country on its feet again. I must wake the country up to its danger—get rid of the Jewish republic, which certainly has nothing for Christianity.'

"We replied that the Church could never tolerate such things as were going on. We could not participate in the destruction of a part of our people; we wanted, rather, to convert them to Christianity. The State we had in mind should be ruled by the principles of Christianity, one of which is love for our fellow men. We insisted that we could not be enemies of the Jews, but must include them in the community.

"To all this Hitler replied, 'When I am Chancellor of the Reich I shall restore the connection between Church and State. The Church will receive financial support from the State, as it did in Prussia. The Church will be permitted to exert its influence in the education of the youth. I am not yet in a position to conclude any contracts. However, I give you my solemn word of honor that I shall do what I say. These are election times. Shootings may occur, but I promise that the Church will be re-established in all its rights.'

"Luther once prophesied that a terrible darkness would come over Germany because of contempt for the Bible.

How little did I realize then that this prophecy would come true in the very near future. For at that time I thought that good was beginning to overcome evil, that the people had reasserted themselves, and that Luther must have had in mind some other period. The last fourteen years under the Democratic republic were the years of darkness, when men could with impunity criticize God and the Church, and refuse to pay their Church assessments. Now, I thought, the years of light were returning, as is always the case after periods of darkness. That is what I told my family and my friends. Today I know that it was altogether wrong that the Evangelical Church should offer its support to Hitler. I was mad to believe him."

When Hitler finally took over the reins of government, the Evangelical Churches, as Pastor Niemoeller told me, were persuaded that their hopes would be realized, and, indeed. Hitler solemnly stated before the Reichstag on March 21, 1933, that the Third Reich would be established on a Christian foundation and would maintain the closest co-operation with the churches. The Evangelical churchmen were jubilant. Not only would domestic peace be reestablished and the country be put upon a sound domestic policy and be once more restored to the comity of nations, but also the former prestige of the Church would be enhanced. Hitler had become the man of the hour. Fears among foreign observers that the shadows again were lengthening over Europe were baseless. Hitler maintained close contact with the leaders of the Conservative Party, and at the first public meeting at Potsdam church bells throughout the country were rung.

"But soon," Pastor Niemoeller told me when we were able to resume our conversations, "we were shockingly awakened from our pleasant dreams. There was no cessation of the propaganda against the churches, as had been promised time and time again by Hitler and his lieutenants. On the contrary, it was intensified. During the time that the Nazis were consolidating their political position they did not attack the churches directly. But when they felt that their position was secure, they put forth a plan for reconstituting the churches that we could not possibly accept. The plan was to unify all the churches in Germany, and to force them to adjust their doctrines to the Nazi ideology. Without waiting for our consent, or even consulting us, Hitler appointed an army chaplain, Ludwig Mueller, as Reichsbishop. The creation of this new office meant the closest supervision of the Church by the State. The Reichsbishop had supreme control of all the Churches of Christ in Germany.

"The indignant protests of the Evangelical and Roman Catholic Churches were answered with the explanation that in the new Germany only one church could be allowed to exist. And if that church expected moral and financial assistance from the State, it would have to conform to the policies of the State."

Here let me interpolate what part, as it turned out, the Nazis designed the German churches to play in the "new order" they were setting up. They maintained that the doctrines of brotherly love, charity, forgiveness, and international co-operation to forward the cause of Christ were in direct conflict with Nazi doctrine, and so had to be discarded. It would be the purpose of the "Evangelical National Socialists" to build up a national church. Therefore the Party demanded:

1. Rejection of the so-called Jewish-Marxist influence in the churches.
2. Rejection of the "humanism" bom of the Jewish-Marxist spirit, with all its ramifications of pacifism and Christian cosmopolitanism.
3. Emphasis on a militant faith in the destiny of the God-given German nation.

4. Purification and preservation of the German race.
5. Opposition to any doctrine which would be hostile to this theory and to all activities which would serve to undermine it.
6. A new spirit in the private and official positions in the management of the Church.
7. Union of the small Evangelical Churches in each province into a strong Evangelical Church of the Reich. All imputations that it was desired to make the Church a political institution were to be rejected. The "Evangelical National Socialists" were not acting as a party, but were following a call of God, heard in the movement of the people.

The document in which this was set forth was signed by Dr. Sieffert.

As early as 1932, Captain Ernst Roehm, the head of the Storm Troopers, who was purged two years later, introduced a rule under which each company of Storm Troopers had to have a chaplain of the rank of a *Sturmbannfuehrer*. Even the purely terroristic groups had their National-Socialist chaplains, who excused and blessed everything the party required of them.

These National Socialist Protestants combined into a group sanctioned by Party and State, called the "German Christians," which soon spread all over Germany. Theirs was the gospel of a German religion, presided over by a German god, whose son and envoy on earth was the Fuehrer, Adolf Hitler. It was the duty of this organization to bring in a majority for Hitler's party in the church elections, and in the spring of 1933, when the church elections were held, after a period of terrorism, the National Socialist Protestants did win a majority, since no one dared to challenge Goering, and Frick, Minister of the Interior, and Kube, all three of whom belonged to the honorary committee heading the

German Christians. At the first national meeting of the German Christians, in April, 1933, *Oberpraesident Kube*, who was arrested later for graft, declared in his capacity as leader of the Prussian National Socialist faction, "This assembly will act relentlessly, and with all the means at our disposal, in reorganizing the nation, even in the field of church politics." At this same meeting Dr. Werner, a lawyer, and later Minister of Churches, proclaimed officially, for the first time, the principle of leadership for the Church: "What the Fuehrer orders, the Church must carry out."

Thus the Nazis assumed control of the Church, and every one who would not swear allegiance to Hitler was discharged from his position. The Christian clergy were horrified, and searched about for measures to save the Church from disintegration. They formed the Pastors' Emergency League, and then reorganized themselves into the Confessional Church. Pastor Niemoeller, of course, sided with the Confessional Church.

The open break came when Ludwig Mueller, who had earned Hitler's favor by providing him with lodging on his tours in East Prussia, when Hitler was unable to pay a hotel bill, was made Reichsbishop. Towards the end of 1933 matters had progressed so far that the Church had to accept the new doctrines or face direct assault. The Jews who had accepted Christianity were the first to fall under the ban.

Hitler's evil enterprise was gaining ground, but obstacles lay ahead. One was Martin Niemoeller.

VI

HITLER, "THE SAVIOR OF MANKIND"

A S WE continued our trudging in the dusty circle in which our lives were circumscribed Pastor Niemoeller took up the thread of the story of his unflagging battle with the relentless Hitler, and I came to see, more and more, that he was made of the stuff of martyrdom. Hitler had all the powers of evil at his command, but Niemoeller's strength lay in his trust in God. His convictions were the sinews of his character.

"When we renewed our protests against his assumption of authority over the Church," Pastor Niemoeller told me, "Hitler didn't think it worth while to give any answer at all. Ignoring all his promises, he appointed ministers for the churches in the several States, and in Prussia gave the office to Kerri, who had no qualification for the office other than excessive brutality. Soon the Church war was at its height. The Old Testament was being vilified as Jewish propaganda, and persecution of the Jews raged throughout the country. Priests and clergy were being placed in prisons and concentration camps. The Gestapo was taking down all sermons in shorthand, and quite literally was tearing pastors from their pulpits to throw them into prison.

"In this hour of peril for the German Confessional Church I decided to resort to a direct appeal to Hitler. I thought that if I could talk to him as man to man I might be able to persuade him of the evil being perpetrated by his henchmen and convince him that they were not only endangering all Germany but also himself. I still believed in his personal honesty and imagined that because of his preoccupation with affairs of State he could not know what was being done to the Church in his name. I requested an audience with him, and he agreed to receive me on January 5, 1934.

"At the Chancellory I had to wait a long time in Hitler's anteroom. Troopers bustled in and out, and secretaries were busy at their desks, but no one took any notice of me. I couldn't help thinking how greatly times had changed. The Church had refused to deal with the Weimar Republic, but now had to go begging to the man whom it had helped to raise to power and who now treated its clergy and membership like traitors or common criminals. I tried to brush away all personal feeling, for I felt that now I represented only the Church and that any untoward action on my part might interfere with the object of my visit.

"Finally, I was led into Hitler's study. He received me with icy coldness. At our previous meetings he had always been cordial and had stressed our mutual interests as soldiers and veterans of the World War. His present attitude disturbed me greatly. He stood as I entered, but did not speak immediately. So, for a few moments, We stood staring at each other in silence. I could see a tremendous change in his expression since I had seen him before."

Here I couldn't help interrupting Pastor Niemoeller and asking him, "But how about yourself? Didn't you feel that you stood before Hitler as a representative of a much greater power than he? Nations will pass; political ideologies are the result only of momentary social conditions. But religion will be always. Your meeting with Hitler seems to me to be of the same historical importance as Martin Luther's stand before the Diet at Worms. You were even braver than Luther, because you knew that you had to deal with the incarnation of inhumanity and injustice."

But Niemoeller waved his hand in dissent. "I didn't even think of myself at that moment," he said. "There was no thought in my mind that I was watching history in the making. I felt very human, and all my thoughts were concentrated on the peril to our faith." He fell silent for a few moments, his head bowed in meditation. Then he continued, more as if talking to himself than to me. The guard was giving us no heed, and I lost my apprehension as I continued trudging behind Pastor Niemoeller.

"Yes, Hitler's face had changed," he went on in his usual subdued tone. "Its air of modesty, honesty and amiability, which I had anticipated, had disappeared. In it now appeared an air of authority, which probably the consciousness of power had given him, and, at the same time, there was something else, something terrible in his features. I can describe it only as an expression of ruthless cruelty, of cunning. Suddenly I knew that I had come on a useless errand, that Hitler had made up his mind. The Church, I felt, was lost, and then, at that exact moment, I felt that I was in the presence of the Antichrist."

Niemoeller paused, and I looked around, wondering whether the guard had heard. But his attention was on the large circle shuffling along in the endless path, heads down, expressionless faces. How quickly sameness can kill the spirit, like a hot wind blowing on a flower.

"Hitler seemed to be watching me closely," continued the monotone, "and I had the impression that he couldn't bear my staring at him.

"His eyelids twitched nervously, and suddenly he began to

talk. His voice was hoarse, with a shrill quality in it. 'You desire to speak to me, Pastor Niemoeller,' he said. 'What is it about?'

"'I know, Herr Reichschancellor,' I said, 'that you are overburdened with work for our Fatherland. I would not have dared take up your time had it not been for the welfare of the Church, whether it is to continue to exist or not under your regime.'

"'A question of the existence of the Church?' he repeated. 'Who is doing anything to the Church? Don't they know that the Church is under my protection?'

"'So you really don't know what is going on. You have been misinformed,' I said. Then I told him briefly of the events that had occurred during the past month, and he frowned and said very coolly, 'I shall have to disappoint you. All this has happened with my knowledge and approval. I have permitted it in order to fulfill my promises to the churches. The measures were necessary to secure the close connection between Church and State that you yourself greatly desired, and to make the Church a powerful institution in the National Socialist Reich.'

"When I heard this answer I knew that all my doubts and fears were confirmed, and that all my pleading would be useless. Also, I felt that it was an insult to my intelligence that Hitler could reduce himself to such a cheap reply. Nevertheless, I determined to say something, to leave no stone unturned if anything could be done to save the Church. So I said, 'Are you aware, Reichschancellor, that what you call "measures of protection for the Church" means that the Church will become nothing but an instrument of propaganda for the National Socialist movement, and that the clergy will be solicitors for the National Socialist government and expounders of the National Socialist doctrines as

religious principles? How can you expect us to do that? Do
you really think that we are so contemptible that we would
surrender the sacred faith given to us by God and accept any
kind of political ideology in its place?'

"'It will be necessary to adjust the Christian dogma to the
ideas which we National Socialists represent,' Hitler replied,
and then he said, 'You are mistaken in believing that this
would be harmful to the Church. The National Socialist ideology is more than a mere political program. It is a
Weltanschauung (world view), comprising everything of
importance for mankind, including religion. An adjustment
of the Christian dogma to the demands of our times will not
weaken the position of the Church, but strengthen it, and
will secure its unconditional backing by the great power of
the National Socialist State.'

"'Christian doctrine is not dependent on any time or
occasion,' I told him. 'It is God's Word, and we believe that
political doctrines should be founded on Christianity, and
not Christianity on political ideology. So we interpreted your
assurances before you assumed the Chancellorship, which
you yourself laid down in your decree of February, 1933.'

"Then Hitler showed signs of impatience [how often he was
to exhibit that impatience later], and said, 'If that is your opinion, Pastor Niemoeller, then our viewpoints are irreconcilable.
What you want to do is to establish an autonomous Church.
That can never be. That is nothing but the revival of the
aspirations of the Church in the first German Empire [the
so-called First German Empire, founded by Charlemagne],
which proved to be a misfortune for the German people. The
Protestant Church never made things difficult for the Prussian
kings. Why are you making matters difficult for me? What pre-
vents you from recognizing that I have supreme power over
the Church and its doctrines? Jesus Christ also was only a man,

and a Jew to boot. Why shouldn't I, who am more powerful than Christ, and who am able to be much more helpful than He—why shouldn't I have the right to establish a new dogma for the Church?'"

Pastor Niemoeller brushed a hand across his forehead. He was under a tremendous strain. It sounded incredible— this thing that Hitler had said, that he should set himself up as greater than Niemoeller's Christ, announce himself as the savior of humanity. But that is the story as it fell from Pastor Niemoeller's lips, and now that I am free, free to think and see and speak my little lines, I know that it is true. I know that this megalomaniac asserts that he has divine right and that the destiny of the German people, and, there-fore, of all humanity, rests in his hands. It has taken the world a long time to realize the satanic gifts Hitler has and the vast egoism that primes his actions and being.

"I reiterated to him," Pastor Niemoeller continued, "that the Prussian State was a Christian State, and that the Prussian kings never attempted to impose a political doc-trine as a religious doctrine. But Hitler screamed at me, 'Now I see what you are demanding. You think, then, that my State is not a Christian State, that it is inhuman and ruth-less. And you dare to tell me this to my face? Let me say this: I may be ruthless. I may be cruel, merciless; but I am so for the good and happiness of our Fatherland. I cannot tolerate deca-dence of any kind, even in the form of religion. My aim is to make Germany the only power in the world. I must, therefore, eliminate any kind of sickness, and I consider the sentimental feeling for Christianity as a kind of mental sickness.'

"Then his voice became suddenly low and calm. He said, 'Let's try to come together. I believe that every human activ-ity is directed by egoism. It is the basis of our National Socialism. And I find it rather hard to see what you hope to gain by keeping up your opposition to me. Wouldn't you rather co-operate with us? I would be glad to give you the position you deserve.' There was an ironic smile on his lips, as if he expected me to jump at his proposal.

"But now I became excited too. I felt the full insult of his words. He really believed that he could bribe me with money and position. When I calmed myself, I said to him, 'You misunderstand my motives entirely, Herr Reichschancellor. I did not come to you in order to ask for any advantage for myself. It is the anxiety for the Church which brought me to you, and my anxiety for Germany. The Third Reich cannot succeed unless it is founded on the principles of Christianity. We live in a Christian age, not in an age of barbarism. And I tell you that you will not accomplish what you are trying to do. You will succeed only in destroying yourself and our beautiful Fatherland.' "Then Hitler completely lost control of himself. The change in him was frightful. His whole body trembled, his eyes opened wide in a ferocious glare, and his voice was pitched in a screaming note of rage. He shouted, 'How dare you talk thus to me? Leave the destiny of the Third Reich to me. It is my work, and I will take care of it. You, as an officer, should have learned obedience. You will all have to obey. I determine what is Christian and what is not. I determine what the Church has to do. I am still the Fuehrer of the German people. God has selected me for that, and my people have called me. I alone am the Fuehrer.'

"The more excited Hitler grew, the calmer I became. When he stopped, I said, 'Then I have come in vain to you, Herr Reichschancellor.' Then I turned in order to leave the room. He screamed after me, 'Pastor Niemoeller, you will either have to come to terms, or you shall die—you shall die, as every one shall die who is in my way.'

"I heard his fists hammering on the desk as I left the room. His words were still hammering in my ears when I reached the street. The fresh wintry air felt like a blessing after that foul atmosphere, that atmosphere of blasphemy and desecration. But I realized that I was now entering the hardest struggle of my life, and I was determined never to give in, never to surrender.

"Afterwards Hitler sent word to me that he regretted his outburst and that a way for negotiations was still open. But when a short time before my arrest I again asked him for an audience he refused to see me."

VII

NIEMOELLER'S COURAGE IN PRISON

IT WAS now nearing the end of summer, when Pastor Niemoeller had been a month in Moabit prison.

Already the leaves of the linden tree were changing to yellow and the flowers were withering on their stalks. It seemed incongruous, sometimes, that a tree should choose to grow in a prison yard, that in such a somber scene little flowers should lift their heads, that birds should flutter above us while they had the freedom of all the skies. Tree and flowers and birds always engaged our intense interest. We noted the changing color of the leaves, the blooming and fading of the flowers, and the inevitable struggle of a few blades of grass to grow and live along the border of the little flower bed. It was as if nature were trying to lavish on us something from her ample store as a token of sympathy. And we knew that here was something beyond the power of evil, that following the decay there would be green growth again, that even the Nazis' hands could not stay the processes of nature. In a way, I suppose, such thoughts stirred the hearts of us all. There is something in the yearly resurrection on which men learn to lean when hope begins to falter and life seems to have lost its purpose. At any rate, I knew, deep in my heart, that there would still be something green and growing when this evil hour was done.

From our cells we could hear the gay blasts of trumpets in the barracks only a few blocks away. Here men and boys were being trained to carry out the "new order" that was old before Hitler was born. Even in prison there is a presage of coming events. One feels it, even though there is no word.

I began to observe a remarkable physical change in Pastor Niemoeller. He seemed to be getting thinner every day. His temples were graying, and the lines in his face were becoming deeper and deeper, indicating the intense mental suffering through which he was passing. Sometimes he complained about his stomach, for he depended entirely on prison food. He was not permitted, as were the other prisoners, to buy additional food with his own money. This was probably to make him feel the full severity of prison life, an effort to break his will power. Nor was he permitted any mental distraction. Each cell was provided with a copy of the New Testament. But Pastor Niemoeller requested a copy of the Old Testament, and his request was denied. When he applied for books from the prison library, literature dealing with the Nazi ideology was offered to him. Among the books he was thus invited to read were a copy of *Mein Kampf* and of Rosenberg's *Myth of the Twentieth Century*, which he refused to accept.

Also, as were the rest of us, Pastor Niemoeller was subjected to the rigid military discipline of the prison. Although a former officer and one to whom the whole country had paid tribute, he had to obey orders of guards who were either former petty officers of the army or young men whose only qualifications were that they were thoroughly imbued with Nazi doctrine. Though there was no actual brutality here, the discipline was such as to inflict mental torture. During his first weeks in prison, probably as the result of a personal order from Hitler, guards would enter Pastor Niemoeller's cell every fifteen or twenty minutes to inspect it. Niemoeller would have to spring from his chair each time a guard entered and rush to the cell window, stand at attention, and report, "Prisoner Niemoeller, charged with high treason against Fuehrer and Reich, reporting respectfully that his cell is in order."

I could hear the rattle of the keys every time a guard opened Pastor Niemoeller's cell. This behavior was unusual, and when I questioned him about the guards' frequent visits, Niemoeller told me of the routine he had to pass through, and added that most of the guards accepted his report with a sneer. Then they would look over the cell, and say, "You dare report this cell being in order! Look, there is some dust on the lamp," or, "The floor is dirty," or something else in the way of reprimand. And sometimes one would add, "Why, weren't you once an officer, and didn't you learn cleanliness and order? If not, we will teach you." Then he would be made to clean the floor or furniture again.

I could see that Pastor Niemoeller was very sensitive to such behavior. He felt the humiliation very deeply. "Yes," he said once, "they make it as hard as possible for me. Their tactics are to make me feel that I am nothing but a common criminal."

This attitude of the guards had another effect on Pastor Niemoeller. Deprived of any sort of occupation or other means to pass the long hours, he became more and more retrospective. What he could not find outside of himself, he found inside. He concentrated his thoughts on God and on the religious faith which had brought him face to face with Hitler's evil displeasure. Alone in his cell, he told me, he found inner strength and even happiness.

"Never before," he once told me, "have I felt the power of prayer so strongly as here in prison. When I pray I feel as if the walls of my cell fall away, and I have a feeling of happiness

I have never experienced before. Sometimes I feel that God has frustrated the evil purpose of His enemies by giving me strength to further His glory. This is God's own means of meeting His enemies."

As I have already said, this attitude of the guards towards Niemoeller was unusual. Towards the other prisoners they were generally correct in their behavior. Some of them were older men, men who did not always conceal the fact that they did not entirely approve of the Nazi regime. Because of my long confinement in Moabit I had become acquainted with some of them. They would come to my cell for a little chat, and, when I had them, they gladly accepted cigarettes and tobacco from me, since they were badly paid and could afford to buy little for themselves. The other guards, who had obtained their positions through their Nazi connections, were younger and were fervent followers of Hitler. But even they were not immune to proffers of cigarettes and tobacco and knew when to relax.

I had a rather special friend among the guards, a man named Klimke, who had served as a petty officer in the Imperial Army and had been wounded in the World War. He had obtained his job in the prison because of his war services, but being a man who had become accustomed to the old order and to whom the caldron of the new must have been rather frightening, he was ready at times to speak his mind. One can still find, I suppose, among the older generation of Germans a nostalgia for the order that existed before Germany became crazed with the Nazi fever, and I have no doubt that they live in fear of the day of retribution.

Klimke would sometimes utter his disapproval of the Nazi regime, and I would admonish him to be cautious, fearing that his opinions might become known and bring to him and his family the reprisals the Nazis knew so well how to inflict. But he would say, "I know that I can talk frankly to you and that you will not betray me." When I asked him one day, during a cautious interview, why the guards treated Pastor Niemoeller with such severity, he told me that on the day Pastor Niemoeller was brought in the guards had been summoned by the prison director for a special interview. The prison director was accompanied by a representative of the Gestapo, who was dressed in the uniform of the Elite Guard. The Gestapo official instructed the guards that Pastor Niemoeller was to be considered as a public enemy of the worst sort because he had opposed the Fuehrer and had intended to try to deliver Germany to her enemies, that he had accepted money from foreign Powers, and had betrayed State secrets. He was in favor of restoring the Empire, which, said the Gestapo official, would oppress the people by establishing a feudal State subject to the authority of the Church. Pastor Niemoeller, therefore, was to be looked upon as an outcast, as a disgrace to the German people, and was to be subjected to the severest discipline.

"This order," said the Gestapo official, "has been signed and sealed by our Fuehrer himself. Every one who disobeys it will be considered as an enemy of the Fuehrer and the State."

Klimke appeared to be laboring under some stress when he told me this. "That is the reason why we treat Pastor Niemoeller so," he said. "We are compelled to do so, otherwise our lives would be in danger. But, in spite of it all, I tell you frankly that I don't like it. I am an old soldier, and I can imagine very well what it means to a man like Pastor Niemoeller to be subjected to such insults. He must suffer terribly. I have never believed all these charges against him, but I am not educated enough to understand the real reason for his being here. But I do feel that even if he has offended the Fuehrer this is a cheap kind of revenge on a helpless man. They always talk of National Socialist chivalry, but this surely is not chivalry, and it couldn't have happened under the Empire, or even in the Republic."

The old fellow seemed genuine enough and I felt that I could trust him. Still, I deemed it to be the better part of wisdom to be careful in talking with him. One could never be sure that he was not talking to a spy, and I knew well enough how easy it was to place a misconstruction on any-thing one might say. I wonder now, sometimes, whether the German people will ever get over their mistrust of one another. Men have betrayed their friends, and sons have betrayed fathers. How, then, could one always be sure of a friend, or a father be sure of his son? What a terrible thing Hitler has done to the most sacred of human relations. To build, he must destroy the hearth, the very family altar itself.

Very cautiously, I explained to Klimke the reason why Pastor Niemoeller had incurred the wrath of Hitler and been brought to his present plight. "So that's it," Klimke replied, somewhat excitedly. "I didn't know that they brought him to prison because he had defended our faith. Is it really true? But I know it must be true," he hastened to add, "because there is something in Pastor Niemoeller's face which shows that he could never be guilty of such accusations. He does not look like a criminal or a traitor. He looks more like a saint to me. I shall never molest him again." He reflected for a few moments, and then said, "My colleagues ought to know all this. But I don't dare tell them, because you can't trust even your most intimate friend these days."

Klimke was of the solid type of German peasant, and his limited education is typical of the masses. During my stay in the United States I have observed that the intelligence and educational standards of the German people are greatly overrated. The truth is, the majority of Germans are too lit-tle educated and trained in politics to be able to form inde-pendent judgments. This was the case under the Empire, and there was little improvement under the Weimar Republic. It was, therefore, relatively easy for the Nazis to gain control of the popular mind. Lacking basic education, the people could have no historic sense, and that was true which was told them. Education in Germany has always been a class privilege, because the average German earns so little money that he cannot afford to send son or daughter to gymnasium (the equivalent of a course in high school and two years in college in the United States) and a university. Also, the class distinction is so clearly marked that even if they could afford it, workers and small peasants feel that they would be overreaching themselves if they sent their children to the higher institutions of learning. It is not as it is in the United States, where educational opportunities are open to all who strive for them. So, even today, the general custom is that the son shall follow the father in his occupation. It is very seldom that a member of the peasant class attends a university. Among all the students who attended my classes there were not more than five or six who came from a family of laborers or peasants. And even they could not overcome a feeling of inferiority, which was not relieved by the continual snubbing they received from students of higher social standing.

The standards of the *Gemeinde Schule* (community school, which corresponds somewhat to the elementary schools here), attendance at which is compulsory, are very low, and those who finish are hardly more than able to write their names. Educational privileges are limited in order to preserve the class distinctions. As Bismarck once said, "There is no need in Germany for an intellectual proletariat, for if there were one the masses would become dissatisfied with their condition and be incited to revolution." Actually, it is their lack of learning that has made it easy for Hitler to promote his fallacies among them.

On the other hand, the standard of education for the so-called privileged classes was very high. At the universities the greatest emphasis was laid on a most thorough training, to the almost entire neglect of sports. A finished education was the *sine qua non* for a government post. Officials were not elected by the people, but appointed by the government. This system made it certain that only the highly trained obtained posts. At the same time, only members from the same clique got into office. This system continued under the Weimar Republic, which not only did not dare to challenge the old legal requirements, but did not have candidates from the other classes fitted for office. Even Hitler was confronted with the same dilemma, and this is one of the reasons why he was not taken seriously by the intellectuals when he first thrust himself on the scene. On his side Hitler had the deepest hatred for the intellectuals. Being himself of humble rank, he put his chief reliance in the masses, and by his powers of declamation and his promises to give them everything they wanted when he achieved power, succeeded in getting them to the polls and voting him into office. Before his rise, forty per cent of the people had never cast a vote, so completely ignorant and negligent of politics were they. Of course Hitler did succeed in gaining converts among the intellectuals, because they saw in his success the fruits of the common aim to restore Germany to her former prestige and also a continuance of themselves as the dominant power in the new nation that was to be. Hitler made promises to both sides, and kept none. Not only did he not raise the living standards of the laboring classes, but lowered them still further by reducing wages. What happened to the intellectuals outside of those he gathered immediately about him is one of the tragedies with which the outside world is now well acquainted.

Herein, I believe, is one of Hitler's reasons for his persecution of the Jews. He saw in them the personification of the intellectuals he hated with such an incredible hatred, and they were easy prey. He could make it appear that they were the chief opponents of his theories, and certainly they were beyond the pale built around his racial doctrine, although before his advent intermarriage was common. He needed a scapegoat, and in the Jews he could find one that had been forced to accept that role in every era. In unifying sentiment against them he could unify Germany and by promoting anti-Semitism throughout the world disengage attention from his real purpose. Also, it aided him in arousing the blood lust which has never been far below the German exterior. Racial hatred, always a convenient curtain for evil design, has served no one better than Hitler.

A short time after Hitler took over, laws were passed by which the educational system was changed considerably. This left the public school system untouched, but the gymnasiums and the universities were subjected to violent "reform." They were ordered to adapt themselves forthwith to the National Socialist ideology. Courses in religion were abolished, and history, philosophy, literature, jurisprudence, and even science, had to be taught and interpreted in the light of the new ideology. Thus Hitler struck at the very roots of German culture and civilization and made fallow the very areas in which Germany had made the most progress. Pure science, in which Germans had made such remarkable advance, was reduced to the lowest possible standard. Indeed, research became a fraud and forgery a science. Professors were at the Nazis' beck and call, and new theories were advanced every day to gull the conscience and allay the national temper for exactness.

Of course, there were professors, some of them inclined to sympathize with the Nazis' national policy, who rebelled against this abasement. But they were soon made to understand that they either had to accept the new teaching or suffer the consequences. Many of them resigned and were replaced by younger men, who adopted the Nazi "science" and wore the SS uniform, and some left Germany before the ax fell. And they were as pure Aryans as any Hitler managed to call to his colors. Students, too, were numbered among the rebels. I recall the story of a student in one of the famous universities who publicly mimicked the manner in which Hitler ate asparagus and thus displayed his lack of breeding. In Germany the correct way of eating asparagus is to take a stalk on one's fork and eat it slowly, in small mouthfuls. Hitler, according to the story, shoved a whole stalk at a time into his mouth and gulped it down like a pig. The student's mimicry was greeted with roars of laughter, and became a subject of widespread talk among students generally. The story came to Hitler's ears, and the student and his friends were arrested by the Gestapo. But because they belonged to influential families. President von Hindenburg intervened and they were released. But Hitler did not forget. Immediately on his taking over of the Chancellorship after Hindenburg's death he ordered all university clubs dissolved. This caused temporary excitement among the students and the older generation to whom the clubs had been part of university life. Among them, for instance, were Von Papen, Von Neurath, and many other men of high military or diplomatic rank. Hitler is as humorless as Satan.

To resume, the guard Klimke apparently had been won over by Pastor Niemoeller, and when he was not under observation by the other guards, treated Niemoeller with the greatest consideration and respect. As I did not notice afterwards that the guards regarded Klimke other than as completely one of themselves, I felt that he had not told them what he had learned from me.

Even in the prison yard Pastor Niemoeller was subjected to humiliation. The guard on duty would suddenly call out his name, which meant that Pastor Niemoeller had to rush towards him, stop within three steps of him, and stand at attention. Then the guard would sneer at him, "Now, Prisoner Niemoeller, how do you feel? How do you like our prison? Do you feel that you have learned something, or are you still a criminal?"

Niemoeller's face would turn to the color of cold ashes, but he would not answer a word in reply. He would continue standing at attention until dismissed, as was the rule, and look at the guard as if not seeing him. This would exasperate the guard, who would continue his insults in the hope of provoking Niemoeller into an angry retort, in which case he could be sent into solitary confinement in a dark cell in the prison basement, without a bed, and with no food but bread and water.

Indeed, Pastor Niemoeller did retort one day. A young guard who had just come straight from the Hitler Youth became so angry at Pastor Niemoeller's attentive inattention to him that he screamed, "If you don't look at me immediately, I will slap your face, you dirty criminal."

Niemoeller stiffened. He became the officer again, and his voice rang out, stilling us all into attention, "You have overstepped your authority. I will report you to the administration for punishment."

Taken by surprise, the guard attempted to speak, but was silenced.

"Attention!" Niemoeller's voice rang out again, "Don't you realize to whom you are talking?" A faint color had risen in his cheeks. He was a commander once more, giving an order and expecting immediate obedience. Every one of the rest of us stood still in his tracks, expecting the guard to lead Pastor Niemoeller away. But he was cowed, and became immediately apologetic. His little authority could not weigh in the balance against the word of an officer. Before Pastor

Niemoeller could continue what evidently he had in mind to say, the young guard pleaded in a low voice, "Will you please go back to your place, Herr Pastor Niemoeller."

Pastor Niemoeller turned on his heels and immediately returned to his place in the ranks. Head high, chest out, he stepped firmly. The guard, his face rather flushed, walked off a few paces, and then turned, trying not to look as crestfallen as he must have felt. I have often wondered, however, if he did not feel then a slight tinge of remorse. He could not but have heard of Niemoeller's reputation as an officer, of his bravery, and of the many enemy ships he had sunk. Even an upstart must feel an atom of respect in such a presence.

I noticed the other prisoners grinning as the guard looked away. They glanced at Pastor Niemoeller admiringly. He had done what they had not dared. His courage gave them courage. Even Mueller, the ghoul, who had behaved hostilely towards Niemoeller, glanced at him approvingly, and whispered, rather loudly I thought, "That was well done, Pastor Niemoeller. You put the swine in his place."

And then Mueller received another surprise. "He is not a swine," said Pastor Niemoeller. "He is a poor, misled human being who knows nothing but to expose his evil side. He doesn't yet know the fear of God." Then, as we continued our interrupted trudging, he fell into a meditative silence.

VIII

FRIEND OF THE FRIENDLESS

DURING his first month in prison Pastor Niemoeller had appeared to be engrossed in his own thoughts much of the time, and the relationship between him and his fellow prisoners was rather vague. There had been several Catholic priests in our cell block before Pastor Niemoeller's arrival, and they had been greeted with indifference, if not hostility, by the other prisoners, most of whom were common criminals, Communists, or Nazis, who looked upon religion only as a refuge for the weak and dependent. But these same men soon began to regard Pastor Niemoeller in a different light. There was no air of weakness about him, rather every indication of an inner strength totally lacking in themselves, and they couldn't fail to show him some respect. They had learned something about him from Judge Preiser, who, of course, knew of Pastor Niemoeller's career in the navy and his subsequent entrance into the ministry. Although Preiser tried to color the story of Niemoeller's arrest in favor of the Nazis, thereby probably trying to aid himself, the prisoners sensed something of the truth, to which I added when opportunity presented itself. I took pains to inform them that Pastor Niemoeller had submitted to ignominy and suffering rather than surrender his conscience to Hitler, and that it was still possible for him to regain his freedom with a

word. That impressed them, for surely there must be something beyond ordinary comprehension in a man who would
stay in prison when he could so easily get out. Not only that,
he faced death itself, for the extreme penalty was meted out
to those who were convicted of high treason, which they
soon learned was the charge against the new arrival.

Now and then, during those first few weeks, Pastor
Niemoeller would inquire of me about the prisoners, but, on
the whole, his attitude towards them was passive. This was
quite understandable to me, who, too, had been too much
concerned in my own affairs to pay much attention to the
unfortunates about me. Niemoeller had just been separated
from his family, his friends, and his life's work, and he was
feeling his position keenly. The humiliation of prison life was
made worse by the refined ill-treatment accorded him, and
the privation was affecting him physically. On top of that was
the uncertainty of his fate. He must now have been fully aware
that he would never receive consideration from Hitler, who
himself had no family ties and no real friends. If I may inter-
rupt myself a moment, that is another fact about Hitler that
has always impressed me, that he had no intimate associates,
that he had veiled his early life, that he could call no man
brother, that, so far as I know, the word *mother* had never been
heard to fall from his lips. And yet the ties of family have
always been a marked characteristic of the German people.

Pastor Niemoeller's trial had been set for the middle of
August, and he had been informed that he would go before
a special court. But his trial had been postponed, for what
reason he had not been informed, and he was kept in a constant state of suspense. This was probably due to deliberate
design. Mental torture was one of the Nazis' favorite
weapons.

One day when he came into the prison yard looking more
than usually pale, I asked him whether he was feeling ill,

although I generally avoided making such inquiries, as there was a sort of silent agreement among the prisoners, especially among the more cultured, not to ask personal questions. Indeed, I used to feel put out myself if any prisoner asked me how I felt or how I had passed the night. But on that day Pastor Niemoeller looked so ill that I could not forbear making a sympathetic inquiry.

"Yes," he said to me, "I don't feel well today. My body is beginning to rebel against all this. I haven't been able to sleep during the past few nights. But I see no reason to be ashamed of it. For suffering is not important, but to overcome suffering. Our Saviour suffered, but did not hesitate to take the Cross. To be a Christian means to suffer. Every one of us has to earn his title of Christian."

At first Pastor Niemoeller's attitude of resignation seemed so far beyond reason that I sought elsewhere for his granite determination. I wondered whether it was not his training as an officer that had made his will so inflexible. This seemed the most plausible explanation, and it is one I often met with after my arrival in the United Stares. But I was not long in learning that it was not Niemoeller's training as a naval officer that made him adamant where his convictions were concerned. He had always been a mystic, had always sought outside of materialism for an explanation of life. Perhaps he was not conscious of this spiritual disturbance in him during his early career; it had overcome him after the World War, and he had found the freedom for which he had hungered. He had passed through the agonizing experience out of which the early Christian martyrs were made. I look upon him now as a religious genius, akin to the saints. Only his faith could have enabled him willingly to sacrifice all hope of earthly success and happiness and to endure the harrowing experiences he endured.

One day Pastor Niemoeller seemed to cease his mental

gropings and to come out of himself. It was as if he had pulled himself out of the deeps and shaken his spirit. One of the causes of this physical awakening to his surroundings was the pitiful plight of a fellow prisoner. This man, Hahnke, who was approximately forty-five years old and the father of a large family, had been arrested for distributing mimeographed copies of Communistic newspapers. He had waited almost two years for his trial. On this day he had just been brought from the People's Court, where he had been sentenced to death on a charge of high treason. He had hoped vainly for a lesser punishment. His fate was certain, for there was no appeal from the People's Court. Following the regulations, he had been returned to his cell in Moabit prison, to be kept there until the prison administration received the order for his transfer to a death cell in Ploetzensee.

He was the picture of abject despair when we saw him. He was seized with a violent fit of trembling while we were walking in our circle, and presently broke down completely. "My poor wife, my poor children, what will they do?" he kept on saying. Pastor Niemoeller looked at him, and an expression of deep concern and pity came over his face. Suddenly he stepped out of ranks, in spite of the guard's warning shout, and walked straight to the condemned man. Placing a hand on Hahnke's shoulder, he said, "Calm yourself. Don't worry about your wife and children. God will take care of them. I am sure there will be many friends who will help them."

Hahnke, who was shorter than Niemoeller, lifted his head and turned a surprised look into Niemoeller's face. He stopped crying, and Pastor Niemoeller spoke again. "Dear brother, think of yourself now. Soon you will behold God. Prepare yourself for it. Death is not the end, but the entrance into eternal life. Whatever you have done will be forgiven you, if only now you will believe in God and His mercy. Be a man; don't show your enemies any fear, for that is what they want. You cannot help yourself on earth now, so take your mind off worldly matters and concentrate on God. Believe in Him, my man, and you will be saved. Don't be afraid. Put your trust in God, and it will be just a step from earth to heaven."

Niemoeller's own face was working convulsively, so great was his pity for the man cowering in mortal terror before him. He must have seen many men die during his time in the navy, but perhaps this was the first time he had seen a man who was weaponless and helpless in the face of coming doom. But his words sank deep into Hahnke's mind. The poor man became calm, and straightened himself. The look of terror passed from his face. He made an effort to control his voice, and then said, "You are right; I behaved like a child."

"I will pray for you, brother, and God will help you," Niemoeller replied.

The prisoners of both circles had stopped dead in their tracks at this scene. I could not help observing the faces of the men. Some of them appeared incredulous, as if they could not believe the drama being enacted in fron of them. Some of them appeared emotionally disturbed Even the guard was so overcome by surprise that he mad no effort to stop Niemoeller. When he finally ordered us to resume our dreary marching, his voice was much softer than usual, and he said quietly, "I have to do this, otherwise I would get into trouble with my superiors." After a while, as if a sudden thought had struck him, he approached Pastor Niemoeller, and said rapidly, "That was good, Pastor Niemoeller. The poor man needed it."

The next morning we did not see Hahnke. A trusty reported that he had been transferred to Ploetzensee. There was no need to tell us more, that another head would roll into the sawdust for Hitler.

From now on Pastor Niemoeller was treated with more

respect and consideration by the other prisoners. Even Mueller, who had been given to uttering the foulest blasphemies and boasted that he had stolen only what the Church had stolen from the people, seemed to be impressed.

When, later on, I asked Pastor Niemoeller whether this change in the prisoners' attitude surprised him, he said, "No, it is only a confirmation of what I have always believed, that religion is deeply rooted in the hearts of our German people. They can be misled by unscrupulous propaganda, but any regime which sets out to destroy religion will in the end be itself destroyed. Loyalty towards the State is most closely connected with devotion to religion, and any attack on religion would be to destroy the foundations of the State. The churches have tried to make this clear to the Nazis, but they refused to listen, and they will pay for their mistake."

A few days later my cell mate, Lauterbach, the man who had written the memorandum on the Jewish question which had fallen into the hands of the Gestapo, committed suicide. Apparently he had convinced himself that death on the block or a life term in prison would be his fate, and he had broken under the strain. When I awoke I saw his body hanging from the window lock. He had made a rope out of his blanket and had managed to secure one end over the lock and so suspend himself. As I usually found it difficult to get to sleep during the early part of the night, he must have watched me carefully to see that I was sound asleep before making his attempt. Being a nervous man, he must have gone through agony in making up his mind to kill himself. On the table in the cell I found a note in pencil, saying, "I couldn't stand it any longer. Please forgive me for bothering you in this way." A sealed letter addressed to his wife lay beside the note. I left it as it was.

I was greatly shaken, not so much by the sight of the limp

body as by the very definiteness of the act. Lauterbach had been alive, and now, suddenly, was dead. He might have been alive and in complete health, going about his daily work, if it had not been for the Terror. And all of us might have been living out our ordinary days and performing our ordinary tasks if it had not been for that thing bred of a nightmare which had stalked us when we thought we were secure. I had always liked Lauterbach. He was a simple man, or he would not have composed that memorandum. Often I had tried to cheer him by expressing the belief that his sentence would be mild and soon he would be able to rejoin his family.

It was some time before I calmed myself long enough to press the button of the emergency bell with which every cell was provided. These bells had been installed chiefly because of the number of suicides in the prison. Prisoners were instructed that the cell mate of a suicide must ring the bell immediately upon discovering such a death, so that the body could be removed before the hour of unlocking the cell blocks. A guard who had been on night duty soon came to the cell, and when he saw the body, he shouted angrily, "Another trouble maker. Everybody here commits suicide in order to give us more trouble. Why couldn't he have waited until he was in the penitentiary, the idiot!" He went away, and in a few minutes returned with another guard and a pair of heavy shears. They cut the rope, and dragged the body out.

When I met Pastor Niemoeller at the recreation hour he had already heard of the suicide from one of the trusties. It was the first suicide since his arrival. He asked me about the details and especially of the guards' reaction. I told him everything, and showed him Lauterbach's note, which I had concealed on my person. He lost himself in reflection for a while, and then said, "I see my task in this place very clearly now. Such things must be prevented. I can understand how desperate people can become. I will do everything in my power to give them more strength to resist."

He asked me if I thought it would be proper for him to make an application to the prison administration for permission to minister to the spiritual comfort of the prisoners, so that there might be fewer suicides. I expressed my doubt that such permission would be granted, and said that, on the contrary, the mere application would be used as an excuse to discipline him further. But he said he couldn't believe it, that it would mean that they were not interested in preventing suicide. He said that he didn't care what action they took against him, that he would carry out his intention. And he did, that afternoon, through one of the guards.

After a few days he showed me a note signed by the director of the prison acknowledging the receipt of his request and saying that authority to act upon it did not rest with him, but with the Gestapo, to whom he had forwarded it. Pastor Niemoeller realized at once that the Gestapo would never permit him to act as a sort of chaplain to the prisoners, and shook his head when I returned the note to him. A few days later he was summoned to the office of the prison director, who read to him a communication from the Gestapo, the substance of which was that his request had been refused and a warning that he should mind his own business and be glad that he himself was still alive. When he had finished reading the communication, the director asked Niemoeller to sign an acknowledgment that he had heard it. The rules forbade any communication from the Gestapo being placed in the hands of a prisoner.

"There must be a way to get into closer touch with the prisoners, and I shall not refrain from trying to do what is right," Niemoeller said to me after he told me of his interview with the prison director. Then he almost shouted, "No threat of the Gestapo will intimidate me." I was afraid that he would attract the attention of the guard, but Niemoeller was not caring then.

"Look at me," he went on. "I am here in this prison because the authorities consider me as the worst type of criminal. My fate is uncertain. I am prepared for death on the execution block at Ploetzensee. I feel desperate at times, like everybody else. But I would never take my own life. For I believe in God, and I know that whatever happens to me happens through God's will. But God does not look out for me only, but for every one. We are all alike before Him. He does not distinguish between the types of crime which society knows, but He looks in our souls. A great man said once, 'We don't live on our deeds, but on the fact that they are forgiven us.' Whatever we receive at the hands of the authorities is imposed by God, for even the authorities are only His instruments, whether they believe in God or not. What might be considered as a punishment might be necessary to clear our consciences for the time when we shall stand before God's face. There can be no greater sin than to throw away one's life, because then you have made it impossible to fulfill God's will. He who throws away his life has committed the worst act possible, for he has frustrated God's will by doing what His enemies wish. They want you to destroy yourself in order to confirm their blasphemous denial of God's existence."

Pastor Niemoeller had lost all the apathy which had marked him when he entered Moabit. There was a new light in his eyes, and I could see behind them the mental energy and spiritual strength which had impressed me when I heard him in his church at Dahlem. What stirred me most now was the note of conviction in his voice. It caught the attention of the other prisoners too, and I marked that they were listening.

It was interesting, too, to note the attitude of the guard.

He had tried to quiet Niemoeller in the beginning, but lost hold of himself in contemplating the man. It was as if he himself had become fascinated by the fire in Niemoeller's words. Whatever it might have been, he let Pastor Niemoeller finish. There was in him such a fire as has set the world ablaze before, and I know that Hitler and all his minions will never be able to put out the flames that one day will destroy all his works. It is impossible for me to believe that the sun will much longer shine on the negation of all that is good, which is Hitler's creed. Some day God will stamp the earth and the thunder of His voice will awaken us again.

After Niemoeller had finished speaking one could feel the silence. Everybody was busied with his own thoughts. And I felt that if some one had spoken then it would have profaned the scene. Niemoeller now had smashed through the wall which had separated him from the rest of the prisoners. Through the connivance of the trusties he began to receive notes from the other prisoners asking him for advice concerning themselves or their families.

IX

NIEMOELLER ON ANTI-SEMITISM

GRADUALLY, and as if by common consent, Pastor Niemoeller accepted the task of comforting his fellow prisoners, and there was no untoward interference from the guards. "I feel as if I have found a new congregation," he said to me once. "My only regret is that I have no means of getting into more direct touch with them."

And, indeed, it was touching to see the devotion of the prisoners towards the pastor. Some of those who had money sent him food, cigarettes, or tobacco by the trusties. Niemoeller always declined to accept any of these gifts for himself, and asked the trusties to distribute them among the poorer prisoners, those who depended entirely on prison food. In the meantime, he had received permission to buy food with his own money. Almost all of this he gave away. He also obtained permission to read a newspaper, either the *Voelkischer Beobachter* or the *Angriff,* which he declined.

Like everybody else, Pastor Niemoeller had to follow the prison routine with clockwork precision. The first bell rang at 7 o'clock, when the prisoners arose and dressed. Then they had to wait for the water for their ablutions, which was given to them half an hour later. Breakfast was at 7:45 o'clock. From that time until the recreation hour at 9 o'clock Pastor Niemoeller prayed.

He would thank God that he was still alive, and ask for strength to keep him through the day. After the recreation hour he read the notes from the prisoners which the trusties had placed in his cell, reflected over them, and prepared answers for them. The rest of the day was spent in prayer and meditation. It seems characteristic of the great souls in Christian history that they have been able to turn themselves inward and there find that peace and solace which are beyond those who are unable to feel beyond the appeal of their physical being. I have been awakened to this fact, and I must confess my belief in the indestructibility of the Christian faith. Men like Pastor Niemoeller are able to reach out into the mystic realm of eternity and draw from it spiritual sustenance. God is real to them, and ever present. Had not the Nazis blinded themselves to this fact and set out to destroy what they had placed beyond their understanding, they might have brought real reform to Germany and given her grace to lead in the pathway to peace. But they gave themselves over to the powers of evil, and for that Germany must die and be born again.

In performing his self-assigned pastoral duties, Pastor Niemoeller did not distinguish among Catholics, Protestants, and Jews. "Here we are all brothers," he said when I remarked to him about it, "and anybody who wants my services is welcome to them."

This encouraged me to ask him one day about his position on the Jewish question. Knowing that he had voted for the Nazis before they took over the government, I assumed that he had once approved, at least in some degree, their attitude towards the Jews. He responded at once. "I have never been what could be called anti-Semitic," he said, "for a true Christian can never be anti-Semitic. From the viewpoint of the Christian faith the so-called Jewish question does not exist, and when I voted for the Nazi Party it was not with any intention of expressing any sort of animosity towards the Jews. I looked upon the anti-Semitic slogans of the National Socialists merely as catch phrases, which were regrettable, but unavoidable in the interest of the ultimate aim. And I was convinced that after they gained power the National Socialists would put a stop to anti-Semitism and restore the Jews to their former status."

But this did not sound quite like the man I had come to know, and I asked him if he hadn't realized that the Nazis' anti-Jewish slogans would promote and intensify anti-Semitism, which would be difficult to eliminate later on. "And, besides," I asked him, "didn't you read Hitler's *Mein Kampf*, in which he states expressly that he would destroy the Jews as soon as he attained power?"

After he had pondered my question for a while, Niemoeller replied, "Yes, I read *Mein Kampf*, but, as I have already stated, we had been assured again and again by Hitler himself and other responsible leaders that *Mein Kampf* represented nothing but a literary ebullition of the leader of the Nazi Party and was by no means to be taken as a political program. To confirm this, we were told also that the future foreign policy advocated in the book would be impossible of execution, so that no one would ever dream of attempting to carry it out. The proposed settlement of the so-called Jewish question was regarded in the same fashion. Its purpose was to show that the democratic system was not suited to the German character, and in naming the Jews, who were, in part, responsible for the establishment of the Weimar Republic, it was the democratic system that really was the object of attack. But, indeed, I certainly am not free from reproach, because at that time certain restrictions against the Jews seemed to me tolerable, considering the great aims the Nazis were driving at.

"At that rime I did not realize that we would have to pay

for these restrictions with our own liberty. I did not fully take into account that equality had been given to the Jews during our epoch of political liberalism, and that any restriction imposed on them now would mean the end of that epoch, and possibly the end of individual liberty, including the right of worship. In other words, to deprive Jews of political equality would mean turning back the wheels of history."

With a self-deprecatory gesture, he continued, "Yes, that is the truth I learned. And I think that it is not sufficiently realized by the anti-Semites in other countries. They still believe that you can put Jews in ghettos again without affecting equality and liberty generally. He who desires liberty for himself cannot deny it to others, lest he lose what he has gained. This is Germany's lesson to the world."

Not having expected such a clear and concise statement on this complicated question, I was very much surprised by Pastor Niemoeller's words. Evidently he had given thoughtful consideration to the subject. "Yes," he said in response to my question, "I have thought it over many rimes since the Nazis started their anti-Jewish policy, particularly as I felt myself guilty to a certain degree for what has happened. I bear the responsibility for my vote for Hitler."

"You mentioned," I said, "that at one time you didn't object to the imposition of certain restrictions on the Jews. What kind of restrictions did you mean?"

"To keep Jews out of political office," he replied. "I thought it would be for their own good. Many of our people identified the Weimar Republic as Jewish, and to a certain degree they were right, without realizing it, for the Weimar Republic was the outcome of the liberal spirit, to the growth of which the Jews had greatly contributed. So, since it was our policy to show that the Weimar Republic was a mistake, the Jews naturally came in for a large share of the discredit. Jews had taken office in the republic, and others had worked for it. It was unwise for us, therefore, to take Jews into the new government of the Reich and of the states, or to employ them in any official capacity."

"The Jews are frequently accused of being a destructive element and of being unable to adapt themselves to the customs and conditions of the countries in which they live," I remarked, more to myself than to Pastor Niemoeller. But he took up the argument.

He shook his head slowly, and said, "I don't think so. I can judge only of German Jews, since I have never lived abroad, and I can state that German Jews do not distinguish themselves from any other Germans. Rather than being a destructive element, they are, on the contrary, generally more conservative than their fellow citizens among the Gentiles. It is generally overlooked, even by educated Germans, that our conservative ideology owes much to Friedrich Stahl, a Jew of great intellectual caliber and a fervent patriot. In the World War Jews fought as bravely as any other Germans, and many were decorated for heroism, and many were made officers. Jews are certainly not destructive in respect to science and the arts. Rather, the arts and science have been greatly enriched by Jews, which is all the more surprising in that they have enjoyed equality of privilege and opportunity only since the beginning of the nineteenth century. During that period they have made use of their educational opportunities with amazing success. They have proved that they can adapt themselves to the surroundings in which they live. Those Jews who have been slow in adapting themselves are recent arrivals from the countries of Eastern Europe, where equality of opportunity was denied them and where it was made impossible for them to adapt themselves. In spite of this, they are of higher intellectual standard than the people of the countries from which they come, and they have developed a great literature. I have read, for instance, some of the works of Shalom Asch, and consider them a most significant contribution to European literature."

Pastor Niemoeller often used to discuss the Jewish question, and I felt that he found relief in unburdening himself to me, a Jew. It was apparent to me that he had been sincere in his thinking and that he had never harbored any ill intention towards the Jews as a people. Because, perhaps, many of them had lost the ties to their ancient faith and so were free from the inhibitions which conservative religion imposes, they were able to move faster towards political and economic change, and thus came to be looked upon as extreme radicals. So it was easy for Hitler to arouse the old conservatives to the supposed danger and lead them in the direction opposite to the new spirit of liberalism which began to appear in the rest of the world after the Great War. Hitler killed reform with reaction, and accordingly Jews were pilloried with Communists. It was Jews who were responsible for defeat in the World War, Jews who were responsible for the ill-starred Weimar Republic, Jews who were responsible for Britain entering the present war, Jews who were responsible for American aid to Britain, Jews, in short, whom Hitler held responsible for all the opposition to his "new order." This in spite of the fact that Jews have fought Jews on every battlefield in Europe and that their ancient history is marked by suicidal struggle.

I would like to digress here a moment to answer a question that has often been put to me since my arrival in the United States.

The question is this: "Do you think that from the viewpoint of realistic policy, or even from a military viewpoint, Hitler committed a fatal error in persecuting the Jews?"

My answer is this:

So far as Germany itself is concerned, and considering the general purpose of the Nazi program, Hitler's anti-Jewish policy cannot be considered a mistake from his viewpoint. By depriving the Jews of their natural rights and plundering them of their possessions Hitler has achieved a twofold purpose. In the first place, he has been able to improve the economic lot of many of his supporters and of many others whom he could thus induce to follow him. Aryans who were unable to maintain themselves in honest competition came into possession of factories, industries, stores, and even homes, for hardly more than a song. It was not difficult to persuade them that they were only regaining what they had been robbed of by Jews. I once asked an "Aryan" lawyer who had taken over the practice of a Jew, "What have you against the Jews? Do you really hate them?" He replied, "I have nothing against the Jews. For me the Nazi policy is merely a matter of economics. I am now able to improve my standard of living. So why shouldn't I approve the ousting of Jews from the German business and professional life? It is a question of survival, and I must take such means as I can to maintain myself." Though this cynicism was common enough—for it was assiduously cultivated—I do not believe that the majority of the German people really hate the Jews. Anti-Semitism is the result of careful and clever propaganda. Hitler had accomplished one of the means to his end—awaking among the masses the instinct to take what one wants, the instinct for self-preservation.

Bismarck was once asked why he had conferred equal rights on the Jews in Germany and protected them in those rights. His answer was, "Because I do not want to arouse the mob instinct to plunder." He feared that if this instinct were awakened there would be no stopping it. Bismarck's attitude towards the Jews, therefore, was not directed by reasons of humanity, but by reasons of realistic policy.

On the other hand, Hitler saw that he could make this instinct serve his purpose. By using the Jews to dull the sense of justice and truth and honor he could train the Germans to believe that they were a superior race and that they owed it to themselves to regard all other races as their servers. Also his destruction of the Jews provided the opening wedge for the contemplated destruction of the Protestant and Catholic churches.

In the second place. Hitler sought by this means to avert the attention of the world from his real aim and to gain the sympathy of anti-Semites elsewhere. Here, too, he was not mistaken. He found this sympathy in Britain, France, and the United States. Anti-Semites, and others, whose motives were equally ulterior, began hailing Hitler as the great crusader against Bolshevism. True, some regarded his persecution of the Jews as a regrettable excess, which time would remove. But it was a domestic matter, with which other nations had no right to interfere.

In the countries of Eastern Europe hatred of the Jews flared up in greater intensity and resulted in organized support of Hitler's policy. In fact, some of them passed new laws to suppress the Jews, and Poland signed a ten-year peace pact with Hitler.

Now, however. Hitler's persecution of the Jews may prove to be a boomerang. For the world realizes that his attempt to destroy the Jewish people is but a means to an end, and that end the enslavement of the rest of the world. For those who agree with Hitler's assumption that the Jewish people are an inferior people can hardly escape the consequence of that assumption, namely, that there are master races and inferior races. If the Jews, who belong to the white race, are considered to be inferior, then there can be no reason to disagree with the Nazi theory that the Poles and Czechs also are inferior. So far, the brand of inferiority has been placed only on those nations or peoples which have been too weak to prove the contrary, the consequence of which is to recognize force as the sign of superiority. The supreme master race, then, would be that nation which was able to display the strongest military power, which would justify the Nazis' claim—if they win the war.

The answer to the question which is the subject of the digression lies, then, in whether Hitler wins or loses the war. If he wins, the persecution of the Jews will have well served his purpose.

If, on the other hand, civilization wins against the power of darkness I firmly believe that the Christian peoples the world will come to realize that anti-Semitism is a two edged sword—a favorite weapon in the Destroyer's arsenal.

X

THE BROTHERHOOD OF MAN

IT WAS now October, and the days were getting visibly shorter. A sharp wind bit into our faces when we went down to the recreation grounds, and one could see that the older men felt the chill penetrating their thin frames. The linden tree in the yard was bare of leaves, and the flowers had succumbed. The earth was going into its annual decline, and our spirits drooped in unison with the decay. Under other circumstances we might have found something sweet and solemn in the autumnal air, but here there was nothing of the quiet glow which braces men's hearts until spring comes again. We could feel only a tightening of the bands, and resigned ourselves to the harder days to come.

One morning we noticed a new arrival at the prison, an aged Catholic priest, Father Lindemann. It was the first time since the arrival of Pastor Niemoeller that we had had a Catholic priest in our cell block, and I wondered how he would fare. He was about seventy years old, and was suffering with a very bad case of dropsy, so that he had to walk with a cane. But the cane seemed to be of little assistance, for it was with the utmost difficulty that he could keep up with the slow pace around our circle. Every movement seemed to pain him, and often he had to stop to recover his strength. I learned that he had been charged with hostility towards

the State and with endangering the morals of youth. Two
fourteen-year-old members of the Hitler Youth had made
depositions against him. He had been arrested by the
Gestapo at his parish in the environs of Berlin, and had
been kept a long time in the Ploetzensee prison. From there
he had been transferred, by order of the District Attorney
General, to Moabit to await his hearing. He was still wearing
his clerical habit when he came to us.

Everybody had to walk when he was brought down for
exercise, and no exception to the rule was made for Father
Lindemann, although it was obvious that he was unable to
keep up. When Father Lindemann told the guards that he
was ill and unable to walk without difficulty, they said that his
trouble was no concern of theirs. The prison doctor had said
that he was able to take the exercise, and he would have to
stay in line. Every time he stopped, a guard would shove him
on and call him names. I noticed that Pastor Niemoeller
turned white every time this occurred. One day a young
guard called the old priest a crook and faker, who was pre-
tending that he was ill when, in reality, he was as well and
strong as any one else in the yard.

This time Pastor Niemoeller lost his temper. "Haven't you
any respect for his priestly frock?" he shouted at the guard.
Stepping out of ranks, he shoved the guard away, and
offered his arm to Father Lindemann. The guard was too
startled to interfere, and Niemoeller walked alongside
Father Lindemann, helping him at every step.

But the next day Pastor Niemoeller was summoned into
the presence of one of the prison inspectors, a man named
Schneider. When I asked Niemoeller the following day what
had happened, he said that Schneider had expressed regret
for having summoned him, and asked him not to make his
own situation worse by interfering with the guards. He said
that Niemoeller had committed an act of insubordination

and merited a reprimand, and warned him that the next time such a thing happened he would be placed in solitary confinement. Then he cautioned Pastor Niemoeller to beware of the guard, that he was a Storm Trooper and considered himself above the other guards who did not have that distinction. "I do not like him myself," he told Niemoeller.

Later on, Father Lindemann was tried and sentenced to seven years at hard labor. The day before he was to be transferred from Moabit to the penitentiary in Brandenburg Pastor Niemoeller walked boldly up to him in the prison yard and embraced him. Even the two guards seemed affected by the demonstration, and both looked away. Fortunately, neither of them was the Storm Trooper who had been so harsh to the old priest. The two men stood thus, in each other's embrace for a few seconds, and then Father Lindemann said loudly enough for all to hear, "I shall probably not come out of the penitentiary alive. But it is God's will. He knows why I have to suffer all this."

"Trust in God," Pastor Niemoeller answered, and he, too, spoke loudly enough for us all to hear. "I am sure that you will not be made to serve your full term. God is merciful."

"Yes, yes," said the priest slowly, and then the guards separated them, but this time not roughly.

While I am at this point I should remark on the rumors circulated in the press abroad that Pastor Niemoeller has become a Roman Catholic. I am able to state that this is not the case, and I feel sure that Niemoeller will never go over to the Catholic Church. While we were together in Moabit prison, and later in the concentration camp at Sachsenhausen, Pastor Niemoeller always stressed his feeling that he was obligated to continue as leader of the German Protestant *Bekenntniskirche*. Nor is it true that Niemoeller has requested in his will that he be buried with Catholic rites. I believe that these rumors were circulated by the

Nazis themselves in order to alienate Niemoeller's followers throughout the world. It is his steadfastness in his faith that has infuriated the Nazis.

Yet there is no question that Niemoeller has a high regard for the Catholic Church, as he often expressed it to me in our conversations. He was a great admirer of Faulhaber, the courageous Cardinal of Munich, against whose life the Nazis once made an organized attempt. The effort miscarried, and apparently the Nazis were afraid to try again. Pastor Niemoeller was especially enthusiastic over Cardinal Faulhaber's sermons against the Nazis. "They show Faulhaber to be a great and courageous man," he once told me. "His sermons are monuments to the Christian faith, and they will be remembered forever." One of Niemoeller's favorite books was the *Imitation of Christ*. "I have again and again drawn from it new courage for my battle," he said.

I often drew him out on Catholicism, and his reply was that the old Germany was under tremendous obligation to the Catholic Church. He said that it was the Catholic Church which impressed civilization on Germany, and once he told me that the Nazis' description of Charlemagne, who introduced the Catholic faith to Germany, as *Karl der Sachsenschlaechter* (Charles the Butcher of the Saxons) was one of the most atrocious lies the Nazis had attempted to introduce into history. "The Catholic faith," he said, "humanized Germany, and it was the chief inspiration of German art." He thought, too, that after the Renaissance of the fourteenth century the Catholic Church became one of the greatest instruments of humanity in the world. And one day he remarked, "If Hitler really had been a Catholic he would not have become the tyrant and ruffian he now is."

On another occasion Niemoeller spoke to me about the Nazi scheme to bring about a union of the Catholic and Protestant Churches. He observed that though the two

128 ¹∕₂ HITLER CAME FOR NIEMOELLER

faiths have virtually the same foundation, they differ in essential points, and that union now was not possible. Besides, he pointed out, the Nazi scheme was not to give Germany a united Christian Church, but to bring about such a fusion of the two branches of Christianity as they could hope to adjust to their pagan ideology. Niemoeller pointed out that despite their dogmatic differences, the leaders of both Churches had taken a united stand against Nazism, and that this unity would be of the utmost significance in the final struggle against Hitler. "We are brothers," he said, "in the battle to keep alive the ideals of Christianity."

As I recall it, this is the substance of what Pastor Niemoeller told me about the struggle between the Nazis and the Christian forces in Germany:

"I think that a union of all the religious groups in Germany would form an insurmountable obstacle against any attempt by the Nazis to destroy the Christian faith in the Fatherland. The Nazis' realization of this explains their wild effort to disparage Christian leaders and thus breach the ranks of the laymen. In the struggle that has ensued the Catholic Church, because of its stronger international position, has done heroic work. And by means of the concordat between the Pope and the Hitler government the Catholic Church was put in position to counteract the Nazis' vicious propaganda against Catholic history and Catholic dogma.*

"Under the provisions of the concordat the Catholic Church published a reply to Rosenberg's *The Myth of the Twentieth Century*. This reply, which appeared in the form of a brochure, was published by the office of the Bishop of Berlin. Of course, it cracked all Rosenberg's theories, and exposed his quotations from history as deliberate misinterpretations or forgeries. All this was written objectively, without personal reference to Rosenberg. Although the brochure was written for Catholics, it found its way into

Protestant circles and was read so widely that it was suppressed as being in violation of the concordat, and the Catholic Church was forbidden to publish anything of the nature in the future."

So the battle continues, and, as I gathered it from him, Pastor Niemoeller counted on the resistance of the Catholic Church to weigh heavily in the ultimate overthrow of Hitler. And, indeed, I myself cannot foresee any other outcome, for though it may be weak in spots, modem civilization has a religious basis, and Hitler has to destroy that foundation before he can hope to erect his "new order." And this fact, I believe, is the source of Pastor Niemoeller's hope.

Often he would recur to praise of the fortitude of the Catholic clergy. He mentioned the example of the Cardinal of Breslau, who, when the Nazis threatened him with internment in a concentration camp, replied, "Nothing would give me greater happiness than to suffer and die for the Holy Church." And the Nazis did not dare to touch him. They feared an uprising of the Catholic population.

Nothing stirred Niemoeller's indignation more than the persecution of the Catholic clergy, of whom the Nazis had a special hatred. At the time of which I am writing now there were a large number of Catholic clergy in the Ploetzensee prison and in the other cell blocks of Moabit. They were charged with being homosexuals or with having violated the strict laws against the transfer of money. Niemoeller ridiculed all such charges, because, he said, he knew too well of the moral qualities of Catholic nuns and monks. Because of a peculiarity in the German law, monks would be

* The concordat provided for certain concessions to the Catholic Church in Germany. The most important was that the Catholic Church should have the right to reply to propaganda against her, provided that all replies were written objectively. This concordat Hitler violated every time it suited his purpose.

charged with homosexuality, and nuns with seduction of boys and girls under the age of fourteen. Under the law only homosexuality in men was punishable. Nuns, therefore, were charged with seduction of minors, because this, too, was a crime punishable by law. This variation in the accusations, Niemoeller said, was sufficient in itself to expose the sinister purpose of the Nazis. In fact, as soon as the Nazis obtained power they began charging Catholic clergy with obscenities and abnormal practices and said that they were a menace to the youth who had been committed to them for education and religious training. In order, then, to give the people an apparent confirmation of these base and baseless charges, they arrested thousands of men and women who had devoted their lives to religion and had taken the vow to preserve themselves immaculate.

No less unjustified. Pastor Niemoeller told me, were charges brought against Catholic clergy of violating the money laws. Severe restrictions against the transfer of money to foreign countries were necessary because of the financial condition of Germany, but Niemoeller pointed out that certain exceptions should have been made for the Catholic Church in order that it could fulfill the obligations it had incurred before the advent of the Nazis. He believed that exceptions were not granted because of ill will towards the Catholic Church rather than to conserve the country's finances. "I am convinced," he told me, "that if the Catholic Church had refrained from opposing Hitler it would have been permitted to handle its money affairs in the proper way. And I agree with the Pope that these laws are unethical. They were seized upon as a means of destroying the Catholic Church's prestige." What Pastor Niemoeller said of the other charges could be no stronger from the lips of a Catholic priest.

XI

NIEMOELLER VIEWS THE NAZI PHILOSOPHY

ONE morning we came down to the prison yard to find it covered with frost, and we shivered, stamping our feet a little in order to start the circulation. The faces of the men were pinched, and some of them needed handkerchiefs. They could do nothing but furtively draw the backs of their hands across their noses. Though Germans are generally clean in their personal habits, the Nazis gave little heed to the needs of their prisoners. They were like chaff, soon to be got rid of.

As we cast our eyes about, seeking signs of the life we had known before, we saw something pleasantly strange and unexpected. It was a big bird house, which apparently had been put up by the prison authorities after we had been returned to our cells the day before. Crumbs had been scattered on the foothold and top, and there was a little pan of water. Pretty soon a sparrow flew down and hovered over the bird house, apparently eyeing it with curiosity and some degree of suspicion. Then it lighted on the ground, hopped slowly towards the bird house, and, finally, with a gay chirp, began picking up the crumbs. The little adventurer was followed almost immediately by a whole flock of sparrows, and all participated of the meal with much noise and happy chattering.

We prisoners gazed on the scene as if we had never before

seen birds feeding at the hands of man, as if it were something absolutely strange and novel in human experience. Traces of smiles lingered on the prisoners' lips as they watched and remarked on the sight, observing how some of the sparrows tried to get more than the others and were chased away with indignant chirps, only to return to the foray for food. It was a great distraction for us, and as long as I was in Moabit the bird house afforded a topic of conversation that drew us a little way out of ourselves. So did little things break the monotony of our life and temporarily at least unloose our fettered minds.

As for myself, I could not help remarking the difference, or, rather, the tremendous contrast, between the attitude of the Nazis towards the fowls of the air and their attitude towards their fellow beings. I think the difference is based on something fundamental in German character and training. Germans have no repugnance to the most horrible cruelties against man if cruelty will serve their purpose. Yet, on the other hand, they display the greatest kindness towards animals. And the strict legislation for the protection of birds and animals was not changed in the least by the Nazis. On the contrary, they imposed the extreme penalty for violation of the protective laws. In fact, if the Gestapo had treated birds and animals as they treated human beings, they would not have been able to stay general indignation.

This strange feature of the German character can be explained, I think, by the centuries-old teaching that man's fate depends entirely on the social structure, which he is supposed to have received from God and from which he cannot escape. Animals, on the other hand, are looked upon as innocent and helpless beings, to torture which would be inhuman. But as there is no man innocent, so there is no law in nature to protect him from his fellows. The German people are deeply imbued with this strange philosophy, and it enables them to meet their fate without question, to die willingly for any cause which is thrust upon them.

When I spoke of this to Pastor Niemoeller, he said, "There is some truth in it, but I don't think that this feature is restricted to the German character, but is inherent in the human race as a whole. All of us are touched when we see the suffering of beings which have not the intelligence to protect themselves properly and therefore must live in a state of dependence. Man, on the other hand, has the power to defend himself, and he knows that the faults of his fellow beings spring from themselves and not from their condition in nature." The conversation led me to bring up the practice of sterilization and emasculation and the mercy killings which had been legalized by the Nazis and which had been brought to my attention in the hospital. When I told Niemoeller of all that I had heard, his pale face reddened, and he became more furiously indignant than I had seen him before. He appeared to doubt my story at first, and made me repeat it and give him the tiniest details. It took him some time to calm down.

"That is nothing but a revival of paganism and the perfect denial of every Christian idea of humanity," he said after he had gained control of himself. "Even if the racial theories of the Nazis had any foundation in science, the great question would be whether society has any moral right to put them into practice. Man cannot be put on the level with animals, among whom the struggle for survival is the only law. Being God's children, we are all brothers. But animals are made to serve the purpose of man. The application of racial theories to man means his degradation to the level of animals. We must look upon every human being as having come from the hands of God, and if there is any deficiency in him he is still our brother.

"And these practices," he went on, "are all the more cruel

and senseless because there is no foundation in science for them. We are not able to look deeply enough into the mystery of creation to be able to explain God's purpose in creating men of different abilities, weights, and measures. We know only that He does have purpose. And the experience of history itself proves that the Nazis' theories are wrong. There have been many men who would have been subjected to sterilization or emasculation, or even killed, if racial theories had been put into effect, but whose offspring have contributed greatly to the arts and sciences and to culture in general. Take Beethoven, for instance. He was the son of a half-crazy drunkard. Or Grabbe, whose paternity was little better. Both were great geniuses.

"What goes into the making of a genius we do not know. Science has made a vain effort to discover the secret. And I think that we shall never know, for here we are confronted with the mystery of creation itself. We know that genius does not depend on the weight of the brain or the formation of the skull. Years ago I read the report of a doctor who had found a man who looked like a twin brother of Goethe. He was of the same height, had a similar skull formation, and his brain weighed exactly the same as Goethe's. But he was an idiot.

"We cannot define the boundaries between genius and madness. Perhaps both are nearer to the mysteries of life than we know or can hope to know. This was the position of the ancients, who had no knowledge of the exact sciences but depended on an instinctive feeling, which made them give the same respect to the madman that they gave to the genius. They believed that both were nearer to the gods than the ordinary man. Also, we know from experience that sometimes men of deficient intelligence have offspring of the highest intellectual rating, and that men of great mental achievement have children who are imbeciles or near to imbecility."

"But the Nazis claim," I interrupted Pastor Niemoeller,

"that they follow these practices in order to breed a healthy race of *average* intelligence. For they believe that the backbone of a strong nation is the average man of average intelligence, and that it would not pay them to tolerate the mentally deficient merely because they *might* produce a genius. They claim that geniuses are rare and that the toleration of the mentally deficient would make for a poorer racial strain and a feebler population."

"Such a theory," replied Pastor Niemoeller, "is, in my opinion, the greatest blasphemy against God. It assumes the right to correct God's will. Like all the other theories which the Nazis have advanced, it is dictated by a selfish purpose, the wish to keep themselves in power and to accomplish their goal to dominate the world. They consider a high order of intelligence, with its tendency to culture and humanity, as an obstacle in their path. This can be seen in every hateful remark Hitler and the other Nazi leaders have made against intellectualism. Their fear of it is implicit in their every speech. So they have made every effort to turn our people from culture and higher education and to establish a uniform educational standard, so that they can create an order of willing slaves, men and women who willingly will submit to the vicious 'new order.' What they understand average healthy intelligence to be is blind and unconditional obedience to the Fuehrer. To bring this about, then, they must eliminate individual thinking.

"But whatever the reason for these practices may be, whether the Nazis sincerely believe that they are essential to the creation of a greater Germany or not, and whether or not there is a sound biological basis for them, I, nevertheless, would oppose them from the standpoint of Christianity. For all this is a violation of the fundamental principle of the Christian religion, which is a religion of love and consideration for our fellow men. The Christian Church concedes the right of the State to punish violation of its laws in order to protect society. But this right does not extend into the field of morals, over which God has placed the Church and which is generally recognized by modern civilization. Sterilization, emasculation, and the so-called mercy killings are not a right or necessary to the existence of the State but a ruthless interference with human rights and the will of God. The purpose of the Nazis becomes even clearer when we consider the fact that so-called political criminals are subjected to these practices without any medical reason at all. Color it as they may, the real reason for the abolition of their opponents' simple human rights is the fear that they might propagate their opinions in their offspring."

In view of the discussion of this problem by doctors and lawyers, which long had preceded Hitler's espousal of the racial theory, Pastor Niemoeller's remarks seemed to me to be of especial significance. The great majority of lawyers and doctors had come to the conclusion that sterilization and emasculation would not be helpful in crime prevention, since crime is not traceable to biological inheritance but to social conditions. A person of subnormal intelligence might not be able to resist temptation and so have to be put under some form of restraint, but beyond this it was admitted that the State would not have the right to go.

No government before Hitler, therefore, had even considered passing such legislation as the Nazis deemed necessary for the preservation of the State. And had such legislation ever been suggested, the effort would have been stalled immediately by the people. It is significant, therefore, that the Nazis have been able to effect such a radical change of opinion and so have altered the concept of justice without encountering any dangerous reaction among the population.

Before I left Germany I had the opportunity to talk with

several families who had been bereaved by mercy killings. These executions had not been restricted to those committed to prison or concentration camp but had been extended to some who had not violated any Nazi law. I recall a case. One of my students, an intelligent and healthy young man, had suffered concussion of the brain in a motorcycle accident. After he had apparently recovered, he still showed signs of mental confusion, which made it necessary that he be put under medical care. His mother, widow of a soldier who had fallen in the first World War, took the young man, who was an only son, to a public asylum for the insane, since she did not have sufficient money to place him in a private institution. The doctor who attended her son frequently told her that he would recover his mind in due course, and she waited patiently for that happy event. One day she was notified that he had been transferred to Grafeneck, a renovated castle in a remote spot in western Germany. It was always heavily guarded and was said to be used to dispose of the insane. Then, some weeks later, without any previous warning whatsoever, she was informed that he boy had died and that she could get the ashes of his body if she would pay for them. Further information was denied her. When, finally, she was able to see the doctor who had attended her boy in the original hospital, he informed her merely that her son had been examined by a government medical inspector, who had come to the con clusion that her son's mental derangement was incurable and not only that, but that his ailment was progressive, a observable in the fact that he had made remarks critical of the Nazi government. I shall not attempt to describe the forlorn condition of this mother. There are times when tears cannot flow, when agony is beyond the power of expression.

Rumors of mercy killings were constantly current. Aryan blood was not a solvent of Nazi fear and hate. It became as clear as dawn to the naked eye that no one was safe who harbored resentment against the Nazi regime. People whose nervous systems became shaky dare not consult a doctor. Under the law any one suffering from a nervous ailment had to be placed in an asylum for the insane if the doctor so ordered. The Terror stalking through Germany was a living thing, for which every careless word was a signal and every door an ambush.

XII

~~~~~~~~

NIEMOELLER ON
THE NAZI CREED

IN THE course of our conversations Pastor Niemoeller made many illuminating comments on Hitler and other Nazi leaders. His remarks seem to me to be all the more interesting because they give a very clear idea of the picture of these personalities formed in the minds of those of the German people of whom Pastor Niemoeller is a typical representative. The world correctly considers Pastor Niemoeller as an outstanding living symbol of Christianity of our time. But perhaps it has been forgotten that he is also a typical German and a representative of the class of Germans from which he springs. In view of this, his reaction to the various personalities of the Nazi movement should, in my opinion at least, be of special interest to the world outside, which I believe to be poorly informed of conditions inside Germany.

Migrant German intellectuals who have written and lectured about Nazi Germany are, no matter whether they are Gentiles or Jews, not entirely competent to tell the story, since they left Germany either immediately after Hitler's ascension to power or a short time before. They have not themselves experienced the change; they have not been eyewitnesses to the movement which has made Germany a madhouse and people refugees even from themselves. They can have only the faintest idea of the psychological pressure to which the German intelligentsia has been subjected. And certainly it is easier to underrate the full effect of the Nazi ideology from the outside than from within. Only those who have been scorched can describe the touch of flame. I do not mean to challenge anybody, but I do wish to say that the usual condemnation of the intellectuals now in Germany is not justified to the extent in which it is being indulged in by their colleagues here. It must be remembered that those who came abroad were either politically involved, or are Jews, while those who remained in Germany either were not politically minded at all or favored the Nazis to a certain extent because of their conservative attitude. The ogre of Communism, whom Hitler later married and then divorced, rallied many to his banner.

Pastor Niemoeller always stressed that in his opinion Hitler is a real German. "Hitler," he said to me, "is as typically German as Napoleon was typically French. The fact that he was not born in Germany itself does not matter, any more than that Napoleon was born in Corsica. It might be doubted that Hitler is of pure German origin, but nobody can successfully deny that he is a German product. He is, in fact, a living example of the falsity of his own doctrine, that only people of pure German blood can be considered as real Germans. But that does not alter the fact that Hitler feels that he *is* German and that he has been able to arouse national fanaticism among all those too weak to think and act for themselves. And I think that Hitler himself realizes this paradox, which may explain his hatred for non-German races, especially the Jews.

"However all this may be, I think that everybody must bsee in Hitler the typical features of German character. He who is unable to see the weaknesses inherent in intellectual dependency on dreams is himself a dreamer, and incapable of realistic action. For Hitler's self-styled policy of realism is nothing but fantasy. He dreams dreams, but there is no vision among them. This side of his character explains what the world has noted with scorn and surprise, namely, his seeming contradictions, the discrepancy between his words and his deeds, and especially his sentimentality, which makes him weep for those he has ordered to die. Here we see the inability of the dreamer to face the realities about him. This predominant German characteristic dictates Hitler's whole course, and his domestic policy, which aims to restore the age of feudalism to Germany—considered by Germans to be their Golden Age and glorified as such by many German poets—is no less fantastic than his foreign policy, which is to conquer the world and enslave all non-German peoples in order that the Germans may live out their dream.

"To accomplish all this, Hitler has adopted the most ruthless means, in which respect he differs from the average dreamer, who is incapable of translating his dreams into action. And this is what has attracted so many people who have the same inherent characteristic but lack the ability to get beyond the dream stage. To them Hitler must be a man of heroic dimensions. He is the ultimate fulfilment of their dreams. Dreamers are not confined to Germany. They are found among all peoples, in all countries, which explains the response Hitler has elicited in some circles outside of Germany.

"So Hitler has become the Fuehrer of the helpless, of those who have failed to make good because of their inability to adapt themselves to the realities of life and to overcome the natural obstacles to pleasant existence. This split in personality explains, in my opinion, everything which the world outside Germany has found strange and hard to understand. Hitler is unpredictable because, as is the case with any other dreamer, he depends on moods. During periods of high exaltation and self-belief he is seemingly honest and truthful. In other periods he will, without scruple, ignore his high-sounding promises and do exactly the opposite of what he has pledged himself to do.

"Another factor in his make-up, which is a common characteristic of all dreamers, is his complete lack of real sentiment. He has in its place a sentimentality which is entirely concentrated on himself. It is the most impressive egotism I have ever known. This makes him see everything in the mirror of his own ego. So he has come to believe that he himself is Germany and that the fate of mankind depends on his will. And what dreamer who sees his dream coming true would not feel the exaltation which so often gives fire to Hitler's words? In reality, there is not an atom of sincerity in him, for, unconsciously, he is the perfect type of the actor who becomes so immersed in his role as to believe that he is actually the character portrayed. His prototype is found among certain of the Caesars, and he is a greater danger to the world than has been any man in history."

This raised in my mind the question whether Hitler, who then had gained control of the destinies of 80,000,000 people, can be regarded as a great man or whether he is merely the end result of a peculiar combination of circumstances. The question has occupied, and will continue to occupy for years to come, the attention of the world. I put it to Pastor Niemoeller during one of our discussions.

"That depends on one's conception of greatness," he replied. "As I look upon it, greatness consists in the ability to be constructive and so contribute positively to the progress of humanity. But I cannot deny that men tend to admire the ruthless power of destruction and to see in it the quality of greatness. From this viewpoint one would have to concede that Hitler is a very great man, greater, perhaps, than all the other destroyers of history. Besides, he has been able to employ all the agencies of destruction which science has invented and developed, and he has perverted to his use even the great implements of peace and construction. The very havoc he has been able to create in the mind and in all the fields of energy seems to have added to his laurels. It has awakened all the primitive delight in destruction, and the more appalling the ruin he has accomplished, the more he has aroused this latent instinct."

I could quite agree with this analysis, and then I pondered another question. "Do you hate Hitler, Pastor Niemoeller?" I asked.

He paused to reflect a while, and then said, "No, I do not hate him. Such men as he are beyond hate. They represent the incarnation of evil. They are like the wild outbursts of the elements, which we cannot hate, but which we must overcome in order to live. One cannot hate a flood or an earthquake, but he must overcome its fury."

"Well," I said, "that reminds me. There are many rumors that Hitler is insane. Do you think that is true?"

"No, no, not by any means," answered Niemoeller quickly. "To think that would be to underrate him, which might well prove to be the final disaster. I think, rather, that his intellect is above the average, and that he has a keen conception of the mentality of the masses, which enables him to feel out their hidden weaknesses and thus bend them to his will. And that is what is most dangerous about him—his ability to destroy the souls of men. No human being has achieved such success in that as he. He has many characteristics which the Bible attributes to the Antichrist. He is, unconsciously, the impersonation of evil."

I have attempted to put down Pastor Niemoeller's observations on Hitler's character and personality as nearly verbatim as possible. Certainly I have put down the substance. To me Niemoeller's analysis of Hitler is vastly important, for after my close acquaintance with him in prison and concentration camp, I have come to feel that this Evangelical pastor has a keener perception of the truth than any man I have met. I find it especially remarkable that Niemoeller could look at Hitler with such objectivity after having been so long under his spell and so long the object of his hare. Not once during this discussion did he indulge in personal bitterness against the man who had brought him to such a pass, who had deprived him of everything but life. And in my opinion his analysis of Hitler's character accounts for everything that has puzzled psychologists. In a succeeding chapter I shall relate the prophetic conclusions which Niemoeller drew from his examination of Hitler's world policy.

I think that Niemoeller's remarks on other leading Nazi personalities also are illuminating.

"When one looks at the men surrounding Hitler," he said to me, "one cannot help feeling that they are suitably and very peculiarly matched. It is hard to say whether each was deliberately selected by Hitler because of his adaptability, or whether they were cast together by an unexplainable fate, for every one of them is an individual of strange, even abnormal, character, and together they form a most surprising unit, each complementing the other, like the cogs in a machine. This unit is the heart of the Nazi regime which has brought the German masses under its spell and which is able to present to the world an impression of unity within Germany which does not exist. As an individual, every member of this unit would be unable to meet the ordinary requirements of society, but in combination they are able to rule a great nation and to interfere with the processes of the whole world. For instance, take Hess, Hitler's deputy, whom, I am informed, he loves as dearly as a younger brother. Hitler has repeatedly stated in private that of all the men around him Hess is next to his heart, and in the event that anything should happen to himself is to be considered as his successor.* A friend of mine once told me that Hitler declared at a dinner, 'Hess is entirely my creation. Mentally, he and I are one. Only he is able to uphold and carry out my ideas and policy for the Third Reich.' Hess thinks only of his Fuehrer and the success of the National Socialist Party. He has no regard for wealth and honor, but is devoted entirely to the cause. Furthermore, I possess certain information that there is ready for publication a law appointing Hess as supreme leader of Germany in case of Hitler's death. Hitler has set this down in his last will.

"Indeed, in my opinion, very seldom can there be found two men so similar in all respects as Hitler and Hess. Each is characterized by the dominating tendency to dream. But whereas this tendency is a heritage in the case of Hitler, it is in Hess the result of the environment in which he was brought up. Hess was born in Alexandria, Egypt, where his German-born father was a merchant. There he fell prey to the brooding spirit of the East and became a visionary. Cultural development in the East has been halted, and the Eastern mind tries to fulfill its purpose not by planning for a greater future but by reliving the past. So Hess lived largely in a world of abstraction, but being German he did not fall into the apathy and fatalism which are so characteristic of the East. What better tool, then, could Hitler have found for the execution of his plans? Here was a man given to illusions but at the same time possessing the German tendency to blind loyalty to a cause and obedience to a leader. And of all the Nazi leaders, Hess, in spite of his absolute ruthlessness, makes the best impression because of his idealism. He is the only one who lives in comparatively modest circumstances, and all this, in my opinion, makes him the most dangerous

* This possibility was removed, of course, by Hess's flight to Scotland and his internment as a prisoner of war by the British Government.

man next to Hitler. In fact, I believe he would be even more ruthless in carrying out Nazi policies.

"The man next in line, Hermann Goering, is much different from Hess. He can best be described as a soldier of fortune, who loves war for war's sake. This, too, is a typical German characteristic, and it helps to explain the fierceness and devotion with which so many German soldiers fought in the World War. They had so adjusted themselves to the conditions of war that fighting had become second nature. Only in battle could they find glory and achievement. And when the World War ended, they found an outlet for their passion in the Baltic wars against the Bolshevists, in the war in Upper Silesia against the Poles, and in the various civil conflicts which developed in Germany itself.

"Goering proved to be an excellent soldier, and he won great fame as a pilot. Only the most reckless of daredevils could become successful pilots in those days, and this gave every opportunity to those who wanted to cover themselves with glory and to become known as national heroes. Contempt for life, his own and others', is one of Goering's outstanding characteristics. He has also a lust for power and splendor which is so strong that no moral restrictions would restrain him. His loyalty to Hitler is merely a matter of convenience, and he would not hesitate to betray the Fuehrer if it could bring him advantage. He has no particular intelligence, and any ideology is good which suits his purpose. Having no moral scruples, he is open to bribery, and Germany is full of stories of his corruption.

"This type of man has no sense of mercy or magnanimity, and I learned that during the purge he was himself busy putting people to death. A friend of mine, who was employed in the Prussian Ministry, told me that during those days people were continually being brought to Goering for questioning. He would fire questions at them for about ten minutes, and then order them to be taken to the Military Academy at Berlin-Lichterfelde, to be shot by SS guards. In not a single case did he show any mercy. On the contrary, he took opportunity to rid himself of personal enemies, as, for instance, General Schleicher. Then they had to kill Schleicher's wife because she had witnessed her husband's murder. Later on, their daughter, who was only sixteen, planned to revenge herself for her parents' death. She managed to get an invitation to a party at which Goering was a guest. She was searched at the door, as was everybody else, and a pistol was found on her. Goering was informed. The girl was taken out, and she has never been seen since.

"Goebbels is another opportunist, and, like Goering, he is completely lacking in idealism. On the contrary, he is cool and calculating, and has the advantage of an education. During his youth he attended a Jesuit school to prepare himself for the priesthood. He was an orphan, and it is a remarkable fact that he was supported in the main by Jews. Therefore, he has no reason to hate either Catholics or Jews, to whom he owes his education and maintenance. But he is remote from feeling, and considers himself as being under obligation to no one. Being physically handicapped—I do not mean to criticize him for this," Pastor Niemoeller added hastily, "as his handicap is an act of God—he probably suffers some psychological deficiency, which inclines him to hate heroes and heroism, while he himself may be a coward. His ruthlessness, therefore, is of the most sinister kind. He is the chief propagandist for the Nazis, and has not the slightest hesitancy in committing the most impudent forgeries in order to forward his purpose. As he pretends to an authority which is too often taken for granted by the uneducated and the careless thinkers, his fraudulent representations of history have had a poisonous effect. Tomorrow though, he would lend his talents to any other regime that might suit his fancy or purpose.

"But the strangest thing about Goebbels is that he is the personified contradiction of all the Nazi doctrines. He is the type of the 'unscrupulous scribbler,' which he himself and Hitler so often denounce in their speeches. And, physically, he is of the very type which the Nazis aim to exterminate. He is corrupt and excessive in his sexual life, and he parades his immoralities with the utmost cynicism and frankness. Goering sees in Hitler the source of his power, Goebbels only a means. No wonder, then, that they are jealous and suspicious of each other, and that they can be tamed only by the supreme power above them.

"No less despicable is Alfred Rosenberg, the doctrinaire of the Nazi movement. He, too, is entirely a product of early environment. He grew up in the Baltic region, between the civilization of Germany and the civilization of Russia, and his horizon was narrowed by the deficiencies he found in both. Hating Russia, he learned to hate the Jews, with the fanaticism exhibited only in those who have lost all sense of reason. That hatred so dominates his whole personality that he refuses to recognize Jesus Christ as our Saviour because He was of Jewish origin. Into the Old Testament Rosenberg reads the manifestation of the Jewish people's will to dominate the world, showing that he does not object to the principle of world domination so long as it is exercised only by the German people, for whom he says it is a natural right. In his opinion Christianity is only Judaism in different form. In fact, he once stated that Jewish propaganda is designed to poison the soul of mankind in order to weaken the non-Jewish nations against the day when the Jews will be ready to put into effect their plan to dominate and enslave the world. Therefore, Christianity must be destroyed. To prove his theory, which the word *mad* cannot even remotely describe, he is writing a history of civilization which is the greatest fraud one man ever has attempted to perpetrate. Rosenberg is a past master in pseudo science, and his book, *The Myth of the Twentieth Century*, is nothing but a chain of forgeries and deliberate misinterpretations.

"It is a terrible thing, a most terrible reflection on the purpose of the Nazis, that a man like Rosenberg should have such influence on the German youth. Young people with whom I have talked told me that they consider him a great man. Lacking the capacity to distinguish between truth and falsehood, they believe him to be a great thinker and scientist, although they do not approve of his fight against Christianity. In normal times Rosenberg would not have dared to set up such theories as have come from his pen, nor would such nonsense have been received with anything but scorn and ridicule. But under the Nazi banner he is permitted to poison the minds of helpless young Germans.

"Himmler, organizer of the Gestapo, is a prototype of the Prussian corporal. In contrast with the correctness of his appearance and manners, which I had the opportunity to observe on several occasions, he is like a bloodhound hunting down men for the sake of hunting itself. People have told me that he prefixes most of his statements with, 'It is my command that,' 'The Fuehrer has commissioned me to,' 'It is my duty to shoot you,' and the like. He is the most feared man in Germany, and his spies have penetrated every corner of the country so deeply that nobody can be sure whether even his nearest relative or best friend is not an agent of the Gestapo. People who have been taken before the Gestapo for questioning have reported later, with every show of horror and terror, that they were asked to betray their parents, their husbands, and their brothers. When one of them replied to such a request with the horrified exclamation, 'But how can you expect me to do such a thing?' the answer was, 'Your refusal merely shows that you are not yet a good National Socialist. Otherwise you would not mind father, brother, or husband. On the next occasion we will put you into a concentration camp in order to teach you complete devotion to our Fuehrer and our party.'"

Pastor Niemoeller told me that he thought Himmler's Gestapo organization was very largely responsible for the moral break-up in Germany. Even high ranking army officers had admitted to him that they were in constant fear for themselves and their families, and, therefore, were compelled to give their approval to things which seared their conscience.* He believed that if it had not been for this instrument of terror, Nazism would have been destroyed at birth.

Pastor Niemoeller's scorn of Streicher, the Jew baiter, was as deep as his scorn for all the other satellites who move around and have the source of their being in Hitler. "The greatest disgrace to Germany," he said to me, "is Streicher's newspaper, *Der Stuermer*, which attacks Christianity under the pretense that it is a low and impudent form of Judaism. He spurns all tolerance and morality based on the Christian religion as being beneath the dignity of man, and does it in such a way as to appeal to the most bestial instincts. He blasphemes God and the Bible by declaring that Jesus Christ was nothing but . . . (the exact words I shall leave out). He has described Catholics and Protestants in words so vile that they cannot even be repeated. His outpourings are so loathsome as to create in me the impression that he is insane. At least, I think he is the most disgusting type of man in Nazi Germany, and from the viewpoint of good taste alone I was always unable to understand how Hitler could endure him and show his friendship for him openly. In private life he is a moral leper. He was one of the few German soldiers who, during the World War, were court-martialed and convicted of raping French women. And that is the man who is

* From reports of the purging of German generals, received as I write, it would seem that they also disagreed with Hitler on his strategy.

intrusted with the training of our youth. His *Der Stuermer* is compulsory reading for the Hitler Youth and for school children. It forms an important part of the National Socialist education."

When he talked about von Ribbentrop, the Nazi Foreign Minister, whom Hitler believes to be a second Bismarck, Niemoeller became sarcastic. He knew von Ribbentrop very well, for Ribbentrop had lived in Dahlem and been a member of his church. "He was one of my most faithful followers— until he went over to neo-paganism," said Niemoeller.

Niemoeller had less to say of von Ribbentrop's character than of the others. He considered Ribbentrop to be a man of average intelligence but of unusual vanity, which is at the root of his ambition. "Add to this a good portion of impertinence and cynicism, which is necessary for a champagne salesman who wants to be successful," he said, "and you have the whole man."

I recall Niemoeller's story of how von Ribbentrop wanted to become a member of his church again. Ribbentrop was then Ambassador to London, and had returned to Berlin for a visit.

"To my great astonishment," Niemoeller told me, "I was honored with a visit from Ambassador von Ribbentrop. When I asked him the reason for such an unexpected honor, he replied, without any show of embarrassment and as if it were a matter of only the slightest importance, 'I have come to you, Pastor Niemoeller, in order to apply for membership in your church again.' For one moment I really believed that Ribbentrop had recognized his mistake and wanted to return to the Christian fold.

"'I am glad to hear that,' I answered him, 'and I take it for granted that your intention is to become a good Christian again.' 'Oh, no,' Ribbentrop replied with an amused smile, 'that is not the point, Pastor Niemoeller. My purpose in rejoining your church is for reasons of State. In my position as Ambassador to London it is necessary for me to be a member of a church. And, of course, I thought of you and Dahlem.'

"'That may be so,' I replied, 'but that is not sufficient reason for me to receive you as a member of my parish again. Membership is only for one who believes in the Christian faith, and is not based on reasons of State.'

"Ribbentrop became furious, and said, 'I wish to inform you that I am here with the knowledge of the Fuehrer. The Fuehrer wants me to become a member of *your* parish again.'

"I understood very well. Hitler wanted to kill two birds with one stone. His Ambassador should become a member of our church again in order to satisfy 'British bigotry,' as British religious feeling is called by the Nazis. And he was to make use of membership in my church as propaganda to deceive the British into believing that Pastor Niemoeller supported the Nazi regime.

"'I'm sorry not to be able to comply with the will of the Fuehrer,' I said, 'as I consider it entirely a matter of conscience, which forbids me to accept anybody as a member of my church who does not believe in the Christian faith.' Apparently, Ribbentrop did not know what to say in reply, for he left in speechless rage, without even attempting the formality of a good-bye."

On another occasion Pastor Niemoeller and I talked about Dr. Ley, leader of the German National Socialist Labor Front. Niemoeller thought that no more unfit person than Ley could have been selected for this job. He saw in Ley one of the most contemptible figures of the Third Reich, and described him as "a man of low moral quality, with impudent street-corner eloquence." Ley's mere personality, he said, was certain proof that what the Nazis called "the solution of the social question" was nothing but a tremendous bluff hiding the most unscrupulous exploitation of the working classes. "The Labor Front represents the Nazi conception of social justice and the fulfillment of the promises Hitler made in his speeches and in his *Mein Kampf* before he was appointed Reichschancellor, for when Hitler came to power they not only got less wages for longer working hours, but lost even the right to dispose of their spare time," Niemoeller said. "The Labor Front prescribed the kind of entertainment the workers were permitted, their reading matter, etc. The Labor Front has duties somewhat similar to those of the Hitler Youth. One of its tasks is to instil in the minds of the working men one idea, to the exclusion of all others, so that their mental level would be so reduced that they would be little more than machines. Hitler's idea of social justice consists in transforming free men into slaves, who would do his bidding and thus enable him to proceed to the conquest of the world.

"But the most vicious instrument of soul poisoning is the Hitler Youth, to which German parents are compelled to surrender their children under penalty of the law. I cannot tell you how bitter I felt when my children were forced to become members of the Hitler Youth. There was nothing I could do to prevent it. Millions of German parents must feel exactly as I do. For membership in this organization means depriving children of all the right of childhood. Our children are taught that there is no natural tie between them and their parents, that their only duty is to live and die for the Fuehrer. If they believe it is in his interest it is their duty to betray their own parents, their brothers, and their sisters. They are trained to spy on their own families. They are trained to abhor the Christian religion.

"Yes, many parents came to me complaining and sorrowing about the unspeakable change that had come over their children. They told me that their children had been taught to use crude and vulgar language, which they were told was the real German language, as used by the Stuermer and the Schwarz Corps. But I could only tell them that there was nothing I could do, that I suffered even as they. I could only advise them to continue to be good parents and to continue teaching their children to love their Saviour.

"These are the men who, for the time being, rule our Fatherland and are leading it into the darkest period of its history. Every one of them is abnormal and mentally deficient, but together they form the most compact threat to our civilization. They have destroyed Germany already. But the greatest danger lies in the fact that the outside world has not yet realized the strength of the menace facing it. If these men should succeed in their evil plans the world will be plunged into darkness more catastrophic than any it has ever experienced. Everything which makes life beautiful and worth living will be destroyed. The world will be ruled by sadistic cruelty, by the mere weight of fists. Slaves will work to satisfy their masters' insane desire for luxury. Still, I can't believe that this reign of terror will come to pass. I believe in the wisdom of God, who permitted this menace in order to show us by its destruction that the good will always endure and that evil will perish forever."

XIII

RELIGION IS NOT DEAD IN GERMANY

DECEMBER came, and over her shoulders the city wore a mantle of snow. It must have been beautiful in Grunewald and in the Tiergarten, where the free would be walking, albeit more quietly than in happier years. But in the prison yard we shivered as we crunched the snow under our thin soles, and the wind bit like a rasp under our equally thin, threadbare clothes. I marked that there were no signs of other life. The birds had taken wing to where food was less scarce and environment more friendly. We, the friendless, walked alone. The guard, too, shivered, thumping his sides with his hands in a vain endeavor to keep warm. His orders came with sharp blasts of smokelike mist from his lips, reminding me of the staccato firing of machine guns, of which I had heard. From the nearby Moabit barracks came the sound of trumpets and the hubbub of men shouting and running hither and yon. Men, I knew, were being drilled. For what? I wondered. Was Hitler really engaged in starting another war, when we were still not finished with the old? Sometimes I wondered how the young men in training felt about it all. Were they looking forward to blood and glory rather than to making homes for themselves and rearing families? If so, could they realize what the future held in store for them, of the desolation they would help to create

155

and in which they would have to live—those of them who would survive? It would not be the bit of pageantry they expected, I thought, as was not the war of 1914-18, to which, as a youngster, I had seen so many march as if they were off for a few weeks' holiday. Perhaps those of us who already were victims of the Nazis' lust for power understood better what lay beyond the shadow. And in these after days, when events begin to take clearer shape, I know that I had a prescience of the evil days to come. I think that all of us who were still capable of thought felt in our chilled bones that the shrieks of fear we heard occasionally would one day be echoed throughout the world.

At this time the *Voelkischer Beobachter*, copies of which we saw occasionally, was bursting with indignation over the German-Austrian question. Reports of atrocities against the Austrian National Socialists, who were described as the real Germans in Austria, filled the pages, and there were fierce editorials calling for action and revenge. We saw such headlines as "Catholic Church Persecutes Protestants," "International Jewry Destroying Germans in Austria," "Bolshevists Gain Upper Hand in Austria," etc., in similar strain. The fervent phrasing was all too familiar, and for me it had a dreadful meaning. The Nazis were building up a war psychology.

The prisoners, too, discussed the Austrian question. Would it come to war? they asked among themselves. Strangely, most of them hoped it would, the Nazis among us because they believed that war would induce Hitler to parole them; the anti-Nazis, because they believed that Hitlerism would be destroyed and they would regain their freedom.

Pastor Niemoeller also showed great interest in the question. As he had declined the privilege of reading the Nazi newspapers permitted in prison, he would ask me every morning for news about Austria. It was apparent that he was observing the course of events with great anxiety. "Austria must not fall into Hitler's hands, for that would mean the loss of the last stronghold of German culture," he said to me again and again. "So long as independent Austria exists, Hitler's power over the German people will not be complete, for there will remain an important group of Germans able to demonstrate to the people of the Reich what real German culture means."

Though all the world is now fully aware of the planned diabolism of Hitler, it may be interesting to Pastor Niemoeller's friends to know what he thought of the possibility of war and of its outcome. When, one day, I put to him the question of what he thought the outcome of war with Austria would be, he said, "That depends entirely upon what the great Powers would do about it, and I think that their policy would be one of realism. Their action would be determined by considerations of national safety, that is, whether they would believe themselves to be in danger if Hitler should march into Austria."

"Well," I asked him, "do you think that the conquest of Austria would endanger the peace of the world?"

"Yes," he said, "for if Hitler succeeds and the Powers hold off, he will take it as an indication that they fear him. That would encourage him to invoke his East European policy and his ultimate aim of overthrowing the whole world."

"But don't you think," I asked Pastor Niemoeller, "that the great Powers would take action to prevent Hitler's annexation of Austria?"

Niemoeller shook his head hopelessly. "Frankly," he said, "I don't think so, for that would depend entirely on England, and I doubt very much that England would see in Hitler's annexation of Austria a threat sufficient to stir her to action. For reasons of national safety she is concerned mainly with preserving the balance of power on the

Continent, and she has already committed herself to strengthening Germany as a counter to France. She won't let reasons of humanity interfere with reasons of State, and in this respect she is backed by history, which shows that the sword has never been unsheathed in the name of humanity."

"But don't you think that the British would try to prevent an act of aggression that would result in spreading National Socialism and increasing German prestige among the smaller nations of Europe?" I persisted. "And, besides, haven't they guaranteed Austria's independence?"

Perhaps I was whistling against the wind in trying to elicit from Niemoeller some encouraging word. I know that I had a dim foreboding of pending tragedy and that I was hoping against hope that there would be some intervention of fate to save us from the two hyenas ravaging Europe. Perhaps I was trying unconsciously to save myself from the spirit of fatalism which had overcome so many of the prisoners. But Niemoeller did not help me.

"Young friend," he said, "the policy of all nations is dictated by self-interest. The British Government, to a large extent, echoes public opinion. And I can imagine that they would find it pretty hard to make their people believe that German annexation of another German country on the European continent would menace the British Empire."

Events, of course, prove Niemoeller's opinions to have been correct. Britain and France did not intervene, and Austria fell into Hitler's hands. It was all so very simple.

As I have said, Niemoeller was very well informed on political matters in general, and, because of his previous connection with Nazi leaders and high army officers, had a keen understanding of what was going on inside Germany. At that time, before the outbreak of war, he was able to outline, with almost perfect accuracy, the events which are now shaking the world. There were, he told me, two plans for world conquest. They differed in pattern only. One plan had been worked out by the brain trust of the Nazi party under the direction of General Haushofer, head of the Military Academy at Munich and editor of the magazine *Geopolhik*. This plan, which was favored by Hitler, was based mainly on avoiding a world war for the intended world conquest. It was Hitler's settled conviction that attrition would succeed better and be less expensive.

This plan, as I gathered from Niemoeller in various discussions, consisted of two parts. The one was the education and preparation of the German people for their future role as masters of the world, and the spreading of the National Socialist ideology throughout the world by propaganda and, when necessary, by military interference in the form of punitive expeditions. But military interference was to be limited in each case. The Nazi leaders, including Hitler himself, did not believe that the world could be conquered by military force alone. It could be accomplished only piecemeal. They were induced to this idea by the facts of history and by their theory that world conquest could be achieved only by melting together the various forms of civilization into a uniform ideology. And since every civilization is founded on some form of religion, be it Christianity, Mohammedanism, or Buddhism, religion would have to be destroyed before the greater aim could be achieved. But as religion is a fundamental necessity of human nature, the old religions would be replaced by a new one—the Nazi religion. In furtherance of this aim, the Nazi ideology has been built up not only as a theory of State, but as a comprehensive *Weltanschauung* (world view). The predominant idea of the State as a mere instrument of society is to be replaced by the idea of a State invested with mystical origin, which derives its power and justification from the Nazi god, personified in the supreme Nazi leader.

"Hitler," Pastor Niemoeller said to me, "has again and again declared that it is not his intention to destroy religion. People have always been surprised by the discrepancies between his assurances and his deeds, especially his persecution of the Christian faith in Germany; but now you can understand his full meaning. Hitler's declarations that he does not intend to destroy religion refer only to his conception of religion. For us religion is not merely something which is derived from the necessity of human society, but something that has been given to us by God, the Creator of the universe, who has created us in His image, so that we are distinguished from mere animals by our capacity to discriminate between good and evil. But the Nazis are nonbelievers. They don't believe in any Divine power at all. To them religion is nothing more than an abstract philosophy, unrelated to any practical theories, as, for instance, the theory of the State. But they do recognize man's inclination to mysticism, and they make the most ruthless use of it in trying to substitute one kind of 'superstition' for another. That is the explanation of the Nazis' attitude towards religion in general and the Christian faith in particular. Looked at from this viewpoint, their position makes sense. They don't want to destroy religion; they want only to give us another.

"The religion they would foist on us would be based on materialism. Love and brotherhood would be replaced by enslavement of the weak by the strong. The survival of the fittest would be the ruling doctrine. Equality among men would be denied in favor of a master race composed of the ruling Nazi clique and their followers. This would not comprise the whole German people, but only those Germans who have accepted the Nazi ideology unconditionally. To reconcile them with their fate they would be given the blessing of illiteracy. They would be schooled only in recognizing the Fuehrer as their god. Yes, incredible and fantastic as it may sound, I am convinced that Hitler considers himself to be the god of a new religion. Only this belief helps me to an understanding of his actions and his ideologies, which he has set forth in *Mein Kampf* and in his speeches. The Nazi movement is not merely a political movement, but a religious movement, like Mohammedanism. From Mohammedanism Hitler derives his idea of the religious State and from Christianity the idea of God incarnated in man. Religion would be practiced with the fist, and the rewards would be the rewards of this world.

"That is the training which German youth destined for leadership undergo. They are taught that the State and the Fuehrer form an inseparable union of mystical origin. The Fuehrer represents the State, and, therefore, all that he does is the action of this mystical power. He can do no wrong. His person is sacred and inviolable. He who dares to insult him commits a blasphemy. You can understand, then, why I must submit to this tyranny of imprisonment rather than surrender my conscience."

Niemoeller's face always grew whiter as he talked, with sometimes a red spot in his cheeks. This time he raised his voice loudly enough for the other prisoners to hear him. They looked bewildered. I wondered whether they had grasped the import of what he had said. Perhaps they were insensible to everything but the cold. I looked upon blue noses and chattering lips. Most of the men had the snuffles. The guard was too busy thumping his sides to pay much attention to us. And I reflected that there would always have to be men like him if Hitler ruled the world—men thumping their sides to serve their self-appointed Fuehrer.

I pondered Niemoeller's talk during the night. Only so could I find release. No prison walls can confine thought; ideas will sprout even in a stagnant world. Otherwise, Niemoeller would never have known Christianity. The world had been stagnant before; it was becoming stagnant again. But Niemoeller still breathed, and from his breath I drew a new lease on life.

By next morning the snow had drifted across our path, but we floundered through it until we made it a hard, compact mass. Little droplets exuded from our noses, and our breath was like the exhaust from a steam engine. When we had circled the path several times and I felt enough sensation in my feet to know that they were still there, I brought up the previous night's discussion. I asked Niemoeller whether he thought Hitler would succeed in the plan he had outlined to me. He was silent for a while, plodding wearily. I thought he hadn't heard me, and repeated the question. Then I saw the muscles in his face tighten, and I knew the answer was forthcoming.

"No," he said, "I don't think he will. He will fail at the right time, by God's decree. I don't know how long the Nazis will last. Maybe much blood will be shed and the whole world go through agony. But the Nazis will be destroyed in time. God will give the people sufficient strength to resist them, and, finally, to destroy them. I feel strongly convinced that the outcome of this struggle will be a triumph of God, religion, and humanity."

The other plan for world conquest which Pastor Niemoeller outlined to me was that prepared by the German General Staff. This contemplated a drive to the East, the old *Drang Nach Osten*, for there, it was believed, the Germans would encounter little, or no, resistance. Hitler reckoned on no intervention by the great Powers. He believed that he could take the small nations like Austria, Czechoslovakia, Poland, and even the Baltic states, one by one, and disguise his real intention by explaining that he was aiming only at uniting the German people into one Reich and restoring former German territory to Germany.

Should this explanation fail, he could then more openly proclaim that his real enemy was Russia and that taking the small buffer states was necessary to his plan, that he could not afford to have enemies or doubtful friends behind him. The Nazis calculated that the antipathy of the ruling classes of the great Western democracies against Bolshevism would blind them to the real purpose of his aggression. With Russia conquered and her vast resources in German hands, the Nazis felt that they then would be ready to take on the world. And, of course, the Nazis knew that the Western Powers nursed the hope that Germany and Russia would exhaust themselves in the struggle and thus remove themselves as menaces to world peace.

This plan did not sound plausible to me, and I spoke my doubt to Niemoeller. I could not conceive that Britain and France would believe that Russia would be able to resist a German march at a time when Germany was not engaged elsewhere and not hampered by a blockade. It seemed to me that they would recognize their peril and would render assistance to Russia, since if Germany conquered Russia and obtained a vast surplus of food supplies and oil, she would be so strong that they would be forced to surrender without a fight. And that, I argued, would open the way to the conquest of the Western hemisphere.

But Niemoeller insisted that this was one of the Nazis' plans. But, he added, the General Staff laughed in private at the idea of launching it now, for they were firmly convinced that Britain and France would fight, that they would realize the danger to themselves if Russia should fall. So, though they were in favor of a vast military adventure to conquer the world, the General Staff maintained that the effort should be postponed for twenty years, when they believed that Germany would be irresistible, even against the whole world. "The German General Staff, a high officer once told me," said Niemoeller, "is the greatest pacifist organization in the world just now, because it desires war only when it is convinced that it has more than a fifty per cent chance of winning."

I asked Niemoeller then what he thought would be the outcome of the difference of opinion between the Nazi leaders and the General Staff, and he said that he thought the General Staff would have to give way, and that he believed that even from their own point of view the Nazis would be making a costly error. He foresaw that the Nazis' policy of piecemeal conquest would finally reach the point when the Western world would open its eyes to Hitler's grandiose scheme and combine against it. "Hitler," he said, "is completely ignorant of the political situation in the rest of the world. He fails to realize the community of interest between the British Empire and the United States. He has forgotten the lesson of the World War, and counts on differences between the United States and Britain to prevent the United States from going to Britain's aid. I think he is mistaken. I believe that the United States finally will join Britain against Germany."

Niemoeller and I ranged through many topics during our conversations. His mind seemed always active, and these talks afforded him relief. Sometimes he talked about the United States. He had a profound admiration for the American people. "They are," he said, "the most progressive people in the world, and religion has played an eminent role in their progress. Their experience is proof that religion does not hinder social progress, but, on the contrary, advances it."

Often he showed his concern about Germany's future. He saw ahead a long process of purification and rehabilitation through which the Fatherland would have to pass after Hitlerism was crushed. Germany, he said, would have to feel her way back along the hard road she had built until she came to the point of penitence. He thought Germany would be lost to democracy for an indefinite period, for democracy had been too thoroughly discredited in the German mind by the Weimar experiment.

"There will be much for the Church to do," he said one day. "Hitlerism has taught it a great lesson by exposing its weakness. For if the Church had had half the influence which we so fondly attributed to her, this madness might not have been. The Church, too, will have to be purified. We have paid too much attention to preaching, too little to the practice of Christianity. Christianity lies not merely in belief, but in action too. We must not merely preach social justice, but also do everything to assure that aim."

"What do you understand by social justice?" I asked him.

"It means an equal opportunity for everybody," he said. "Higher education should be made possible for all who desire it; it should not be made dependent on financial ability. Every one should have the opportunity to establish a home and family, so there will have to be a minimum wage and a minimum standard of living. On the other hand, there should be recognition of talent and enterprise, for there will always have to be leaders, else civilization would lag to the step of the slowest. Everybody should be thoroughly grounded in the fact that he is a child of God, that he has been put into the world for a definite purpose, and that his work is as important as the next man's. The world does not need the elite breed that Hitler fancies; it has no place for supermen. The world is tired of all this talk of supermen and super-races. In God's eye there is no such thing. What the world needs is brave men who are humble, who will bring up their children in the fear of God and with love for their fellow men. The Church will have to begin all over again, begin right at the bottom."

And after a pause to blow on his hands, "But don't believe that religion is dead in Germany. The German people really are religious at heart, but many of them have fainted at the Terror. But they won't be crushed. Many of my colleagues are still in the fight. Some have given their lives; others, like me, are wasting away in prison. But their example will bear fruit. You may live to see it. And remember my words. The world is going to be shaken by moral revolution. Watch and pray."

I think Pastor Niemoeller is right. The great sickness will pass; civilization will recover.

So the month dragged on—a succession of long cold nights in cheerless cells, with short interims of somber days and monotonous rounds in the exercise yard. Christmas was approaching, and memories of happier days flooded back among the prisoners. One could mark a stronger stirring of nostalgia for hearth and home. The great Christian festival has always been marked with elaborate ceremony in Germany, and the Christmas tree is Germany's contribution to the observance. In the better days there was never a home that did not have its decorated tree and never a family that did not make merry with exchange of gifts. And now even those of the prisoners who had been outspoken in their anti-religious views showed a marked change in attitude, a strange softening in demeanor and disposition. Almost as if by common accord, the talk turned to Christmas, and reminiscences poured from lips blue with cold. Even the guard seemed less sullen. Each tried to outdo the other in telling how Christmas was observed in his home, how wife or mother would decorate the tree, and how, with much shouting and laughter, the members of his family would exchange gifts. So the talk was of home, of father and mother, of wife and child, of friends near and of friends far away.

On Christmas Eve morning, before we were let out of our

cells for our exercise, we heard an unusual commotion and loud talking in the hall below. When we were taken down we saw that guards had erected a tree in the center of the hall. So there was to be some observance of the greatest of Christian festivals. Yes, there was more. We had frankfurters and potato salad for our dinner that night.

Shortly after Christmas two of our fellow prisoners received their sentences. Preiser, the former judge, was sentenced to seven years at hard labor—a heavy fall for a former favorite. Mueller, the ghoul, received a life sentence. He seemed to have expected it, and not to mind, because he would fare better in a prison for habitual criminals than in a concentration camp. The regular prisons were under the jurisdiction of the Department of Justice; the concentration camps were under the jurisdiction of the Gestapo.

During the first weeks of January preparations for Pastor Niemoeller's trial on a charge of attempted high treason were begun. Several times he was summoned to appear before the inquiring judge, who was busy gathering evidence for the trial. Niemoeller exhibited no signs of fear when I would see him on the mornings following his appearance before the judge. Rather, as the fateful hour of his trial drew nearer, he became more mentally alive, and became fired with the old fighting spirit. "I shall never weaken " he told me once. "Even if they sentence me to die on the execution block I will fight to the last minute not for my life, but for the cause."

Nevertheless, Niemoeller would discuss with me, from time to time, the question whether the charge of attempted high treason could legally be maintained against him Under the law as it existed before Hitler assumed power an act of high treason was punishable by death, and attempted high treason, by imprisonment. That is, the law distinguished between an act that succeeded and an act that failed. But the

Nazis had changed the law to include the death penalty for attempted high treason also. The only comfort I could offer Niemoeller, then, was that the evidence against him would be insufficient. Otherwise, it seemed, he would have to die.

Now, the charge against Niemoeller was based entirely on his sermons, which the Gestapo agents had taken down stenographically. But in none of his sermons did Pastor Niemoeller exhort his congregation to overthrow the Nazi regime. He merely raised his voice against some of the Nazi policies, particularly the policy directed against the Church. He had even refrained from criticizing the Nazi government itself or any of its personnel. Under the former government his sermons would have been construed only as an exercise of the right of free speech. Now, however, written laws, no matter how explicitly they were worded, were subjected to the interpretation of the judges. The totalitarian principle which governs Nazi Germany, as I have indicated before, includes religion as a function of State. Therefore, by recognizing Christ only as his Leader, Pastor Niemoeller was denying the right to divine leadership to Hitler. His offense was all the more serious because he had exhorted his followers to do likewise. Under the Nazi interpretation, then, all this could be construed as a direct assault on the government.

Niemoeller fully appreciated the peril of his situation, and I could not but marvel at his determination not to surrender but to assert his belief to the last. He was perfectly aware, too, that for his defense in court he would have to depend entirely on himself. His lawyer, though he was "a man of good will," as Niemoeller expressed it, would not be allowed to take an active part in the defense. Most lawyers now were little more than tools of the court, and in many cases they would actually confirm the evidence against a client. They themselves might get into trouble if they were regarded as too active in a client's behalf.

In the days before the trial, which was now rapidly approaching, Niemoeller concentrated all his energies on preparing himself for the duel. He walked with firmer tread, head up and shoulders back, and occasionally took deep draughts of air. Often he was lost in thought, as if going over in his mind what he would say in his defense. When he talked with me it was to reassure me that he was fit and ready, that he would not budge from the position he had taken. "I am going to let the Nazis know," he said, "that a man who fights for his religion cannot be broken." The People's Court, before which he was to be tried, generally held its sessions in secret, so that there could be no publicity concerning the evidence. Thus the victims of the Nazis had no chance to air their cases before the court of public opinion. They could be convicted out of hand and the public be no wiser. Exceptions were made in the trials of Catholic priests charged with sex crimes. In this way the Nazis hoped to embarrass the Catholic Church in the eyes of the world. Pastor Niemoeller knew all this and, therefore, that he would not have the opportunity of winning public support to his side. On one occasion, he told me, the inquiring judge had urged him to admit his guilt, promising him leniency if he did. Again, it was hinted to him that if he admitted his guilt and so justified the measures that had been taken against him, he could expect a pardon from the Fuehrer. But Pastor Niemoeller was adamant against all temptations. "I am seeking justice only," he told me. "I am not concerned about my safety."

I could not help thinking on these occasions that the Nazis, if they decided to kill him, would find Niemoeller dead more dangerous than Niemoeller alive.

XIV

IN THE HANDS OF
THE GESTAPO

IN THE meantime, my own affairs were still hanging in the balance. I had been summoned repeatedly for questioning, but the judge appeared to be having difficulty in preparing the necessary evidence against me. All the witnesses except one denied having heard me utter any word which could be construed as an insult to the government. I began to feel encouraged a little. Then, one day, I was summoned to appear again before Judge Walter. He greeted me with his usual affectation of punctilio and politeness, behind which I could detect the sardonic gleam in his eyes. He informed me, with ill-concealed reluctance, that there was not sufficient evidence on which to convict me, and that, therefore, I would come under the general amnesty which Hitler had proclaimed in celebration of his birthday on April 17. Under that decree all guilty of insults to the government, and all charged with this offense, were to be pardoned, provided, however, that the offense did not demand a penalty of more than six months' imprisonment. I was told that I could expect to be released as soon as the necessary formalities had been complied with. I tried to conceal my elation as I walked with lighter step behind the guard who led me out of the room.

When I informed Pastor Niemoeller of the good news the

next morning, he felicitated me, and a gentle smile loosened his taut features. "You will have the chance to go abroad and begin a new and better life there," he said, and then, after a moment or two, he added, "But tell them what is going on here." I reminded him that this might make his own condition harder. But he waved away my objections, and said, "That does not matter. It is not I that am important, but that the world should know the truth. It is our only hope." So we parted in the exercise yard, each to return to his own cell. Niemoeller turned to look back at me as we separated, his face again relaxed for a fleeting instant.

After breakfast the next morning, the guard on duty entered my cell and sharply ordered me to pack my things and to prepare for my dismissal from Moabit prison. He gave me ten minutes to make ready. I had to clean my dishes, pull the bedclothes from the cot, and pack all in a bundle, together with the few things I had been permitted to keep in my cell, such as toothbrush, hair brush and comb, etc. I trembled with excitement as I worked. Finally, the hour for which I had longed for almost two years had come. Within a few minutes I would be outside the prison walls, free to go home and to my wife. I revolved again plans I had been forming to get out of Germany and to go anywhere that the air of freedom still blew.

The ten minutes had just elapsed when the guard reappeared at my cell door. He let me out, and then led me down to the administration room. There some of my belongings, which had been kept in a little suitcase, were handed to me, and I signed a receipt for them. "Do you know where you are going now?" the prison inspector asked me.

"Certainly," I said, "I am going home."

"Good luck to you," he answered, and there was an ironical smile on his face. But I was too far gone with glad anticipation to grasp its significance.

A guard led me to the prison door. Another man, on guard at the door, pressed 1 button, and the door opened wide, almost noiselessly, to let me out. Now had my hour come.

But I had no sooner passed through the door than I felt a heavy hand fall on my shoulder. I looked up in surprise, to see two heavily built men, one of them in plain clothes, the other in the uniform of the Elite guard.

I was in the hands of the Gestapo again. All feeling drained from me.

"Follow me," said the man in plain clothes, "and don't try to resist."

They put me between them and led me to a car waiting for us at the next corner. Sandwiched between them, I walked the fifty yards, silently and without looking up. It was very cold. Snow lay on the ground. People were passing along, going about their business. I could see their legs and feet, but I did not look into their faces. My escorts walked very fast, and I had great difficulty in keeping up with them. I was pushed roughly into the car, and the door was slammed behind me. Neither of the guards talked during the ride. I did not know where we were going, and I did not dare ask. Soon, however, I glanced out at the street, and realized that we were headed for the police headquarters at the Alexanderplatz.

As soon as we arrived I was hustled out of the car and taken immediately to the police prison, familiar to me as the place of my confinement before my transfer to Moabit.

But this time I was a prisoner of the Gestapo. Before, I had been put into a cell by myself, but now I was shoved into a large hall-like room, already crowded with prisoners. The air was filled with the odor of sweating bodies, and a thin film of smoke floated about. The room was provided with a number of wooden cots, which were already occupied, while the other prisoners had to stand or lie down on the bare floor. I soon found out that this was the collection point for prisoners who were to be taken to concentration camps. This was all I could learn then. The other prisoners were too apathetic to give me any information, even if they had had any. I knew only that we were to be distributed among the concentration camps. At the supper hour a small piece of bread and some thin soup were given to each of us. But I was too sick at heart and too nauseated by the fetid atmosphere to eat.

There was no cot for me, so I lay down on the hard, cold floor, sleepless throughout the night. Men going to the toiler, behind a thin partition in the rear, stepped over me, around me, and sometimes on me. I could not protest. They were as helpless as I.

Strange to say, I was not afraid. I felt keenly curious about the unknown that was awaiting me. It seemed to me that I was going forth to meet fantastic adventure, for up to this time I had not become aware of what went on in a concentration camp. Rumors and stories of terrible mistreatment and killings in the concentration camps had come to me, but I had refused to believe them. I could not imagine that even the Nazis would do such things. The press always described the concentration camps as educational centers, where the prisoners were schooled in Nazi policies. People released from a concentration camp either said nothing about their experience or admitted that it had not been too bad. Later, I learned the reason for this cautious policy. Every one who is released is required to pledge that he will never say anything that might reflect on the conduct of the camp. The penalty for violation of this pledge is to be taken back and tortured to death.

Men snored, sighed, and moaned about me. There was a constant sound of shuffling, tossing and turning. It seemed to me as if I were in a place of departed spirits. At four o'clock in the morning a guard ordered us to make ourselves ready. Men scrambled to their feet, tumbling over each other in the darkness, and got in each other's way for a last trip to the toilet. Then we were marched to the yard, where we were lined up as if for military inspection. An official called off the names. As each man answered, he was ordered to go to a certain place in the yard, where he became one of a group. Finally, the group to which I had been assigned, comprising about sixty men, was led to another yard, where we saw *two* trucks awaiting us. We were informed that we were to be taken to the *Schutzhaft Lager* (protective camp) at Sachsenhausen, and then were ordered into the trucks. It was bitterly cold, and we were not protected, for the trucks were covered only with canvas. We had to wait a long time before the trucks moved from the yard. We huddled together and shivered as one man. Finally, two guards mounted each of the trucks, and we moved out. The canvas top flapped in the wind.

We rode through the night-darkened streets of Berlin, which were almost empty at that hour. Now and then we encountered a vehicle, or passed a lone pedestrian, with his overcoat collar turned up. Soon the business district was behind us and we entered a seemingly endless avenue in the eastern part of Berlin, inhabited mostly by workers. I had not been in this district for a long time, and I was struck now by its melancholy aspect. There were the same low-class apartments I had seen during the Empire and the Weimar Republic. Hitler had done nothing to improve the homes and living conditions of the working class. His armament had taken precedence over everything. More people were on their way to work, their heads bowed to the cruel wind and always their coat collars turned up. Soon we were on the outskirts of the city and entering the open country. Dawn had broken through the gloom of night, and we were able to see each other and to take better note of our surroundings. But we were too utterly miserable and chilled to try to talk. We swayed together with the swaying of the truck, which was now moving fast on the frozen highway, whose monotony was interrupted now and then by small houses with little gardens in front of them. I glanced around at my companions. They were pasty-faced and their lips were blue. No one had been able to make any preparations for the trip, and the effect of general uncleanness was heightened by scrubby beards and mustaches. Nothing serves to abase man more than personal filth, and it is difficult to maintain morale under a dirty shirt.

After a while we entered another town. "This is Oranienburg," the man next to me muttered. Perhaps his home was here, for he searched the faces of the people we passed. There were more on the streets now, and when we stopped for a traffic light a crowd gathered at once to look us over. There was pity in some eyes. Some lips moved with unuttered imprecations. But in no face did I see a sign of contempt for us—only apparent sympathy. Our driver snarled at them as the light changed and we moved off, and, looking back, I saw a fist raised in the air. Perhaps it was as well that neither of our guards saw the gesture.

Beyond Oranienburg great forests began to appear. We drove deeper and deeper into them, until we reached a cleared space. It was the entrance to the concentration camp at Sachsenhausen. A big gate swung open, and our trucks moved swiftly through and came to a halt. An order from the guard, and we tumbled stiffly out. My feet felt like iron weights, and my hands were numb. Again we were lined up. Scattered about were a great number of Elite guards, wearing a uniform different from any that I had seen before. It resembled somewhat the uniform of the American army. The men wore regulation caps, but on their breasts and on their upper arms were insignias of skulls. They were members of Hitler's most infamous Elite guard division, men who had sworn a special oath to his person and to do his every bidding.

Our lines were ragged, and the guards came up and struck us with their fists or rifle butts to force us to correct our positions and assume a stiff military attitude. Those who moved slowly were bludgeoned on head and face. The guards enjoyed striking us and laughed among themselves. Finally, they tired of the play, and left us, with the injunction to remain as we were until they returned. "Any one who moves from his position," said the leader, "will be shot by the guards on the watch tower." The watch tower was over the entrance to the camp, and I looked up and saw men with rifles in their hands. So we stood, stiff and straight, not daring to move even a finger or to turn our heads. It was still bitterly cold, for the sun seemed not to have warmed the air, and an icy wind cut our faces. Mucous oozed from every man's nose and ran down his lip, but no one dared to use his sleeve. There was no sound save that of the heavy footsteps of the guards on the watch tower. From where I stood I could see three machine guns trained on us from the tower. The stillness affected me strangely. It was as if I were no longer in the world but already disembodied and on another planet. I was weak from hunger and confinement, and it was all I could do to keep my balance. The man in front of me swayed drunkenly, and I shrank into my coat, expecting a shot. The sick man leaned heavily against the man on his right, and there was a wave through the rest of the line. My own knees trembled violently, and I felt that I could not endure another second, that I must go down.

But suddenly the stillness was broken by loud, scolding voices on our right. I turned my eyes furtively in that direction, and for the first time noticed a great pile of wood. The voices were from behind it, and were coming nearer and nearer. A group of men, each bending beneath a heavy load, appeared from behind the pile of wood. They made a grotesque spectacle. They were wearing a strange uniform made up of rags of different colors sewed together, and on their heads they wore high caps, tapering to a point, which resembled the foolscap of the Middle Ages. The ridiculous costume enhanced the tragic bearing of the men. As they came nearer, I noticed that each had on his right breast and on his left trouser leg a red, green, or black triangle, below which was a number. The men were frightfully emaciated, and so weak that they staggered rather than walked. They moved in absolute silence, heads bowed and eyes downcast. They did not attempt to look up as they passed us. Accompanying them were SS guards and men wearing old police uniforms, all armed with long sticks, with which they were continually belaboring the prisoners, the while scolding them to move with faster pace. It was as if we were looking into a corner of hell suddenly exposed. It was a foretaste of what we could expect.

We were still under the eyes of the guard and standing at attention when this motley array passed us. Involuntary groans escaped us, as if in answer to the feeble wheezes of the burden carriers. There was, too, an involuntary shuffling of feet, for we had been moved too deeply to maintain our rigidity. The guards on the watch tower fingered their rifles menacingly as one called out, "Attention! Keep still, or we will shoot you down, you swine." We straightened, stood stiffly again, numb in body and heart. It seemed so unreal, the sight of these men, so like a disordered dream.

Later on, I learned that I had seen one of the labor columns made up of men who were sick or physically incapable of hard labor, who worked in the inner camp, performing "easier" tasks than were given to the men in the outer camp. Their uniform was the usual camp uniform, and they were of the type of weak unfortunates who had not had the intelligence to escape the vigilance of the Gestapo. They were easy marks for the humiliating and degrading practices of the Nazis, useful victims on which to practice the finer arts of sadism.

Finally, after many hours of standing rigidly at attention, an Elite guard, heavily armed and carrying a long stick, appeared. He whacked the man nearest to him, and ordered us to fall in behind him. He led us to a room in which the uniforms to be distributed among the prisoners were kept. There we had to undress and to surrender all our possessions, including such money as we had brought with us. Then our weights were taken, and each received a camp outfit, consisting of a coarse shirt, a suit of underwear, a pair of socks, shoes, a jacket, trousers, and a foolscap. Everything was made of ersatz material. One part of the jacket was red, the other green. One trouser leg was black, the other red, or some other vivid color. The uniform was too thin to afford any protection against the cold, and it proved to be extremely uncomfortable in the summer time.

In contrast with the custom at Moabit prison, every one who had sufficient money with him was allowed to keep ten marks at a time, with which he could buy additional food or cigarettes. Those who had them were allowed also to keep their pocket knives. This was permitted to prisoners in concentration camps because they are looked upon as prisoners of the police and not as criminals in the generally accepted meaning of that word. In effect, the Gestapo is a branch of the police, though their powers are far wider than any the police could exercise before the Nazis assumed control. In normal times one could appeal to a court of administration against any act of the police, but in 1934 the Supreme Court of Administration ruled that there could be no appeal from an act of the Gestapo. This ruling, of course, conferred extraordinary powers on the Gestapo, which, however, preserved the fiction of legality by describing the concentration camps as *Schutzhaft Lager* (protective camps) and the prisoners as *Schutzhaeftlinge* (the nearest to which I can give in English is "protective prisoners"). The Gestapo may arrest any one and imprison him without giving any reason for the arrest.

After we had donned our uniforms we fell in line outside for a hair cut. A number of barbers, themselves prisoners, were awaiting us. Taking turns, we sat in ordinary chairs while the barbers passed clippers rapidly over our heads, cutting as close to the scalp as possible. With the guards lounging about and uttering coarse jokes, the operation was over in short time, the barbers seemingly as anxious to get the job done as the guards were to get us away. Then we were led off and made to fall in line again. I don't know whether all this delay and shunting about was to sample our powers of endurance or was the result of confusion and overcrowding; but certainly it gave extraordinary delight to the guards. Authority is dear to little minds, and all the sense of frustration these men might have felt in civilian life now found an outlet in orgiastic cruelty.

We stood and shivered until nearly 10 o'clock, when blankets were distributed among us and we were led off to our quarters for the night, without food, though we had had none for three days. The barracks room into which my group were herded was overcrowded and all of us had to sleep on the bare ground, covered only with our thin blankets. We pressed against each other for warmth and the comfort of contact. There were no barriers of caste or profession. I did not know those between whom I lay down. They were merely buffers between me and the cold. And so with the others. All doors and windows were closed and securely locked, and the atmosphere soon became foul. Men snored in terrible discord. There was a continual hawking and clearing of throats above subdued moaning and groaning. But the day had been too long and hard, and sleep came at last.

So ended my first day in a concentration camp. I woke to

the sound of the harsh voice of the block senior shouting to the "swine" to get up. Men stirred sluggishly, sat up stupefied, rubbing their eyes with grimy hands. Clothes were wrinkled into grotesque shapes. The odor was beyond words. Some more shouting at the "swine," and we pulled ourselves to our feet. Some had to make the effort twice before they could stand. The laggards were beaten with sticks. We were supposed to wash in the yard. But there was no water. The pump didn't work, nor was there any breakfast. So we had to answer roll call—tired, cold, and hungry. Working columns were lined up, but all the newcomers were ordered to stand where they were. Then we were taken to the building where we had received our uniforms, and there had the identifying insignia sewed on our jackets and trousers. I received a red triangle and a yellow one, the latter placed over the other so as to make a star, which identified me as a Jewish political prisoner. This done, the man in charge of us, known as a block senior, marched us back to where we had answered the roll, and ordered us to stand at attention.

This time we had not long to wait. We saw a tall, heavily built man, wearing a resplendent uniform, approach. He was the Commandant of the camp. Vanity and arrogance exuded from him. He eyed us contemptuously, and in a disdainful voice told us that any attempt to escape would be punished with death. It would be useless to make the attempt, he said, because it would be impossible for any one to pass through the gates or get by the guards.

"I assume," he said, "that none of you will risk his life in an attempt to escape. But I tell you also that failure to appear on time for roll call also will be considered an attempt to escape."

Those who had funds, he informed us, would be permitted to receive ten marks a week until their money was exhausted or more was sent to them, but that the ten marks would have to be spent within the week. A prisoner who was found in possession of more than ten marks would be deemed guilty of planning to escape, and would be dealt with accordingly. As I soon learned, inspections were held regularly to enforce this rule. We had to undress, place our clothes on the floor, and stand a certain distance away from them. On one occasion a prisoner was discovered to have twelve marks in his possession. He was beaten on the spot and then taken away to a dark cell. We never saw him again. Death was the punishment also for disobedience to an officer, and even to a foreman or block senior. "These men," the Commandant warned us, "have been personally selected by me because of their toughness. And don't think you can get out of work. You will work or die." Physical disability was no excuse, and to plead it was taken as a refusal to work.

Being prisoners of the police, we were allowed to smoke, but we were cautioned that if a building caught on fire its doors would be locked and prisoners trying to escape be machine gunned. Then the Commandant went through a long list of other things *verboten*, which would be punished by whipping, hanging on a tree by the thumbs, or wrists, or confinement in a dark cell.

"Don't mistake this camp for a prison or a workhouse," the Commandant finished. "You will not get along here with your prison and workhouse manners. Remember, this is not a sanatorium but a crematorium. You will soon find out."

Then we were dismissed. Back to the grim, dark building that unfortunate men had made little better than a sty we were taken, to remain there in pain and misery until we were led out again. Those who still had some shred of will and purpose left whispered among themselves. The rest sank within themselves, lost to hope and feeling. There was the constant snuffling, now and then a sigh as of wind in the distance, or of a half uttered imprecation. Men went frequently to the large pail in the middle of the room, some from necessity, some merely from the desire to move, like that of animals in a cage. At last we lay down, those on cots who had them, the rest of us on the bare floor, beneath the wafer-like blankets.

It seemed not long before there was the hoarse shout from outside again, again addressed to the "swine." Perhaps we looked not much better, and we could hardly feel so, as there was no water for washing face and hands. Our slim breakfast swallowed, we were taken to a large administration room, where we had to fill out long questionnaires concerning the personal history of ourselves, our parents, and our grandparents. Then back again to our quarters. The next day we were taken before the political department, where we were questioned by men in plain clothes about our political convictions. We were required to state whether we had ever been members of a political party, and, if so, to what party, and for whom we had voted during the period from 1918 to 1933.

Then, on the following day, was medical inspection, which was no more than a sham. After we had undressed, the doctor gave each a casual examination, and pronounced each "fit for any son of labor." It did not matter that some of the prisoners were old men, men who had seen more than seventy years. And it did not matter that some were ill, and some still suffering from wounds they had received in the first World War. The doctor was as callous towards them as towards the younger and stronger men.

After roll call the next day we were marched to the labor director and by him assigned to labor columns.

I was assigned to a column which had to carry stones from the quarry to a building site, and was ordered to report for work after roll call the next morning. I wondered how big the stones would be.

XV

DEATH HITLER'S ONLY MERCY

SACHSENHAUSEN lies deep in a beautiful forest, and as one approaches it the outward aspect of Germany's most notorious concentration camp looks like that of a park or vast estate. It was still in process of construction when I was imprisoned there, and prisoner details were working everywhere when we entered through the main or central building.

The camp consists of two areas, one inclosing the other. The inner area is approximately a mile square, and is surrounded by an electrically loaded wire fence. Immediately outside this fence are watch towers, fifty yards apart, each manned by a guard armed with rifle and machine gun. The guard is changed every two hours. The strip of ground within six paces of the inner side of the fence is marked off as forbidden territory, to enter which is to invite sudden death, for the guards are ordered to shoot a trespasser without challenge or warning. It was not infrequent that prisoners stepped into this forbidden zone in a final—and successful—effort to escape by suicide.

On the right of the main building is a wing which is given over to dark cells used to confine prisoners who have violated the camp rules, and on the left a wing in which are the administration headquarters. Beyond are the prisoners' barracks, arranged in streets. Each building forms a block, which is under the immediate supervision of a block leader and a block senior. The block leader is a SS guard, and the block senior is a trusty appointed by the Commandant. The block senior is assisted by several other trusties, also appointed by the Commandant, and together they form the so-called service staff. These trusties were selected from the ranks of habitual criminals when I was there. Sometimes Communists also were so favored. Prisoners were required to obey the block senior and his assistants without question. Violation of this rule was punishable with a severe beating, or even instant death, or the culprit was reported to the Commandant, who ordered what was called a disciplinary measure, for which various forms of torture had been devised. The duty of the block senior was to keep order in the barracks under his supervision, and as he and his assistants were relieved of all hard labor their offices were much coveted. In order to remain *personae gratae* with the Commandant they refined themselves in methods of cruelty towards their fellow prisoners, and even sometimes resorted to mutilation or murder.

The barracks buildings were constructed to accommodate two hundred men each, but because of the constantly increasing influx of prisoners, sometimes three or four times that number were confined in them. Prisoners could sleep in them only during the "rest" period, between ten o'clock at night and three o'clock in the morning. As the building was unfinished, we had to lie down on the bare floor, packed together like herrings in a net. One could not move without disturbing his neighbors. There was no latrine, and in lieu of one, pails were distributed about the floor. Sometimes there was only one large pail. Doors and windows were securely locked. The filth and stench can better be left to the imagination than described.

In the outer square were the barracks of the SS guards

and the elegant homes of the administrative officers. Here the prisoners were engaged in quarrying stone, erecting buildings, opening streets, and laying water pipes. Drinking and bathing water was brought in for the guards and officers. Prisoners could drink ditch water, and did. The outer square was well posted with guards, placed twenty feet apart. Many trees and bushes had been left standing, and as I shall tell later on they were frequently used to ambush unsuspecting prisoners. The henchmen of the devil inherited much of the paternal ingenuity.

There were many thousands of prisoners in Sachsenhausen when my name was entered on its rolls. They were divided into various groups—political prisoners, professional criminals, homosexuals, and so-called shirkers, who were classified as anti-social elements. During the beginning of my stay there, there were only a few Jews classified as political prisoners, and they lived in barracks with the "Aryans." But, later on, thousands of Jews were brought in at one time, and special Jewish blocks were formed, and all contact between them and their Aryan fellow prisoners was strictly prohibited.

Each prisoner was identified as to his classification by the color of the insignia on his jacket and trousers. Political prisoners wore a red triangle; professional criminals, green; shirkers, black, and homosexuals, lilac. Jews were classified at first under the general categories. Later, the rule was changed to classify them all as shirkers. In addition, Jews were required to wear also a yellow triangle placed over a black triangle so as to form the Star of David.

It did not follow, of course, that one had been a shirker because he was so labeled. It was a convenient method of classifying those, including Jews, against whom no real charge could be laid, and it pleased the Nazi officials to add this insult to injury.

Also in this group were Aryans who had refused "voluntarily" to separate from their Jewish wives. And Aryans were often so classified because they had incurred the enmity of Nazi officials. A large number of the "shirkers" were workers who had refused to labor under conditions imposed by the Nazi regime, or who had changed jobs in order to get higher wages. Under the Goering plan this was considered sabotage. As the Nazis had decreased wages and increased working hours, this may be taken as an answer to those who still are under the delusion that labor conditions in Germany improved under Hitler and that he clothed the naked and shod the barefoot. In truth, he robbed the working classes to provide for his war machine, and the lot of the working man steadily deteriorated under his "efficiency."

The workers, then, who had tried to better their condition were classified as shirkers and anti-social and placed in concentration camps to correct the idea that they had any individual rights and also to make good National Socialists of them.

Political prisoners were in a somewhat similar situation. Among them also were many cases of men who had become involved in personal quarrels with local Nazi officials. The "political crime" of others consisted in having read illicit newspapers and magazines. Still others were men who had offended because of their religious views. Besides Catholics and Protestants, there were Witnesses of Jehovah and Christian Scientists, who, like those of other religious persuasion, had committed the terrible crime of not believing that Hitler had been sent of God to the German people. Most of these were pacifists, and probably only remnants of their creeds, for many were shot out of hand when war broke out. The larger number of these, too, were men of the skilled labor class or small peasants. Hitler cheated the nation of their skill and labor because they had proclaimed that his assumed divinity was a blasphemy against God. Again, this is the man who was going to improve the economic lot of the German people.

Then there were the Communists, and former Nazis who had broken faith or defaulted in some respect. Those who escaped one net were caught in another.

Professional criminals formed a separate group. The police had judged them to be incapable of reform, and they had been brought to Sachsenhausen because there was no room for them elsewhere. Yet, despite their supposed incorrigibility, it was from their ranks that most of the block seniors and their assistants were selected, the officials assuming, and evidently correctly, that habitual criminals would use their authority to revenge themselves against the society in which they had been unable to find a place.

The homosexuals formed the fourth group. Since it was generally known that many prominent Nazi leaders were homosexuals, I often wondered why others of this type of abnormality were kept in "protective" custody.

What other system could have gathered together, under one roof as it were, such a heterogeneous mass of perverts, incorrigibles, political offenders, and men of varying religious views? What a field of study and research for criminologists and psychologists! But for the Nazis it was a means of revenge and for political and religious perversion. Can any one doubt, then, that the Nazi system is itself a perversion of all that man has learned to hold dear?

Let me show you what life was like in Sachsenhausen. Roll call was at 5 o'clock, which meant that the prisoners had to be awakened at 3 o'clock, since it took about two hours to form the thousands of men into the various working squads. There was no need for the men to dress, as they had slept in their clothes. And as there was no water they didn't have to wash. They simply had to get up and steady themselves on their feet when the first call was sounded. Breakfast was a matter of only a few minutes. It does not take long to swallow a black liquid called coffee. Then there was a last minute scramble for the latrine if there was one, or for the pails if there was not, as no opportunity would be allowed during the day.

The roll, called through loud speakers, took about forty-five minutes. The number of prisoners was checked at the same time. The prisoners then had to remove their caps and stand motionless while an officer reported to the Commandant, a former officer of the Imperial army named Vierkant, that all was in order. Then the working columns were formed. As their names were called, the men had to run to the columns to which they were assigned. When all were ready, the columns were marched to the outer camp. Up to a designated point we stiffened our legs for the goose step. Beyond that point we marched in ordinary fashion.

Every working column was accompanied by a number of Elite guards armed with long, heavy sticks, with which they continually belabored the prisoners, especially to force the weak to keep pace with the stronger. Special foremen and their staffs assisted the guards in "keeping order."

The work was very hard, too hard even for well-fed common laborers. While some quarried the stone, others broke it into suitable sizes, and still others carried it to where the barracks and officers' quarters were being erected. I was one of those who had to carry blocks of stone. Often we had to carry our loads at the double quick, which was done for the amusement of the guards. Also they took particular delight in forcing the weak to load themselves to the point where they could hardly fail to collapse under the burden. Those who did collapse were beaten with sticks, rifle butts, or fists. Often the guards kicked them or stamped on them with their iron-shod heels. Sometimes prisoners died under these attacks. They were left where they fell until later in the day, when there was time to move the bodies. Prisoners became so used to the sight of dead bodies lying about that they hardly noticed them. Their senses had so often reeled under the shock of continued assault that they could no longer feel. Death was escape. It could hold no terror for those who were dying under the heels of their fellow men.

Frequently the guards who watched us in the outer zone hid behind bushes and trees, which seemed to have been left for the purpose. Prisoners who failed to see these guards and accidentally went too near the place of concealment were shot down. They had trespassed into a forbidden zone. Sometimes a prisoner, with his back bowed under a heavy load, would scream shrilly as he was shot and collapse, with the stones he was carrying falling from his back. If we turned we could see a grotesque, misshapen thing lying dead amid a pile of stones. The guard who had fired the shot would jump from behind his place of concealment and laugh uproariously. His comrades would yell their congratulations, for the murderer had earned ten marks and three days' leave. So it went until four o'clock in the afternoon, when we were marched back for the evening roll call.

Often a number of prisoners would be missing. Sometimes sick prisoners who had been assigned to lighter tasks in the inner camp had been unable to drag themselves back for the roll call, and there would be men who had remained away deliberately, knowing that absence from roll call meant certain death.

The Commandant had a pleasant little formula for such an occasion. "Guards, to the forest," he would shout. "Look for the 'birds.' " Yelling uproariously, a number of guards would rush to where the missing prisoners had been working and make search for the "birds." Then we had to sing, generally "Die Lore" or "Mein Schlesierland." Sometimes the men added this refrain of their own as a timid appeal to the commandant:

"Wir wollen gern die Sterne tragen,
Doch bitten wir uns nicht so ban zu schlagen." *

A whistle sounding above our discordant voices was notice to the Commandant that the "bird" had been found. "Louder," the Commandant would shout at us, "louder!" But we could never sing loudly enough to drown the screams of the "bird" dying under the beating of the guards. So we had to stand and continue singing until the guards returned, dragging their victim or victims by a leg. Sometimes a "bird" would still have a little life left in him. The guards finished him off among the trees at the back of the inner camp. Then came the command, *"Aufhoeren zu singen"* (stop singing), and we were dismissed.

In order to keep a thorough check of the number of prisoners, the dead were counted along with the living. At each roll call, morning and evening, the bodies of those who had died or been killed during the day or night, as the case might be, were dragged out in front of the assembly and laid out in rows. The block seniors reported to the camp leader the number of dead in his charge, together with the name of each of the dead, and the camp leader checked off the list and counted the bodies. The camp leader then reported to the Commandant, who could tell at a glance whether the total of the living and the dead corresponded with the number of prisoners who should appear at any particular roll call. While this was being done the prisoners had to stand at attention, with their heads uncovered. If the count at the evening roll call was correct the guards in the outer camp were ordered withdrawn and the prisoners were marched

* "We are ready to carry the stones,
But we beg you not to beat us so hard."

off to their barracks. After the roll call the bodies were piled into trucks and taken to the crematorium to be burned.

Formal notification of death was sent to the families in each case. It ran: "Protective Prisoner X has died." That was all. Accompanying this was a notice that the family could obtain the ashes of the body upon payment of 250 marks. In all cases this ghastly tax on love and affection, unique in history, was paid. If a family was too impoverished by the loss of the bread-winner to pay for the carton of ashes, help came from friends, church, or synagogue. This procedure, followed in every concentration camp in Germany, provides the Nazis with an enormous additional revenue, now probably several hundred million marks a year, which they claim is used for improvements in the camps, but which actually is used for purposes of war. This explains why the Nazis muster the dead as carefully as they call the roll of the living. They are nothing if not ingenious. Goebbels even appointed committees to investigate conditions in the sepulchers of the living. And the committees invariably reported that the stories of atrocities were baseless and that camp conditions were constantly being improved.

What will the families of the murdered do when they learn the truth, as some day they must?

Every night prisoners died in the barracks from hunger and exhaustion and the results of beatings. We saw their bodies dragged out for the roll call. One morning I awoke to find that I was lying pressed close to a dead man. I was not startled. I had then been in Sachsenhausen two months, and the sight of dead bodies had become too common to affect me deeply.

After evening roll call we worked in the inner camp, usually felling trees and clearing away the branches and limbs, carrying the trunks to where they were needed, and cleaning up. We worked until eight o'clock, when we were permitted to return to our quarters. There we stood in line, often nearly an hour, to receive our dinner-thin soup, a piece of bread and a little oleomargarine, and sometimes thirty grams of sausage or cheese. *We* were not permitted to "go to bed" until ten o'clock. That gave us five hours' "rest." The intervening time we occupied with our thoughts and occasional whispered conversation. Men moved about among the pails. There was no light, and there was much stumbling, with awkward consequences.

Sundays and holidays meant nothing in the life of the camp. We worked as usual. Those who were devotionally inclined were a little longer at their prayers on Sunday mornings and evenings. It was an impressive sight to see them on their knees and the Catholics crossing themselves. If Hitler had read history he would have known that he couldn't crush religious faith or substitute a pagan creed for Christianity.

Prisoners were not permitted to receive visitors except under special dispensation, in which case the prisoner was taken to Moabit. Only a near relative was permitted to visit a prisoner, and the visit was limited to half an hour, in the presence of a guard. Every other Sunday we were allowed to write post cards to our families. We had to say that we were "well," so as not to "annoy" our families. On these Sundays work was not required of us after evening roll call.

In addition to the "punishments" inflicted to satiate the lusts of the Nazi officials, there were the official disciplinary measures. For the more serious violation of the camp rules the penalty was death, as I have stated before. Prisoners, therefore, had to be very careful lest they commit some infraction unwittingly or be trapped into a violation. For instance, I once saw a guard beating a prisoner in the face with a stick. The victim instinctively raised his arm to shield himself from the blows raining down on him. "You are resisting me," yelled the guard. "You are resisting me, you dirty dog," and he drew his pistol and shot the prisoner dead. Another time a very sick prisoner had collapsed under his burden. A guard came up and asked in an apparently friendly manner, "Don't you feel like working any more?" "No," answered the prisoner in a weak voice. "May I rest a little while?" "You are refusing to work," shouted the guard in reply, immediately dispatching the man with a shot through the head. There were no inquiries into these murders. The guard's report was sufficient. Day after day I saw the murderers return to duty. We learned to beware of them as best we could.

But it was always hard to keep within the rules. Everything was *verboten*. It was forbidden, for instance, to go to a latrine during working hours. I will not describe the frequent consequences. I was once badly beaten for breaking this rule. We were not allowed to seek shelter during a heavy rain. If one crept beneath the eave of a roof for a moment he was punished. Most of these violations were reported by the members of a secret force of camp police made up of prisoners. They bore no mark to distinguish them from the rest of us, and were frequently changed, so that it was difficult to know who was friend and who was not. The method was for a member of these secret police to take note of the number of an alleged violator and then report the offense to his superior, who, in turn, would see that it was brought to the attention of the Commandant. Other prisoners, too, most of them habitual criminals, former Nazis, or Communists, would volunteer information to the camp authorities. There was no hearing for the accused man, no opportunity whatsoever to defend himself. Few escaped this espionage.

The penalty for offenses reported by the spies consisted of whipping or hanging in a tree and confinement afterwards in a dark cell. The punishment was inflicted at evening roll call, in full view of the prisoners.

If the victim was to be whipped, his feet were tied together and then fastened to the whipping post. A guard on each side held him in position. Two other guards, one on each side, beat him on the back with long heavy whips, using all their strength. The minimum punishment was twenty-five lashes; often there were one hundred. After the beating, the man was forced to stand at attention and report to the Commandant, "Protective Prisoner X punished with— lashes because of disorderly conduct." Then he was led off for confinement in a dark cell. The cells used for close confinement were very small, and their little windows were darkened by planks nailed across them.

Frequently prisoners were tied by their wrists to the limb of a tree. The method was to have the victim's fellow prisoners pull down a limb of a tree, tie the man by the wrists to the limb, and then let it go, so that the man swung clear of the ground. He had to swing there twenty-four hours. Sometimes the victim would be forced to climb up into the tree for the hanging. Often prisoners died under this treatment. Not infrequently they were sentenced to several days of this cruel punishment. In that case they were untied every twenty-four hours and allowed to rest for a time, and then tied up again.

One day I was reported for violating the smoking rules. In a moment of forgetfulness I had lighted a cigarette just before the hour in which smoking was permitted. At the evening roll call I was placed in the line of those who were to be punished and heard my sentence—twenty-five lashes. I had to watch the other beatings while waiting my turn. I managed to avert my eyes at times without being detected. Then two guards tied my feet together and dragged me to the whipping post, to which I was fastened. A guard on each side held my arms and forced me to a bending posture. Two other guards applied their whips to my bare back. The whips fell—once, twice, three times . . . I lost count. After the first few blows the pain was not so intense. I suppose I was only partly conscious after that. When it was over I had to make my report to the Commandant. Then I was dragged to a dark cell, to be confined for three days.

The guard forced me to remove my shoes and ordered me to stand as I was. There was a cot in the cell, tied against the wall, but I was forbidden to use it. Constantly guards peeped in to see that I didn't. My back hurt horribly. Finally, I could stand no longer, and I lay down on my stomach. It didn't matter to me then whether the guards came in to finish me or not. Perhaps they were too busy in adjoining cells, for now and then I could hear prisoners screaming shrilly under the guards' sticks. Some of them had become insane, and their maniacal outcries had angered the guards. Beating did not silence them, of course, and they only shrieked the louder. Some of them died that night. In the mornings my fellow victims and I were allowed to go to the toilet for a few minutes, after which a tiny piece of bread and a little water were given to each of us for breakfast, the only meal of the day. This continued for three days and nights. Each night I lay down on the floor, not caring whether the guards saw me or not. Strangely, I longed for the "peace" of Moabit prison.

But there was no improvement in our lot, despite the reports of the investigating committees. There was no water for the prisoners, and the sanitary conditions were terrible. We had to drink dirty water from ditches, and there was too little even to wash our hands and faces. We could get a change of under clothing only once in three months. In consequence, there was much disease, especially inflammation of the eyes and of the skin. There were few accommodations for the sick, for there was only one building used as a hospital, and that accommodated only fifty patients. And there was only one doctor, a brutal young man who wore a SS uniform. He seemed to regard every case of sickness as a personal offense. A few of the prisoners had received superficial training as *Sanitaeters* and they were called upon to treat major illnesses, as for instance, pneumonia. The patients did not linger long.

Those who were regarded as not being ill enough to be sent to the hospital formed a *Schonungs* company, that is a company receiving "special consideration" and required to do only "light" work in the inner camp. Others who could not walk and still were not in the hospital were allowed to sit on the bare ground at the back of the camp, and if they could not sit upright they were allowed to lie down. The doctor would use his stick on them to see if they were malingering, and they were a convenient target for passing guards. Jews were not permitted to see the doctor, and in no case could one get into the hospital.

This savage and senseless treatment resulted in a strange and most horrible psychological phenomenon—the physical and mental debasement of the prisoners. They became animalistic in appearance and habit, and their deterioration was enhanced by filthy clothing. Many were unable to endure the daily torture, and it was not uncommon for prisoners during their first days in camp to commit suicide by banging their heads against rocks. Others who did not have the strength or will power to end their lives in this fashion deliberately trespassed on forbidden territory, hoping to be shot down by the guards. But the guards, who otherwise frequently called prisoners into forbidden zones to shoot them down for sport, refused to fire at those whom they suspected of suicidal intent. To these they would shout, "Get off, you swine. You want to be shot in order not to work." Once an old man who apparently had reached the limit of endurance deliberately entered a forbidden zone, and when the guard hesitated and ordered him away, he opened his jacket and, pointing to his bared breast, shouted, "Why don't you kill me, you cowardly Nazi swine?" The infuriated guard then fired point-blank at him and he dropped in his tracks.

When I first saw such a scene it seemed to me as if civilization had been only a thin veneer which was now washed away in blood. In my ears rang the retort of the Roman Emperor Tiberius when the victims of his torture begged of him the mercy of death—"I am not reconciled with you yet." Today, nearly two thousand years after Christianity was given to the world, death still is the only mercy Hitler knows.

But the spirit of rebellion against this daily cruelty was only of short duration. The will of most prisoners soon broke under the strain, and they became like dogs cowed by the lash and fighting among themselves for a bone. At times I came near to succumbing to this degradation myself, and it was only by supreme exercise of will and by daily engaging my mind in observation and reflection that I escaped.

Often we were glad to eat chestnuts that we were able to pick up from the ground, and gladder when we could get a few raw potatoes. Frequently starved and unnerved men got into bloody quarrels with each other on the slightest provocation—for a piece of bread men committed murder. The guards never interfered on such occasions. On the contrary, they would stand by and encourage the famished men to continue their quarrels.

"Now, let's see who is stronger, who is the best man," they would jeer. They knew that they would not be called to account for permitting these murderous quarrels, for it suited the Nazis' purpose to stir up animosity among the prisoners lest the concentration camps become breeding grounds of hostility to Hitler. It would look better in the record, too, if ever there is one, if it could be made to appear that all the killings in the concentration camp were by the inmates themselves. These quarrels often led to mutual denunciations to the officials. For instance, a prisoner was whipped and then confined in a dark cell for four weeks because he had told a fellow prisoner that he would rather serve in the French Foreign Legion, of which he once had been a member, than exist in a Nazi concentration camp. This was almost treason, for no military organization in the world is so deeply detested in Germany as the French Foreign Legion, to which many Germans had fled in order to escape hardship and poverty in their own country. Another man who had become half crazed by the ill treatment applied to the Commandant to be placed under the law protecting animals because they were treated so much better than human beings. At roll call the next morning he was ordered to report at the Commandant's office, and none of us ever saw or heard of him again.

Thus the prisoners were forced to become victims of their own primitive instincts and so made to serve their masters better than if they had been able to live together in a spirit of friendship and camaraderie.

Another method of undermining the morale of the prisoners was to tell them that they could regain their freedom if they could prove that they had become good Nazis. Thus they were tempted to denounce each other, but the only reward was a package of cigarettes or a piece of bread. It was very seldom that Aryans were released from camp, no matter what the plea.

Jews were treated worse than the Aryans. Fifteen hundred of them who had been caught in a mass round-up were brought in one day, and were immediately put into separate blocks and working columns. Among them were many scholars and professional men, such as rabbis, professors, lawyers, and doctors, all of whom had to wear the Star of David on their arms to distinguish them from the Aryans.

They were forbidden to talk with the Aryans, and received only a third of the bread ration and half of the soup ration. Every third day they had to go without food altogether. That became my lot, too, of course. Yet, in spite of this, the Jews were the envy of the Aryan prisoners because, at that time at least, Jews could obtain their release from concentration camp whenever they could show that they had the means to leave the country. As all the "means" save the actual expense of getting out of the country was confiscated by the Nazis this was another source of revenue. They not only got rid of Jews but got most of their money too.

As time went on, the slavish submission of most of the prisoners increased, and gradually they lost all sense of the tremendous wrong that was being done them. They became immersed in the trivial details of existence. Their bellies became their gods, for hunger was never satisfied. They talked of the cruel cold, and when they could, nursed themselves in a ray of sun. They looked forward to the hours of "rest," and complained in whispers of their aching backs and tired feet. They would talk among themselves of the guards, saying of this one that he was less cruel than another, of that one that he did not use his stick so often, and of a third that he would sometimes permit a man to go to the toilet. They could no longer think, save to remember that the stretch from dawn to night was a measure of eternity. Many of them stopped writing to their families. They seemed to have forgotten home, wife and children. They lost their dread of death, for life no longer had any meaning. If they were doomed to hell it would be a change at least, and if there were neither heaven nor hell, then there would be the eternal peace of the grave.

Some became insane. But this was not considered sufficient cause to release them. Besides, where could they have been sent when asylums, hospitals, and prisons were already full? So a company of "idiots" was formed of those who were harmless, while the violently insane were taken into the dark cells, where, in time, they were beaten to death. The company of "idiots" worked in the inner camp, under the supervision of one of their number who was found still sufficiently intelligent. They were very quiet, and, strangely enough, they regained some of their former human qualities. Into their befuddled minds came some sense of responsibility for each other, and they even shared their food and money. Was this an act of Providence, or can it be explained in human psychology?

But I must not fail to relate that one group of prisoners were a sublime exception to the general rule. They were the religiously devout. These martyrs to faith did not lose even their dignity in this place of torment. Perhaps it was because they had undertaken their martyrdom voluntarily that they had such supreme fortitude. For they could have regained their liberty if they had agreed to make obeisance to Hitler. Instead, they determined upon resistance to the end. They would share their last piece of bread with the sick and the weak. They offered comfort when they could. They prayed at night and in the morning, and they remembered the Sabbath to keep it holy so far as they could. Among them were clergymen of every faith—Catholics, Evangelicals, Christian Scientists, Jehovah's Witnesses, and others.

Another phenomenon which has impressed itself indelibly on my memory was the unabating cruelty of the SS guards. They seemed never to grow weary of exercising their ingenuity to inflict torture. How these tall, well-built men, dressed in elegant uniforms, could treat helpless, miserable fellow creatures as if they were fiends from hell puzzled me. Personal motives could not have been the reason, for there were too many prisoners, and, besides, they were constantly being changed. Fresh prisoners filled the places of those who went out in little containers. Nor could racial or class hatred have been the reason, for most of the prisoners were Aryans like the guards, blood of their blood, and mostly from the same social strata.

From their various dialects and from their general manner, it was plain that most of the guards were representative of the lower classes. But I was struck with the fact that the majority of their officers were of better education and social standing. Among them were even many officers of the former Imperial army. Up to this time I could not have imagined that men who had served under the late German Emperor could be party to such cruelties. I had always refused to believe the atrocity stories about the German army during the first World War, but now I saw the proofs, and I soon learned that those who claimed to represent the best German tradition were no better than the most ruthless Nazis.

These men were able to live in their own homes, together with their families, and bring up children, and yet in the camp they knew only one thing—the destruction of the very things by which they lived themselves, and that by the most infernal means that ingenuity could devise. They were types of the men who chilled the blood of refugees beyond the Rhine with the cry, "The Fuehrer is coming," who machine-gunned women and children in the roads of France.

What can the world expect from such hordes if ever the Nazis are victorious?

Even the wives and grown-up daughters of the officers were often despicably cruel. Frequently, with our heavy loads, we had to pass their homes in the outer camp. In the summer the women would sit in their gardens at a *Kaffeeklatsch.* Sometimes I would glance at their faces. But not once did I see in them an expression of sympathy or horror at the sight of the living dead. I saw only hardened indifference. They were untouched by the sight of the most terrible human misery. Yet they knew that their homes were built of the blood and pains of the bent, white-faced creatures who passed their gates. One day an officer's wife noticed a prisoner approach her garden fence too closely. She took down his number and reported him. He was punished with fifty lashes and three days in a dark cell.

These are the conditions to which half of the men of Europe will be subjected if Hitler wins. Already he has imprisoned in camps no better than Sachsenhausen thousands of men from France, Holland, Belgium, and other countries. And be sure that he will wreak his vengeance on all the others who have resisted him if he has the chance.

In reports dealing with conditions in concentration camps which I have read in this country there was always an optimistic note. Correspondents prophesied that the camps would become focal points from which rebellion against the Nazis would start, that they are breeding places of an opposition which will prove most dangerous to the Nazi regime. I am unable to agree. What I saw was a force of such inhuman monstrosity as to make resistance impossible and hope a vain thing.

Since the concentration camps are used also to provide forced labor they give a clear idea of the system of enslavement planned by the Nazis after the consolidation of their conquests—should that evil day come about. The part these camps are playing in Hitler's grandiose scheme for the conquest of the world has not been fully realized by his intended victims. Not only are they used to provide slave labor and a means to crush all opposition, but they are also made to serve as garrisons in which the Nazi armies are schooled in the fiendish ruthlessness which is necessary to the kind of warfare the Nazis are waging. Here Hitler's men are taught to despise and hold in contempt the rights of others, to harden themselves against any sentiment of pity or mercy, and to make themselves dynamos of destruction. And here, in my opinion, lies the secret of the successes Hitler has achieved so far—the spirit of ruthless ferocity he has inculcated in his followers.

Just as this chapter was being finished the Western hemisphere was awakened from its lethargy by Japan's treacherous assault on Hawaii and the Philippines and the declaration of war upon the American people by Hitler and Mussolini, when, finally, it became abundantly clear that the world must either submit to dictatorship or destroy it. If Nazism is to be destroyed spiritual force is as necessary as tanks and guns, for there are still people on this side of the Atlantic who continue to believe that there is a positive side to Hitler's "new order." They continue to look upon Hitler as the leader of a new dispensation. Nothing could be farther from the truth, nothing more dangerous in its consequences. For, in reality, the world is faced with a movement it has never before experienced. Whereas conquerors in other times have generally surrendered to and tried to adopt the cultural standards of the peoples whom they have conquered, Hitler has set forth to destroy the culture and civilization which gave him birth and to erect in its place a universal system of slavery. He is the true nihilist, a representative of the powers of evil which our civilization has been trying to overcome for nearly two thousand years. The evidences of this are already writ large on the face of Europe. They appear in broad detail in the concentration camps Hitler has set up in the path he has blazed. He has destroyed where even he could have had no need to destroy. He has strewn his way with havoc and deluged a continent with blood. And he must go on. He cannot stop. Each new conflict must begin another. Civilization must destroy him and his imitators or be destroyed by him. Let those who still hold the belief that he is a man of destiny, an angel of reform wearing the disguise of man, reflect on what he has done to his own people. He has taken from them all the hard-won standards of Christian culture and sacrificed them on the sword of destruction. He has taught the German youth that the only virtue is to believe in him, that the future of Germany is bound up in his success, and that they must wait on his word. With my own eyes I have seen the evil transformation he has effected, and what I have witnessed is warning of worse to come if Hitlerism is not utterly and forever destroyed.

I hope that what I have written may contribute to a true understanding of the character and intentions of Nazi Germany.

XVI

TOGETHER AT SACHSENHAUSEN

WEEKS passed, interminable, terrible weeks of existence in this Nazi hell. Even now they come back to me in my dreams, and I wake sometimes in the night with my body in a cold sweat of fear. I start at a sudden step behind me and shrink at the sound of a loud voice. The Terror will never entirely leave me.

As I have indicated, induction into the routine at Sachsenhausen was cruelly abrupt. On my first day I was assigned to a carrier column, with which I marched out to the quarry in the outer camp. At a certain point near the main building we were ordered to fall into *Parademarsch*, and while goose stepping through the main entrance we had to turn eyes left, towards a window behind which a guard sat to count us as we passed. When we passed through we ceased goose stepping, but still had to march in military formation, with lines three feet apart. Those who could not keep the proper distance were beaten by foremen or guards. It was very difficult for me to keep up, for the column, urged on by the sticks of the foremen and guards, marched at an extremely rapid rate, entirely too fast for one who like myself had never had any military training. In addition, the shoes which had been given me were much too large and were in such a bad state of wear that they chafed and cut my feet until the pain was almost unendurable.

At last we arrived at the quarry, in front of which there was a great heap of stones. We had to climb to the top of this pile and there each shoulder a stone. Then we had to rush back to our places in the line below. There we were inspected by a guard to see if each one of us had a sufficiently large stone. If his stone was considered too small, the carrier was beaten and ordered back to the pile, where a guard would point to a very large stone and order him to carry it. I was ordered back to the pile on the very first trip because, in my innocence, I had picked up a stone which I thought I would be able to carry, and which I found heavy enough, considering that this was the first manual labor I had ever attempted in my life. Up to this time I had spent my working hours at a desk, doing research, writing, or teaching law—work that I enjoyed because it brought me into contact with young, intelligent minds and gave outlet to my own inclination.

When a guard pointed to a large stone and ordered me to pick it up, I found that I could not even budge it.

"He does not want to work, *der feine Herr* (the fine gentleman)!" the guard shouted at me, and blows from his stick rained on my head and shoulders. "He is accustomed only to exploiting the German people, the dirty Jew! But now I will show him what honest work means."

But all this did not help. I simply was unable to pick up the stone and place it on my shoulder, and when the guard ordered the foreman to pick it up and put it on my shoulder I dropped under the burden. The guard forced me to get up by stamping on me with his iron heels. But still I could not lift the stone. Realizing, finally, that I was physically incapable of lifting the stone to my back, the guard allowed me to pick up a smaller one. Even that was extremely heavy for me, and it required all my strength to lift it. Then I had to go back to my place in the line. When all the backs were found to be sufficiently loaded we were ordered to march at the quick to a place approximately a mile distant. How I made that first trip has always been a mystery to me. I know only that when I reached the goal I was thoroughly exhausted, with pains shooting through every joint. And though it was an icy cold February day I was burning with thirst. But there was no water, not even a drop from a ditch, which I gladly would have swallowed. Nevertheless, back and forth we went, carrying and delivering stones for an officer's home. Each stone seemed heavier than the last. Our pace finally slowed down, for even the lash could not put new life into our legs and backs, and the guards finally desisted from attempting to force us to faster pace. It was not from pity but because they feared to kill off all the beasts of burden while there were yet stones to be moved.

One day I collapsed under a heavy stone, and was unable to get up. The guard kicked me and stamped on me, which, of course, only rendered me the more helpless. An officer came up, and I heard the guard say to him, "He refuses to work." Then the officer, a tall, heavy man, leaned down and hammered on my skull with his knuckles. This hammering on the skull sometimes made prisoners go insane. It hurt terribly, and I was already in agony from the kicking and stamping. The officer continued thumping on my head for several moments, and then he ordered the guard to get me up and chase me towards the chain of guards posted near by. This was a ruse to have me shot down. Prisoners frequently were shot down in this way. The guard kicked me again, but I simply could not get to my feet. I think I must have screamed, for the officer finally said, "Well, let him lie there. Give him another chance."

Why he accorded me this mercy I don't know. Perhaps they were both tired of beating me. The officer left, but the guard stood by, and at length I was able to get up, shaky and unsteady. Fortunately for me, it was at the end of the work period, and I was taken back to the barracks. I had to return to work as usual the next morning.

Afterwards I learned from my wife that she had been told by Jewish prisoners who had been released before I was that I had been killed. It was not the first time that she received such news.

After I had spent a week at this excruciating labor I was in no wise distinguishable from any of my fellow prisoners. My jacket was torn at the shoulder from the wear and tear of the stones. My body was covered with sores caused by the sticks of the guards and the stones' sharp edges. Besides being physically exhausted, I felt the tremendous mental strain caused by this cruel, incessant toil. We never had sufficient rest from one day to the next, and there was little or no nourishment in the food we were allowed.

I observed two changes coming over me. First, I was becoming completely indifferent to the cruelties practiced against my fellow prisoners, of which I was as much a victim as they. Every day men of our column and of other columns were beaten to death and left lying where they fell, like dead dogs. When I noticed this for the first time I was greatly shocked and was unable to understand the indifference of my fellow prisoners, who did not even glance at the dead bodies as they passed by. but very soon I began to experience this same indifference myself, and I realized that this was the natural consequence of the tremendous strain on mind and body. There came a time in the personal suffering of each when he became insensible to that of others. There were exceptions, of course, most of them being the religious. But most of us could not help trying to shut ourselves in from all this unbelievable hurt.

The second change I observed about myself was a diminishing capacity to think. I had always been able to think clearly and logically before. But now I noticed an increasing confusion in my mind. I was unable to concentrate long enough to think anything through. It was strange that I could make even this self-observation. I was shocked at the thought that it might not be very long before I sank to the same mental level of those around me. The fear nerved me to greater exercise of will power, and I concentrated on saving my mind if not my body. This may explain, in part at least, the indifference I developed to what was going on around me.

I was not permitted to have my wounds treated at the hospital, the guards saying, "These are only the marks of honest labor." In my desperation I determined one day to drop a heavy stone on one of my feet or my hands and so mutilate myself as to become unable to carry stones. But an accident proved to be my salvation.

The forefinger of my right hand became infected, and when I showed it to the guard he, for some reason, let me go to the hospital. There a prisoner superficially trained in first aid lanced the wound and removed the finger nail, without giving me any local anesthetic. But I did not feel much pain, probably because of my general weakened condition. Then my finger was dressed, and I received permission to join the *Schonungskompanie* (company of the sick), who were permitted to do easier work in the inner camp. For me it consisted of carrying bricks on my left shoulder. I had to go to the hospital every morning to have the dressing changed. During this period I came into closer contact with the camp senior, who was a Communist and former secretary of a labor union and a well educated and decent man. When he saw my condition, he said, "You won't be able to stand this much longer. If you have money I can help you." I replied eagerly that I had money with me and some on account. "Then you don't have to worry," he answered. "Everything can be straightened out for you. You can become a member of the *Klub der Zahler* (club of money payers)."

When I expressed my astonishment he informed me that a prisoner who had money could have his life made easier, even in a concentration camp. I learned from him that there was in existence a well organized paying system by which some prisoners who had succeeded in getting appointed to a camp office shared the booty with the Nazi guards.

I was receiving ten marks from my personal account. It was a very small amount, equalling, according to the official price of exchange, four American dollars. With this money I was permitted, as were all other prisoners who had funds, to buy additional food and cigarettes. The prices of these were excessive, and the quality very poor; but even such small amounts as my account played a tremendous part in the concentration camp. For the great majority of the prisoners, especially those who had been imprisoned a long time, were without private means, and had, therefore, no chance to buy extra food or to get anything to smoke. They were glad to get from some fellow prisoners a few pennies with which to buy the extras they wanted. Money in the concentration camp was, therefore, worth much more than its real value. Ten marks in the concentration camp equalled in buying power many times that number on the outside. Not only prisoners, but guards too, were always anxious to obtain extra money, for they were so poorly paid that they could not afford anything beyond their immediate necessities. And so there had been created an underground system profitable for the guards and some favored prisoners, and of inestimable value to those prisoners who were able to pay. It helped to save the lives of many of them.

When I learned all this I eagerly agreed to the camp senior's proposal. I handed eight marks to him, leaving only two marks for myself, for I was glad enough to renounce the purchase of additional food for the chance to get out of the working column of the outer camp. A few hours later my new friend told me that everything had been arranged. He had spoken about me to the guard in charge of the inner camp during working hours. The guard had accepted my money * and had no objection to my staying in the inner camp. I was told that regardless of any special permission or not, I should join the *Schonungskompanie* every morning after roll call. The camp senior, who was under the supervision of the guard who had received my money, had the task of sifting out from the *Schonungskompanie* those who did not have special permission to be in it, but I was told that there would be no interference with me. So, although my special permission had expired, I joined the *Schonungskompanie* every morning. The majority in the column consisted of very old or sick prisoners, but every morning many of them were arbitrarily sifted out and put back in the regular working columns. Those of us who belonged to the *Klub der Zahler* were not troubled. Most of the members were men who had held responsible positions in Germany, scholars, high officials, big business men, etc.

My life was easier now. I was relieved virtually of all work. Most of the day the *Klub der Zahler* spent in the laundry, or if that was not possible, we were assigned to some easy work, as, for instance, carrying things from one building to another. Since the inner camp was watched very casually during the working period, we enjoyed comparative freedom, which meant that we could walk through the camp streets, enter some of the barracks, and chat with the so-called "barrack service" left behind to clean the barracks.

One afternoon when I was strolling near the building

* Some of this may have gone to the guard who sent me to the hospital, as he knew I had funds. I have been informed since that prisoners are not now allowed to keep funds on account or on their persons and that this form of bribery no longer exists. Therefore, I am not betraying the prisoners now in concentration camps by relating this experience.

from which the camp uniforms were distributed I noticed a prisoner standing in front of it, with his back turned towards me. I became very curious, for I knew that a prisoner standing in front of that building at this time of the day must be a newcomer, and I wondered why he was alone, because usually prisoners were transported to the camp in groups. But before I could approach nearer, he turned around and faced me. It was Pastor Niemoeller.

Yes, there he stood, clad in the grotesque camp uniform, a foolscap on his head. The lines in his face were deeper, but he still wore the same gentle expression with which I had become familiar. I was horrified to see him here, for I had always hoped that he would be acquitted by the court and would regain his freedom. I couldn't imagine that the Nazis would have dared intern him in a concentration camp.

But there he was, in the flesh—a World War hero who had risked his life a hundred times for his country and then had tried to save her spiritually. Now, as a reward, the Nazis had reduced him to the status of a slave. It seemed to me that in enslaving him the true Germany, which I have loved all my life, had itself become enslaved.

Pastor Niemoeller returned my gaze, apparently in great astonishment, on account of my appearance I suppose, for although I had not been out with the working column for several weeks I must have looked terrible enough. There were no mirrors in camp, and no one would have wanted to look at himself even if there had been one, and I could have only a vague idea of what I looked like. He did not know me at first, but when I approached nearer, he recognized me.

"Is this you?" he said, startled. "I thought you had already left Germany."

"No, no," I answered. "But what of you? Why are you here? What has happened? I thought that the court would have released you and that you would be free."

Briefly he told me what had happened after my departure from Moabit. The court had dropped the charge of attempted high treason against him, but had sentenced him to seven months' imprisonment on a charge of violating the *Kanzel Paragraph* (the pulpit law, which prescribed punishment for clergymen who offended the government in their sermons. This law was introduced by Bismarck during the time of the famous *Kultur Kampf,* the conflict between the German government and the Roman Catholic Church). But the court had ruled that the prison sentence had already been made up by Niemoeller's stay at the examining prison at Moabit, and he was, therefore, released from prison.

But his dismissal from Moabit had been of no avail to Niemoeller. He, too, had been subjected to the same procedure used by the Nazis if the sentences of their own courts did not satisfy them. He was arrested by the Gestapo when he emerged from Moabit, and was taken to the Gestapo headquarters, where again he was offered his liberty if he would pledge himself to refrain from preaching. Again he refused, whereupon he was immediately rushed, alone, in a fast car (not a prison van) to Sachsenhausen. When I met him he had just received his camp uniform.

"But do you know what you have done, Pastor Niemoeller?" I could not help saying. "Do you know what you must expect here?" and I told him a little about the conditions at Sachsenhausen. "You see," I added, "Moabit prison was a paradise compared with this camp."

"I know," he replied, "but I am ready to see it through to the bitter end. Perhaps I am lost. I may never be released. But I will keep my conscience clear to the last. God will give me the strength. He always reveals Himself in time of trial."

In my eagerness to save him from the tortures I feared would be his lot I told him of the opportunity offered to those who were able to pay. But he refused to consider it. "I will not have a better fate than any other man in this camp," he said. "For it is by God's will that I have been brought here, and if it be His will I shall get out of here." I felt as if my soul were naked before him.

We were interrupted by the coarse voice of a Nazi guard who stood suddenly besides us. We had not heard him approaching. "What are you doing here, *Saujude* (Jewish pig)?" he shouted at me. I was frightened, for I did not know this guard and feared that I would be returned to the working column. When I tried to stammer an excuse he slapped my face and ordered me to accompany him to the guard in charge of the inner camp. "And you, too, you dirty dog," he said to Niemoeller, "follow me."

We followed him through the empty streets of the camp, his heavy boots kicking up the dust in our faces. Finally, he found the guard in charge of the inner camp, and, pushing me towards him, said, "I found this swine in a place where he had no business to be. You know what to do with him." Then shouting to Pastor Niemoeller to follow him, he turned in the direction of the main building, evidently with the intention of taking Niemoeller before the authorities. I watched the saint in foolscap and grotesque uniform until he and the guard turned the corner.

As for myself, I knew that I had nothing to fear from the guard in charge of the inner camp, whose name was Gehring, and who had the rank of a troop leader. His palm had already been well greased. He merely admonished me to be more careful in the future and told me to go back to my place. So ended my first meeting with Pastor Niemoeller in Sachsenhausen.

I hoped to see him at the evening roll call, but was disappointed. I learned later from my friend the camp senior that

the pastor had been "accommodated" in one of the punishment cells and that the planks used to darken its little window had been removed. This was unusual, and I was much
worried, for I feared that he had been placed in this cell in
preparation to kill him.

XVII

WOULD HITLER HAVE LAUGHED?

I DID not see Pastor Niemoeller again for some days, but my friend the camp senior brought me news that he had been relieved of the necessity of answering roll call, though the camp senior did not know why. Although a Communist and professing no religious belief at all, the camp senior seemed very much interested in the newcomer and remarked to me that the Nazis were heaping curses on themselves by their treatment of Niemoeller.

"Do you mean to say," I asked him, "that a Communistic regime would have behaved differently towards Pastor Niemoeller?"

"Yes," he answered, "for Communists always recognize the value of human worth."

When I reminded him of the persecution of the Church in Russia, he replied, "That is a different story, and can be judged only by the special situation existing there. In Russia the Church was more or less a feudal institution and was too closely connected with the former ruling class. A German Communistic government would not try to destroy the Church so long as it restricted itself to its special mission and did not meddle in politics."

I could not help questioning the correctness of this view, for it reminded me of similar statements that had been made by the Nazis before they attained power. They too had said that they really had no intention of persecuting the Jews and the Christian Church. But when *der Tag* arrived and the persecutions began, those same men approved the attacks, and when I reminded some of them who formerly had been my friends of their promises, they said, "Oh, at that time we did not understand the real situation. After all that has come out now, you yourself must admit that the government is right and is following the realistic policy which the situation demands." So I had no reason to place any credence in the camp senior's statement, though I could not doubt his own sincerity.

One day, while we were carrying planks to a new stable that was being built, I heard some one shouting, and turned my head to see Pastor Niemoeller coming out of the main building under escort of two SS guards. "Quicker, quicker, *altes Pfaff ens chwein* (old swine of a priest)!" I heard one of them shout. "Can't you walk any faster? You are faking. You aren't sick." Both guards were beating the pastor with their sticks. The sight made me sick.

As we passed back and forth I noticed later that the guards had resorted to one of the favorite games at the camp. Standing about a hundred yards apart from each other, they beat and chased Pastor Niemoeller between them, laughing hilariously the whole time. "He needs exercise, that *Schweinehund* (pig dog)," they shouted back and forth, belaboring him every time he came near.

Niemoeller himself did not utter a sound during this scene. His face was very white and drawn, and his lips tightly pressed together. Perspiration streamed from his forehead. After a while he slowed down, panting for breath. The guards continued to beat him, but he had reached the limit of his strength. "Look at the weakling," one guard shouted to the other. "Such a weak swine! Yet he dares to oppose our Fuehrer!"

"Right you are," the other shouted back. "What would become of Germany if all Germans were like him?"

Then they desisted. Niemoeller's hour of "recreation" was over.

I had been pretty well squeezed dry of all emotion, but this harrowing sight wrung me to my very marrow—two, callow, cynical, ignorant young men, who probably were as little acquainted with the history of the Fatherland as they were with kindness, hilariously torturing a man whose name had once thrilled every home in Germany! If American people can imagine one of their heroes being treated with such foul ignominy by two of his own countrymen, then they can understand the depth of the degradation to which Hitler has brought his hirelings. Neither previous valor nor present virtue is proof against the cultivated heartlessness of the Nazis. This is the gang whom statesmen once thought to appease—thieves, liars, traitors, assassins. Nothing beyond the grasp of their mercenary minds is sacred. Hitler must answer not only for wrecking the world as we knew it but for befouling the German cradle for generations to come. The thousand years of "peace" he was to give to Germany will be a thousand years of suffering, penance, and regret. The mark of the beast is upon him.

The two guards who were making sport of Niemoeller were hardly more than nineteen, both of stolid appearance when in their natural pose. It was plain that they had been "educated." From their dialects I judged that one must have come from Bavaria and the other probably from the Frisian islands and therefore, in origin, both of the purest German strain. Both were more than six feet tall (membership in the SS guards is limited to men not less than five feet eight inches), and so considerably taller than their victim. The Frisian was fair, with even features, and the Bavarian dark, with irregular features, large nose and mouth.

Both youths enjoyed the torment they were inflicting, laughed as Niemoeller panted for breath. I had to turn my head. The other prisoners took little heed. I think they did not know that the two youths were torturing a former U-boat commander, whose name once had rung familiarly in their ears. Hitler took personal part in the bloody purge of 1934. I wish that he could have witnessed this bloody scene—he the former corporal who fraudulently wears an Iron Cross. I wonder whether he too would have laughed at this sportive beating. Sometimes I picture him in varicolored tatters and foolscap being chased back and forth by two merry guards.

I saw Niemoeller almost daily now while we were passing by where he was being "exercised," but, of course, had no chance to speak with him. One day I saw him being led away with an ax on his shoulder, two guards with him. He had been ordered to cut wood, and I often heard the guards shout at him to cut faster. Cutting wood was considered easy work, suitable for the old and infirm and the sick. But it was as hard as other labor, for the prisoner was not allowed a single second in which to draw breath or relax weary arms. I could hear the fall of his ax sometimes. It sounded like the knocking of fate reverberating against the walls of the inner camp. For a long time Niemoeller had to submit to this daily ordeal. I caught occasional glimpses of him and saw that he was a little more bent, a little grayer where I could see his hair below his foolscap. Still there was no chance to speak with him. But I got news of him from the camp senior, who had to visit Niemoeller's cell to see that it was in order. He told me that every time he entered it he found the pastor praying. When he asked Niemoeller how he felt, the latter would say, "I have nothing to complain about." His cell was always in perfect order. I wanted to send him some message, but feared that it would be an intrusion.

One day I learned that Niemoeller's routine had been

changed. He was relieved of all work and allowed to return to his cell after his "exercise." I did not know the reason then, nor, I think, did Niemoeller. But after I regained my freedom I learned that Field Marshal von Mackensen, who had received an estate from Hitler, had intervened with him on behalf of Niemoeller.

Nevertheless, the select specimens of Nazi culture continued to torment the victim of Nazi scorn. They even invented new means of torture during the exercise hour. Sometimes they made him hop on one foot between them, sometimes crouch and hop. They beat him at the same time to make him more agile. One day he evidently used the name of God (though I could not catch it), for I heard one of the guards shout, "The *Schweinhund* is calling his *Drecksgott* (dirty god). I would like to see if He will help him out of here."

Sometimes the Commandant or other officers would stop to watch the play. Then the guards would outdo themselves as they received approving laughs. "I think he will never wish to preach against the Fuehrer again," said the Commandant one day, and turning to Niemoeller, "What do you think, Herr pastor?"

I became apprehensive lest this continued abuse affect Niemoeller's mind. But when I had opportunity to talk with him again I found him mentally unchanged, and as determined as ever never to surrender. This opportunity came about in a strange way.

One evening, at roll call, a prisoner was found to be missing, and immediately there was an uproar. Search by the guards in the inner camp was without result, and it was apparent that the missing man must either be hiding in the outer camp or have escaped altogether. All who had been relieved of attending roll call were ordered to be brought out, and among these was Pastor Niemoeller. Then the Commandant announced that all the prisoners would have to stand at attention until the missing man was found. How long that would be no one could guess. A detachment of guards was sent to the outer camp to search for the fugitive. Hours passed, and there was no sound of a whistle to indicate that the search had been successful. Finally, the guards returned, reporting to the Commandant that their search had been in vain. The Commandant became wild with anger, and shouted to us, "It will go hard with you if the *Galgenvogel* (gallows bird) is not found! I will make you stand there until you die of hunger and exhaustion." Then he called for prisoners to volunteer as a searching party. "I will recommend that whoever finds him be set free," he shouted. "But if he is not found I will decimate your ranks." And, strangely, many prisoners volunteered to search for their fellow prisoner, each hoping for the reward of freedom.

They marched out, escorted by guards, who now had been reinforced by the SS garrison.

Hours dragged by, and we still stood at attention. Most of us had already been exhausted by the day's work and trials, and no food was given to us while we waited. Night fell, and still there was no sign that the fugitive had been found. The Commandant and the officers had retired after leaving an order that they should be informed immediately the missing man was brought in. Many of the older and weaker prisoners collapsed, but nobody was permitted to give them assistance. "Let the swine lie where they are," the guards would shout if any one made as if to help a comrade. All of us began hoping that the missing man would soon be found. Better that one be punished than that all of us be made to die in our tracks. Dawn had lighted up the camp when we heard the whistles blowing. The unfortunate man had been discovered. Soon we saw him being led into the inner camp. The upper part of his body was naked and blood was streaming from his head and shoulders. The guards had begun on him as soon as they found him. Guards standing at the entrance laid their sticks on him as he passed. He made no outcry, but as he came nearer where we were all standing silent I could hear him moan like a wounded animal. When he was directly in front of us, he was ordered to stand at attention.

The Commandant and other officers came to receive the report. As I learned later, the fugitive had climbed to the top of a tree in the outer camp and hidden himself there. How he hoped to escape I don't know, for he must have been aware that the guards would continue their search until he was found or that it had become certain that he had succeeded in getting away. In which case he certainly would have been recaptured.

The Commandant and the officers accompanying him were now in high good humor. It was evident that they had been drinking, for they were laughing boisterously. They did not even glance at the unfortunate man. After a short conference among them, the camp senior was ordered to bring a wooden box. Presently they brought it. It was a narrow box, considerably longer than it was wide, and about as high as a man's shoulder when standing on end.

When the guards had placed the box on the ground the Commandant ordered the camp senior and his assistant to bring the prisoner before him. When the man was brought forward the Commandant struck him in the face. Already weak from the beatings he had received, the victim tottered under the blow, and had to be supported by two fellow prisoners who had been among those who had volunteered to take part in the search. The Commandant gave the camp senior another order, which we couldn't hear. We knew what it was in a minute.

The camp senior and his assistant dragged the victim to the wooden box and threw him in, head first. Then they nailed down the lid. During all this the victim did not utter a sound. His silence was more terrible than if he had screamed. The Commandant was laughing.

Then he addressed us: "Now, you *Galgenvogel*, you know what will happen if any one dares try such a thing again. Even this is too good for him. We should have skinned him alive, like the pig that he is."

But we were not dismissed, as it was already past the time of the morning roll call. We were permitted to sit down for a while before the working columns were formed.

And the man in the box? I don't know what his original crime had been. Perhaps some one had seen him read a foreign newspaper and reported him. Perhaps he had said something that he should have kept to himself. Perhaps he had worshipped God instead of bowing down to Hitler. Anyway, he was now nailed in a box—alive.

In the meantime the sun had topped the trees, and the birds and insects were beginning their busy day. But we had eyes only for the box. It was difficult to look away. Presently men began to stir and get to their feet. The ground was cold, and one could keep warm better by stamping his feet and slapping his body. Then I saw Pastor Niemoeller, a group of men around him. It was apparent that some of them were clergymen like himself, both Catholic and Protestant. They presented a strange sight, with their wise, grave faces beneath their high foolscaps, some unconsciously set at a rakish angle.

I approached the group in time to hear Pastor Niemoeller exclaim, "It is unbelievable." His mouth twitched. He had been beaten again, and there were welts on his face. Sometimes the guards of those in "protective custody" struck high. I think most of us there in that gathering were physically numb. All of us were sore from beatings and carrying heavy burdens, and some were bruised beyond healing. Then there was the box. Pastor Niemoeller was saying something. It sounded like, "God forgive us." Then some one spoke up from the group. "Pastor Niemoeller, what shall we do, what shall we do?"

For a few moments Niemoeller was silent, his eyes roving the group and beyond them to the box. His mouth twitched again. His face held me, and I waited for him to speak. And so the others. Here was a man upon whom they could depend. He had been through it all, and, besides, he had fought in the war, and there must be people in the outside world who still remembered him.

"Brothers in Christ," he said at length, "don't despair. Let us show them"—and again his eyes roved to the box—"that in spite of all these foul things we shall remain firm. We must not weaken even for a second. God will give us strength to show His power to His enemies. We may lose our lives, but we shall save our souls. Let us pray for our friend."

He meant the man nailed in the box. And he prayed, quietly. He asked God for mercy on that other one, who was beyond praying for himself. He asked God to reach down His everlasting arms to save that one—and us all. A low *Amen* rumbled through the ranks.

The guards ordered us to attention. The working columns were formed, and we were marched off, though we had had no food or water since the evening before. Often during that day's work I had to pass the box. It was as it had been, and there was no sound from it. I caught sight of Pastor Niemoeller too. He was passing the box, and I heard one of his guards say, "Do you see this? Some day, maybe, the same thing will happen to you. What have you to say to that?"

Then they recalled an old trick. "Say 'Heil Hitler,'" they ordered him. He was silent, and they struck him. Then they said, "Who are you?" Now, it was a rule that when a guard asked a prisoner his name the prisoner had to stand at attention and answer promptly. Niemoeller drew himself up and replied, "I am Pastor Niemoeller."

"Who did you say you are?—Pastor Niemoeller? Don't you know yet that you are nothing but a swine? Say at once, 'I am the swine Niemoeller.' "

Niemoeller did not answer, and the guards resorted to their sticks. "Will you repeat what we told you?" they demanded. "That is an order, and you know what will happen to you if you disobey orders." Whereupon Niemoeller said, "I am the swine Niemoeller."

I was told afterwards by some of the prisoners who had worked in the outer camp that day that the guards were more than usually cruel, probably because of what had happened the night before. The number of deaths was especially high, and many suffered terrible beatings. It was announced afterwards that the Commandant had issued an order that all prisoners were thereafter to be held accountable for the act of any one prisoner and that it would be for the prisoners themselves to eliminate any of their number who caused trouble. This was a revival of the method followed by the Prussian army. To give immediate effect to his threat, the Commandant ordered that we go without food for three days, that permission to smoke be revoked eight days, and that we not be permitted to write to our families for four weeks.

For six days the box remained in full view. Sometimes when I had to pass by I thought I heard moans issuing from it. But this must have been due to an overwrought imagination. The victim must have died from his wounds or from suffocation long since. On the seventh day I noticed that the box had been removed. And, of course, the family of the man must have received the usual message—and the customary carton.

XVIII

"TELL THE WORLD" —NIEMOELLER

LIFE in the camp became even more unbearable in the summer months that followed. We had suffered enough during the winter, when our ersatz uniforms gave us no protection against the cold. And now they proved much too warm. But there was no relief. Under the camp rules we had to continue wearing every piece of the outfit given us, including even a scarf. So we were always running with perspiration. To make our condition worse, there was still a shortage of water, which, of course, we felt more terribly now than we had during the winter. We had no opportunity to wash ourselves, and our drinking water was still what we could get out of holes and ditches filled by rain or from dirty cans used to carry water for camp purposes. The "coffee" given us had, of course, no effect on our thirst. Anyway, we received this only once during working hours, and then hardly more than a few drops.

But the guards met this emergency with their customary forethought. Perhaps, indeed, they had helped create it. They began smuggling in water in cans and selling it to the prisoners through the block seniors. Prices were high. The only thing we could get in quantity for nothing—and that only during the day, for the cells were always suffocatingly stuffy at night—was air. And the guards would have sold that if they could have arranged it.

226

In the middle of June of this year thousands of Jews were brought into the camp to add to the already large number there. They were the victims of the latest mass round-up of Jews in Germany, carried out in reprisal against the "Jewish press campaign" in Czechoslovakia. As a prelude to annexation of that country, Hitler had ordered a vicious press campaign against the Czech people. When the Czech press retaliated, it was hailed as an "impudent campaign of Jewish lies" and as justification for the arrest of thousands of "dangerous" Jews in Germany. Even Jewish Homes for the Aged were raided and their inmates carried off to concentration camps.

Sachsenhausen became so overcrowded that the Jews had to be quartered in unfinished stables. There were no floors, and we had to lie down on the damp and stony ground. We were allowed only a third of the bread ration, and one-half of the soup ration, and every third day we went without food altogether. A considerable number of the Jewish newcomers were intellectuals—rabbis, doctors, lawyers, teachers. They were singled out for the most exhausting work.

Among them, I recall, was a young rabbi who was a marvel of patience even among those who had long since learned that even patience was no protection against the brutalities of the guards. One day, which had been unusually hot and humid and when thirst had become well-nigh unbearable, we had just returned to the barracks from our daily chores when we were called for assembly. The Commandant, yelling and gesticulating, complained that we did not work hard enough, long enough, or fast enough.

"You shall long for death, you dogs," he roared. "This is not a sanatorium, it is a crematorium." It was his favorite phrase.

The young rabbi, who was standing next to me, slowly turned his head, and, without changing his expression in the slightest, looked at me sadly, a world of pity in his eyes. I think his pity was for the Commandant and the guards as much as for us, for there were some in this Nazi concentration camp whose pity for those who had lost their souls overreached horror at their brutalities. It was hard, I suppose, for the young rabbi to believe that our tormentors were German. A few minutes later, when we were on our way back to our primitive quarters, he turned to me and said, "Life is like a dream. Sometimes it is a good dream, sometimes a frightening one. But isn't it true that one always passes through a dream to something better?" He pondered a moment more, and then: "At least, we have been chosen to suffer for a good cause."

He was a typical example of the fortitude exhibited by the rabbis in the concentration camp. Though the Nazis might kill them—and did—they could never vanquish their spirit. Neither their arrest nor life in camp or prison, neither brutal lashings nor severe discipline; neither hunger nor thirst could undermine their faith. Like all the religious prisoners, who by their very tolerance incited the Nazi guards to brutal excesses, they were given the hardest sort of work, making roads and breaking rock.

Not long after this little incident the rabbi fell victim to an "accident." Two storm troopers in a small car came down the road at breakneck speed and swerved at the exact spot where the rabbi was bending over his pick. The car went over him, and he was mortally injured, dying that afternoon. Of course, there was no investigation of the "accident." And it goes without saying that the family of the rabbi received a letter informing them of his death and saying that they could have his ashes upon payment of 250 marks. That was the price of the remains of one whose greatest sin was that he would never seek his place on a stable floor without first making sure whether there was any one in need of the spiritual consolation he had to give.

However, all the hatred and brutal treatment by the Nazi guards did not succeed in driving the Jewish prisoners into anger or open rebellion. Of course, it would not have helped them anyway; they would have been shot down like dogs. On the contrary, the Jewish labor columns marched in good order and observed the strictest discipline. Sometimes the Nazis gave them credit for it, albeit unwillingly. One day a Storm Trooper officer met a Jewish labor detachment on the road. "What the devil," he exclaimed, "these are Jews! They look more Aryan than the Aryans."

Another officer, named Lange, looking for an explanation of this phenomenon, offered this solution:

"You Jews are all actors; we know that very well. You act as if you were orderly and disciplined like good Germans. In reality you are nothing but dirty pigs; you stink. You can't fool us."

I think the answer to that is in what a well-known rabbi once said to me when we had returned to our stable:

"I have never been prouder of being a Jew than here at the concentration camp. I am proud of the great moral force that is alive in the Jew and that makes him able to endure all these tests and still preserve his dignity."

Many of the new prisoners were well-to-do and had brought money with them, and, in addition, they occasionally received money from their families. And here I might add that I believe it is not too much to assert that in no people in the world is the family relationship more tenderly regarded than among the Jews.

The camp Commandant soon found means of tapping the Jews' funds as a new source of income. A short time after the arrival of the "recruits," and after they had been properly "disciplined," the Commandant announced at an evening roll call that the camp was much in need of a library for the use of the prisoners in their "spare time." This was astounding news. Spare time! The only hours which could be called "spare time" were between eight and ten o'clock at night, during which we had our evening meal and then "cleaned" our uniforms. And there were no lights to read by.

The purpose of the announcement was made clear to us when the Commandant continued, "The Jews have brought a lot of money with them, and it is only fair that they should contribute to the welfare of their fellow prisoners. I therefore expect them to give as much as possible for our library. I emphasize that no one is compelled to give. Whether one does depends on his own free will."

Afterwards our block senior informed us that we in our quarters were expected to contribute two thousand marks to the library fund. His tone and gesture indicated what would happen to us if that amount was not forthcoming. Special permission was given to those of us who wanted to write to our families for more money, but we were forbidden to mention the purpose for which it was wanted. Of course, the money was raised, and thereafter our "voluntary" contributions were collected with unfailing regularity every four weeks. But there was never a library.

Then came news for me. A letter from my wife brought me word that my relatives in the United States had procured and sent the documents necessary to permit my immigration to this country. I could hardly contain myself, and let word drop to my immediate friends in the camp. They were nearly as overwhelmed as I with vicarious joy. It would be necessary for my wife to consult with me, and she had applied to the Gestapo for permission to visit me. Under the rules, she could not visit me at Sachsenhausen, and I would have to be taken to Moabit. One evening, at roll call, my prison number was called out, and when I ran forward to answer, as was the rule, the officer in charge ordered me to be ready the next morning to leave for Moabit.

No sleep came to me that night. I was too busy fashioning my future. Soon, if all went well, I would be on the way to freedom and to all that freedom meant. After roll call the next morning and we had been shaved and had put on our civilian clothes, I joined a small group of other prisoners who also were going to Moabit, and we were led into the outer camp, where we were herded into a truck. Just before we started, Pastor Niemoeller climbed in with us. He had just been brought up. Two SS guards took seats next to the driver, and the truck began moving towards Berlin.

I noticed great changes in his appearance since we parted from each other at Moabit. He was greatly shrunken, and when he removed his foolscap I saw that his hair had turned white. He had become very old.

As there was plenty of room in the truck I moved to a seat beside him, and spoke. He turned and looked at me doubtfully. I, too, had changed greatly. Then he recognized me and returned my greeting. We learned that each of us was going to see his wife, and when I told him of my anticipated good fortune, he ejaculated, "Thank God. If you do succeed in getting out of here, tell the world everything you have seen and heard. Warn the people of the world that Hitler is the enemy of mankind!"

I was surprised at his vehemence, for he had never spoken of Hitler in such terms at Moabit, and when I expressed my apprehension that he might be made to pay for his words, he became almost violent. "But I have learned that he *is* the enemy of mankind," he said. "The world does not recognize his power for evil. You must tell it everywhere."

As we bumped along at a rapid pace, he told me he was convinced now that a long and terrible war would break out in the near future, and he said that he was unable to understand the attitude of the British Government. "At Munich," he said, "any chance for peace was destroyed. The British

Government's policy of appeasing Hitler has demonstrated that they are afraid of him. Now he will proceed relentless towards his aim, until it comes to the point where the British and French will have to fight for their existence."

Again he insisted that I make my experiences public if I escaped, that I report all I had seen and heard.

"But don't you think that if I did, it would make matters worse for you?" I asked him.

"Do you believe that matters could get any worse for me than they are now?" he answered. "But, at least, the world will learn the whole terrible truth and be warned. And remember," he added, raising his voice, "I shall never commit suicide."

Then he told me of the various terrible means the Nazis had resorted to in an effort to break his will. When cajolery and brutal treatment failed, they attempted to get him to commit suicide. "Do you want to finish yourself, you *Schweinhund?*" they would ask him. "We are ready to help you. You have only to tell us what method you would like best, and we will give you a rope, or a pistol, though you are not worth a bullet, or anything else you want."

Niemoeller raised his hands in a gesture of determination and set his lips tightly together. Then he said, "But I tell you again, I shall never do them the favor of committing suicide. I shall never end my life. If ever you hear that I have committed suicide you will know that I have been murdered by the Nazis."

The other prisoners had been listening, and they knew now who it was that was speaking.

"What shall we do?" one of them asked. Then all joined in. "What shall we do? What is going to become of us? Has God forgotten us?" It was a chorus of despair. They were all pale and emaciated, and their clothes hung on them like bags. It is what you good American people will see—hundreds of thousands like these—if you let Hitler win. All *your*

Niemoellers will be arrested and persecuted as enemies of the "new order."

Pastor Niemoeller hushed them with upraised hand. "No," he said, "God hasn't forgotten you. God never forgets. We are all equal in His eyes." (He was thinking of me, the Jew.) "Great suffering has been imposed on us, but it is better to perish here than to submit to the beast. Remember, it is more important to die as Christians than to live in cowardice. Remember what Christ said, 'If any *man* will come after me, let him deny himself, and take up his cross and follow me.' This means that we shall have to *earn* our salvation. The Saviour bore His cross. But this does not absolve us from bearing our crosses, from suffering for our faith. Believe on Him, and ye shall never perish but have everlasting life."

There was a long, low *Amen.* I don't know whether the other prisoners were Christians or not. But I do know that Pastor Niemoeller had reached down into the souls of us all. It was as if heaven had breathed on us. I do not know how to describe it, but such is the power of example. And I hope that when the hour of reckoning comes many will be remembered for Martin Niemoeller's sake.

We were in the open country now, somewhere between Oranienburg and Berlin. Trees were in leaf, and flowers bloomed along the roadside. Fields of waving grain broke the lines of little forests. We saw peasants tilling the soil, cows and goats grazing peacefully in their pastures. We gazed at it all, fascinated. We had forgotten that such things could still be, had ceased to believe that anywhere there still could be such signs of peace. For so long we had known only the Terror. For so long we had seen only the vileness inside Sachsenhausen camp.

But here was the dead come to life again. Here God still moved and had His being.

Soon the fresh country was behind us, and we were clattering over a street. A little later we were at Moabit prison. We climbed out of the truck, and were led inside, where we were distributed among the various rooms allotted to visitors.

My wife was awaiting me. A look of terror came into her eyes when she saw me. I was down to eighty-five pounds. But she managed to control herself and keep her poise. She herself did not look well, but thin and very pale. We were permitted only to shake hands, and our conversation was limited to the business that had brought us together. I signed the documents necessary for my emigration, and we clasped hands again. Then she was ordered from the room. A guard was with us the whole time, and he was suspicious of every word and gesture.

The rest of the day the visiting prisoners had to spend waiting until the guards were ready to take us back to Sachsenhausen.

Pastor Niemoeller had seen his wife and oldest son, he told me on our way back, with a touch of happiness in his voice. "Now," he said, "I shall count the days until I can see them again." This was the first time that Niemoeller had mentioned his wife to me, and I ventured to ask him how she took his imprisonment. "Very hard," he said, "but she, too, knows that God comes before all."

She must have been worthy of the man who had left all to follow his Lord. There is a martyrdom at the hearth as well as in the concentration camp.

Prisoners were encouraged by news that opposition to Hitler outside of Germany was stiffening, for it was understood now that if help came it would have to come from the outside. The camp authorities were quick to note the change in the prisoners, and resorted to more violent methods to quell the spirit of "rebellion." There were more deaths, more "accidents," more cartons of ashes for sale to those who would buy. But hope persisted.

One Sunday morning, when the roll call had been completed and the working columns were about to be ordered out, a prisoner stepped suddenly from the ranks and turning to face us, called out loudly:

"Don't despair, brothers in Christ, and don't give in to the enemy of God. God sees our misery and He will liberate us when the hour is at hand. Pray to Him, and He will help you."

He stood there for a moment, his right hand raised as if imparting a blessing, and then stepped back into place and faced about. We waited for the fury to break. This was a defiance of Hitler himself. Men had been shot down in cold blood for far less.

But the Commandant stood silent, his face drained white. He stood like that for seconds. The only sound was of men breathing heavily. The stillness was terrifying.

Then the Commandant recovered himself, and barked the order for us to march out.

Why didn't he break into a rage and order the prisoner who had defied him to be punished? I don't know, unless that spark of good which is said to be in every man had at last been touched. I learned afterwards that the prisoner who had called us back to the memory of God was a Protestant minister. He was never disciplined.

News of Nazi victories reached us. Hope died again.

The guards became more arrogant, more viciously cruel. And the Commandant evidently armored himself anew.

At the evening roll call of the day following another Nazi victory he addressed us. For a moment he let his eyes rest on us contemptuously, and then he said:

"Even you gallows birds will understand now what sort of man our Fuehrer is. Soon the whole world will be ours. But you, you swine, tried to sabotage our victory. The German people want to get rid of you, and they will. That's all."

However, for me the light was beginning to break. I had received news that the negotiations for my release and emigration to the United States were proceeding favorably, and I resigned myself to patience. I was not able to see Pastor Niemoeller again. But I had occasional word of him, and one was that the guards who came into close contact with him were beginning to sympathize with him, and even to be converted. I am unable to confirm the information, but I cannot doubt it. No one could long associate with Niemoeller without coming under his influence. After my release, I heard that even Rudloff had said privately that Niemoeller was a man whom one was bound to respect.

One evening, at roll call, the glad news came. I was ordered to be ready for my release at five o'clock the next morning. That night I could not sleep. I was nervous and excited and fearful lest some other barrier be raised against me.

There were eighty of us the next morning—all Jews—who were to be freed on condition that they leave Germany. We were marched to the uniform building, where we changed to our civilian clothes, and where such money as was left from our accounts was paid to us.

And now something strange happened.

Nazi guards came up to us, begging for money. The very men who had beaten and tortured us now were humiliating themselves to ask us a favor. Every one received a tip. That is to what Hitler has reduced even his own guards.

Then each of us had to sign a paper renouncing any claim against the Reich.

When this was done, we were ordered to stand at attention. It was to listen to the Commandant. This is what he said:

"You will go soon abroad. Remember that you are forbidden to report anything you have seen or heard here. Whoever disobeys this order will be brought back and placed in a concentration camp again. If this should be impossible in any given case, the man will be liquidated wherever he is. We have agents in every country in the world. Nobody can escape us. Also we will revenge ourselves on the families and relatives left in Germany."

Trucks were awaiting us, and we were taken to police headquarters in Berlin, where we were dismissed to go our separate ways.

It is not necessary to tell of the long negotiations that remained to be finished before my wife and I could leave Germany. Finally, I had to appear at the American consul's office. He was very courteous and considerate. I had to undergo an examination by a doctor, also an American. He was shocked when he saw my body. He said so.

The last words my wife and I heard in Germany were from a customs guard as we crossed the border into a neutral country. He said:

"Glueckliches Ehepaar, das Deutschland verlassen kann." *

* "You are a lucky couple to be able to leave Germany."

APPENDIX A

HITLER ON RELIGION: EXCERPT FROM *THE VOICE OF DESTRUCTION*

Hermann Rauschning was the president of the Danzig senate. Danzig was a free city and Hitler learned it had no extradition treaty with Germany. Before he came to power, he was constantly fearful of arrest, and Danzig was to be his sanctuary. He cultivated the officials of Danzig and, after he gained power, frequently sent his car for Rauschning, who spent extended time as Hitler's houseguest. Hitler did all his planning through oral monologues, and Rauschning wrote many of them down and published them as *The Voice of Destruction*.

ANTICHRIST

I REMEMBER in every detail the conversation to be recorded in this chapter. It made an indelible impression on me. From it dates my inner revulsion against National Socialism. For now I began to understand the true nature and aims of this movement.

I can still feel today the narrow, restricted atmosphere, the smell of new furniture, the meaninglessness of an outworn day. The familiar blend of narrowness and bohemianism, *petit bourgeois* pleasures and revolutionary talk. I can still hear the ubiquitous and abstruse Puzzi Hanfstangel manhandling the piano in the next room. He had just composed a march which seemed to appeal to Hitler's taste—a bastard product of Wagner *motifs*.

A small sofa, a few chairs, a table: Frau Raubal, Frau Goebbels, Forster, Goebbels, and myself sitting in the room. Behind us the "leader," the newly appointed Reich Chancellor. He was leaning across his desk, turning over the pages of documents. Facing him were Julius Streicher and Wagner of Munich. Tea was being served, and small cakes. Frau Raubal, whose manner suggested motherly kindliness, was trying help a harmless conversation on its way. We were listless. Frau Goebbels, her face in very un-German make-up, was watching Hitler, and I, too, was unable to drag my thoughts away from the conversation that was being carried on behind me and moving me to a growing excitement.

It was late at night. Hitler had been to the cinema—some patriotic rubbish glorifying Frederick the Great. We had preceded Hitler to the Chancellery and had waited for him there. Goebbels had been the first to arrive.

"A magnificent film," he said, "a remarkable film. That's the sort of thing we shall need." A few minutes later Hitler came up in the lift.

"How did you like the picture?" Forster asked.

"A horror—absolute rubbish. The police will have to stop it. We've had enough of this patriotic balderdash!"

"Yes, my Führer," Goebbels exclaimed, pushing forward, "it was feeble, very feeble. We have a great educational task ahead of us."

Prince August Wilhelm of Prussia, who had come back with Hitler, and was now taking his leave, remarked as he went:

"It's about time some sort of cruelty-to-animals law was passed against this abuse of historical memories." The date of this evening is recalled to me by the following day, which was of special significance. I had dined with Hitler, after having brought him my report. It was a momentous day, for the post of Reichsstatthalter (lieutenant-governor of the Reich) had just been created. The sole purpose of this measure was to suppress in time the independent aims of the provinces. In Bavaria, an independence movement of the greatest danger to National Socialism had been successful. Had Bavaria made use of its opportunity, and had Crown Prince Rupprecht, above all, been firmer, a Bavarian monarchy would have put an early and decided end to all National Socialist strivings. The German renaissance would have come from a different quarter and in an essentially different form.

Our nocturnal conversation arose out of our anxieties regarding such a development. The two Bavarian *Gauleiter*, Streicher of Franconia and Wagner of Munich, had brought us the tale. It was Streicher who gave Hitler his cue in the conversation. I had not listened to the beginning of it and became attentive only when I heard Hitler's voice behind me getting louder.

"The religions are all alike, no matter what they call themselves. They have no future—certainly none for the Germans. Fascism, if it likes, may come to terms with the Church. So shall I. Why not? That will not prevent me from tearing up Christianity root and branch, and annihilating it in Germany. The Italians are naïve; they're quite capable of being heathens and Christians at the same time. The Italians and the French are essentially heathens. Their Christianity is only skin-deep. But the German is different. He is serious in everything he underrtakes. He wants to be either a Christian or a heathen. He cannot be both. Besides, Mussolini will never make heroes of his Fascists. It doesn't matter there whether they're Christians or heathens. But for our people it is decisive whether they acknowledge the Jewish Christ-creed with its effeminate pity-ethics, or a strong, heroic belief in God in Nature, God in our own people, in our destiny, in our blood."

After a pause, he resumed:

"Leave the hair-splitting to others. Whether it's the Old Testament or the New, or simply the sayings of Jesus, according to Houston Stewart Chamberlain—it's all the same old Jewish swindle. It will not make us free. A German Church, a German Christianity, is distortion. One is either a German of a Christian. You cannot be both. You can throw the epileptic Paul out of Christianity—others have done so before us. You can make Christ into a noble human being, and deny his divinity and his role as a savior. People have been doing it for centuries. I believe there are such Christians today in England and America—Unitarians they call themselves, or something like that. It's no use, you cannot get rid of the mentality behind it. We don't want people who keep one eye on the life in the hereafter. We need free men who feel and know that God is in themselves."

Streicher or Goebbels made some remark which I did not catch—a question perhaps.

"You can't make an Aryan of Jesus, that's nonsense," Hitler went on. "What Chamberlain wrote in his Principles is, to say the least, stupid. What's to be done, you say? I will tell you: we must prevent the churches from doing anything but what they are doing now, that is, losing ground day by day. Do you really believe the masses will ever be Christian again? Nonsense! Never again. That tale is finished. No one will listen to it again. But we can hasten matters. The parsons will be made to dig their own graves. They will betray their God to us. They will betray anything for the sake of their miserable little jobs and incomes.

"What we can do? Just what the Catholic Church did when it forced its beliefs on the heathen: preserve what can be preserved, and change its meaning. We shall take the road back: Easter is no longer resurrection, but the eternal renewal of our people. Christmas is the birth of *our* savior: the spirit of heroism and the freedom of our people. Do you think these liberal priests, who have no longer a belief, only an office, will refuse to preach *our* God in their churches? I can guarantee that, just as they have made Haeckel and Darwin, Goethe and Stefan George the prophets of their Christianity, so they will replace the cross with our swastika. Instead of worshiping the blood of their quondam savior, they will worship the pure blood of our people. They will receive the fruits of the German soil as a divine gift, and will eat it as a symbol of the eternal communion of the people, as they have hitherto eaten of the body of their God. And when we have reached that point, Streicher, the churches will be crowded again. If *we* wish it, then it will be so—when it is *our* religion that is preached there. We need not hurry the process."

Hitler paused. Frau Raubal asked me a question about my family, and I failed to catch what followed.

"Let it run its course," I presently heard Hitler say. "But it won't last. Why a uniform religion, a German Church independent of Rome? Don't you see that that's all obsolete? German Christians, German Church, Christians freed from Rome—old stuff! I know perfectly well what is coming, and we shall take care of it all in good time. Without a religion of its own, the German people has no permanence. What this religion will be we do not yet know. We feel it, but that is not enough."

"No," he replied to a question, "these professors and mystery men who want to found Nordic religions merely get in my way. Why do I tolerate them? Because they help to disintegrate, which is all we can do at the moment. They cause unrest. And all unrest is creative. It has no value in itself but let it run its course. They do their share, and the priests do theirs. We shall compel them to destroy their religions from within by setting aside all authority and reducing everything to pale, meaningless talk. Shall we succeed? Certainly irresistibly." The conversation took a quieter turn. Goebbels sat down at our table, and Hanfstängel came from the other room to join us. The two Bavarian leaders related a few cases of uncompromising resistance from the Bavarian Catholic Church.

"They had better stop deceiving themselves," said Hitler menacingly. "Their day has passed. They have lost."

He would not, he went on, do the same as Bismarck.

"I'm a Catholic. Certainly that was fated from the beginning, for only a Catholic knows the weaknesses of the Church. I know how to deal with these gentry. Bismarck was a fool. In other words, he was a Protestant. Protestants don't know what a church is. In these things you must be able to feel and think with the people, know what they want and what they dislike. Bismarck stuck to his legal clauses and his Prussian sergeant-majors. That was not enough. And least of all shall I institute a cultural struggle. That was a blunder. Naturally the monks were anxious to shine before their poor little woman with the martyr's crown. But I shall know how to deal with them, I can guarantee that.

"The Catholic Church is a really big thing. Why, what an organization! It's something to have lasted nearly two thousand years! We must learn from it. Astuteness and knowledge of human nature are behind it. Catholic priests know where the shoe pinches. But their day is done, and they know it. They are far too intelligent not to see that, and to enter upon a hopeless battle. But if they do, I shall certainly not make martyrs of them. We shall brand them as ordinary criminals. I shall tear the mask of honesty from their faces. And if that is not enough, I shall make them appear ridiculous and contemptible. I shall order films to be made about them. We shall show the history of the monks on the cinema. Let the whole mass of nonsense, selfishness, repression and deceit be revealed: how they drained the money out of the country, how they haggled with the Jews for the world, how they committed incest. We shall make it so thrilling that everyone will want to see it. There will be queues outside the cinemas. And if the pious burghers find the hair rising on their heads in horror, so much the better. The young people will accept it—the young people and the masses. I can do without the others."

"I promise you," he concluded, "that if I wished to, I could destroy the Church in a few years; it is hollow and rotten and false through and through. One push and the whole structure would collapse. We should trap the priests by their notorious greed and self-indulgence. We shall thus be able to settle everything with them in perfect peace and harmony. I shall give them a few years' reprieve. Why should we quarrel? They will swallow anything in order to keep their material advantages. Matters will never come to a head. They will recognize a firm will, and we need only show them once or twice who is the master. Then they will know which way the wind blows. *They* are no fools. The Church was something really big. Now we're its heirs. We, too, are a Church. Its day has gone. It will not fight. I'm quite satisfied. As long as youth follows me, I don't mind if the old people limp to the confessional. But the young ones—they will be different. I guarantee that."

At the time, I regarded this whole speech as sheer braggadoccio, and as a concession to the pornographic Streicher. Nevertheless, it shook me to the depths. I had not supposed Hitler capable of so much cynicism. Later I was to remember many times—at the time of the currency trials, and then of the immorality trials of Catholic priests, the purpose of which was to brand them as criminals in the eyes of the masses and thereby deprive them in advance of the halo of martyrdom. It was a cunning, and as has since transpired, long planned scheme, for which Hitler himself is solely responsible. I heard little more after this. The only thing that interested me further was the Führer's ostentatious contempt for the Protestant church. Hitler by no means shared the hopes and desires of many militant, anti-Rome Protestants, who thought to shatter the Roman church with the aid of National Socialism, and establish an essentially evangelical, German, united church of which Catholics would be expected to form a subordinate section. I have spoken many times since then with the Reich Bishop Müller, who was very nearly my predecessor as President of the Danzig Senate. His ambitions lay in this direction.

"The Protestants haven't the faintest conception of a church," I heard Hitler saying. "You can do anything you like to them—they will submit. They're used to cares and worries. They learnt them from their squires. The parsons, when they were invited to the Sunday roast goose, had their place at the foot of the table, amongst the children and tutors. It was even an honor that they were not asked to sit at the servants' table. They are insignificant little people, submissive as dogs, and they sweat with embarrassment when you talk to them. They have neither a religion that they can take seriously nor a great position to defend like Rome."

The conversation ebbed again into unimportant details and mere abuse, and rose only once more to higher levels of interest. Hitler was speaking about the peasantry, claiming that under their Christian exterior, the old eternal heathendom still lurked, and broke out again and again.

"You're a farmer," he said, turning to me. "What can you tell us about it? How are conditions in your district?"

I rose and joined the group. In our district, I said, we had highly rationalized farming where there was little of the old customs left. But no doubt it was true: if you scratched the surface, ancient, inherited beliefs were revealed.

"You see," Hitler returned triumphantly; "that is what I'm

building on. Our peasants have not forgotten their true religion. It still lives. It is merely covered over. The Christian mythology has simply coated it like a layer of tallow. It has preserved the true contents of the pot. I have said this to Darré, and told him that we must start the great reformation. He has suggested means to me, magnificent means! I have approved them. The old beliefs will be brought back to honor again. In our 'Green Week' and in the 'Traveling Agricultural Exhibition' he will allude to our inherited religion in picturesque and expressive language that even the simplest peasant can understand.

"It will not be done in the old way, running riot in colorful costumes and dreaming of a departed, romantic age. The peasant will be told what the Church has destroyed for him: the whole of the secret knowledge of nature, of the divine, the shapeless, the daemonic. The peasant shall learn to hate the Church on that basis. Gradually he will be taught by what wiles the soul of the German has been raped. We shall wash off the Christian veneer and bring out a religion peculiar to our race. And this is where we must begin. Not in the great cities, Goebbels! There we shall only lose ourselves in the stupid godlessness propaganda of the Marxists: free sex in nature store and that sort of bad taste. The urban masses are empty.

Where all is extinguished, nothing can be aroused. But our peasantry still lives in heathen beliefs and values.

"The same is true of all other countries, Sweden, France, England, the Slav agricultural countries. The renaissance of heathendom has always broken against the mischief done by the literary, those urban ranks of the totally uprooted, those mental conjurors. Unless we give the masses something in exchange for what we take from them, they will later fall a prey to every kind of swindle. But it is through the peasantry that we shall really be able to destroy Christianity because there is in them a true religion rooted in nature and blood. It is through the peasantry that we shall one day be able to act as missionaries to the urban masses as well. But there is plenty of time for that."

With that the conversation ended. We sat on for a time round the table, where Hitler joined us. Frau Goebbels was solicitous for the well-being of the Führer. It was time to break up, she said.

"You have had a hard day behind you, my Führer, and another before you tomorrow."

We took our leave, and I went to my small hotel near the Friedrichstrassen Station.

It was all fulfilled later, even to the last item Hitler had hinted at. Attempts were and are being made to make use of old folk-customs to de-Christianize the peasantry. I have seen pavilions at the agricultural exhibitions subtly planned with this end in view. I have seen a picture-series, prepared with the greatest pedagogical skill, representing the struggle of the Steding peasants against the Church in Bremen. I noted how all visitors reacted, in the midst of the objective representation of our agricultural calling, to the terrible accusations wordlessly raised against the late medieval Church in regard to her bloodstained repression of surviving heathen beliefs and of the peasant's love of liberty. We agricultural leaders were regularly invited to the new type of godless meetings of the National Socialists, "religious" evenings on which the new religions were paraded. There were Professors Hauer and Wirth and many others. It was clear that these invitations, which were personal ones from Darré, were designed to ascertain how far we might be regarded as belonging to the true *elite* and how serious we were about the total revolution of National Socialism.

In other words, they were a test of our trustworthiness. That was the first step. The second was pressure on us to give up membership in the Church. How quickly the whole process moved became clear to me from the case of an acquaintance of mine, the Westphalian farmer Meinberg, a splendid fellow who was unmistakably solid and loyal. He was a *Staatsrat* (councilor of state) and a leader of the peasantry, Darré's deputy in the Reich Labor Ministry, and a most apt pupil. A new fireplace appeared in his ancient peasant homestead, its walls decorated with runes and heathen maxims. The crosses had disappeared to make room for other sacred symbols. Woden, the ancient huntsman, was in the place of honor. And on the hearth burned the new, eternal flame. Was Hitler right in saying that the Christian crust was a thin one in our peasants? What happened to us happened also to the men of the S.S., especially to the higher ranks—the ranks of the Hitler youth. Thoroughly and systematically, with iron logic, the war of annihilation against Christianity was being waged.

Here is what Hitler thought when words of concentration camp conditions, and the brutality toward the Jews, began to circulate.

THE TERROR

HITLER dismissed us. His adjutant Brückner had entered. Time was getting on. That afternoon a National Socialist school for leaders was to be inaugurated in a former Social-Democratic school, and Hitler had promised to attend. The interrupted conversation, however, had a kind of sequel later in the autumn. Complaints as to the horrors of the concentration camps had begun to reach Hitler. I remember a particular instance in Stettin, where, in the empty engine-rooms of the former Vulkan docks, respected citizens, some of them of Jewish parentage, were brutally maltreated. Vile things were done in an unmistakable enjoyment of brutality for its own sake. The matter had been brought to Göring's attention, and he had been unable to evade an investigation. In one case, reparation was made.

In those days the routine excuse was that a revolution was taking place in Germany which was extraordinarily bloodless and lenient. It was not justifiable, we were told, to draw general conclusions from a few isolated cases. But the truth was very different. The cruelty, of a nature increasingly refined, dealt out then and later by the S.S. and the S.A. to political opponents was part of a definite political plan. The selection of asocial, abnormal types to guard the concentration camps was carried out with conscious purpose. I had occasion to see something of this myself. Notorious drunkards and criminals were selected from the military organizations of the party and placed in special sub-divisions. It was a typical example of specially selected sub-humans for definite political tasks.

I happened to be present when Hitler's attention was

called to the Stettin incident and other similar occurrences. It was entirely characteristic that Hitler was by no means indignant, as one might have expected, at the horrible excesses of his men, but on the contrary roundly abused those who "made a fuss" about these trivial matters.

The occasion was my first experience of Hitler's paroxysms of rage and abuse. He behaved like a combination of a spoilt child and an hysterical woman. He scolded in high, shrill tones, stamped his feet, and banged his fist on tables and walls. He foamed at the mouth, panting and stammering in uncontrolled fury: "I won't have it! Get rid of all of them! Traitors!" He was an alarming sight, his hair disheveled, his eyes fixed, and his face distorted and purple. I feared that he would collapse, or have an apoplectic fit.

Suddenly it was all over. He walked up and down the room, clearing his throat, and brushing his hair back. He looked round apprehensively and suspiciously, with searching glances at us. I had the impression that he wanted to see if anyone was laughing. And I must admit that a desire to laugh, perhaps largely as a nervous reaction to the tension, rose within me.

"Preposterous," Hitler began in a hoarse voice. "Haven't you ever seen a crowd collecting to watch a street brawl? *Brutality is respected.* Brutality and physical strength. The plain man in the street respects nothing but brutal strength and ruthlessness—women, too, for that matter, women and children. The people need wholesome fear. They *want* to fear something. They want someone to frighten them and make them shudderingly submissive. Haven't you seen everywhere that after boxing-matches, the beaten ones are the first to join the party as new members? Why babble about brutality and be indignant about tortures? The masses want that. They need something that will give them a thrill of horror."

After a pause, he continued in his former tone:

"I forbid you to change anything. By all means, punish one or two men, so that these German Nationalist donkeys may sleep easy. But I don't want the concentration camps transformed into penitentiary institutions. Terror is the most effective political instrument. I shall not permit myself to be robbed of it simply because a lot of stupid, *bourgeois* mollycoddles choose to be offended by it. It is my duty to make use of *every* means of training the German people to severity, and to prepare them for war."

Hitler paced the room excitedly.

"My behavior in wartime will be no different. The most horrible warfare is the kindest. I shall spread terror by the surprise employment of all my measures. The important thing is the sudden shock of an overwhelming fear of death. Why should I use different measures against my internal political opponents? These so-called atrocities spare me a hundred thousand individual actions against disobedience and discontent. People will think twice before opposing us when they hear what to expect in the camps."

No one ventured to put any questions.

"I don't want to hear anything more about this," Hitler said in conclusion. "It's your business to see that no evidence about such cases leaks out. I cannot allow such absurd trifles to break in on my work. Anybody who is such a poltroon that he can't bear the thought of someone nearby having to suffer pain had better join a sewing-circle, but not my party comrades."

APPENDIX B

OFFICIAL REPORT OF THE NAZI WAR ON RELIGION BY WILLIAM DONOVAN, DIRECTOR OF THE OSS

25 October 1945

MEMORANDUM

Subject: Relationship of the German Churches to Hitler

To: General Donovan

1.) Introductory Note:

Besides small sects, there were and there are only two Christian churches of importance in Germany: the Protestant and the Catholic churches. The Catholic Church was politically represented by the Center-Party (Zentrumspartei), the Bavarian People's Party (Bayerische Volkspartei), and the Christian Trade-Unions (Christliche Gewerkschaften). Since these three groups stood in opposition to Hitler from the beginning, the Catholic Church, before 1933, found itself in quite an obvious enmity toward the Nazis. As for the Protestant Church, this was not true in the extent it was in the Catholic Church, because there are no politics in the Protestant Church. Therefore, it may be said that before 1933 there was no relationship, either of a friendly or of an enemy nature, between Hitler and the two churches.

2.) Relationship of the Catholic Church with Hitler since 1933:

Immediately after Hitler had seized the power, National Socialism showed itself as an ideology plainly opposed to Christianism. Only a minority among the princes of the Catholic Church, like Bishop Berning from Osnaabruck and later Cardinal Innitzer from Vienna, tried to show a friendly attitude toward Hitler. The majority of the princes of the Catholic Church left no doubt in their declarations and pastoral letters that there was no bridge between Naziism and the Catholic Church. As the years went by, the attitude of the Catholic Church became ever clearer. The rejection of Hitler became more and more obvious. Because of the hierarchic organizations of the Catholic Church, the denunciation of Hitler was propagated by the majority of the Catholic clergy in the land. The result of this was that the enmity toward Hitler was promulgated not only by the high clerics but was also carried to the masses by the low clerics. The decisive credit for this attitude ought to be given to Cardinal von Faulhaber from Munich, whose personal sermons branded Naziism as the enemy of Christendom. Both princes of the church did not shun the gravest danger but managed to voice their opposition to Hitler in such a way so clever that the Gestapo had no opportunity to silence them. By their example, these two dignitaries of the church have swept along with them those groups within the Catholic Church that still hesitated. On the other hand, quite a number of the lower clerics ended up in prison or in a concentration camp. Also, in the political resistance movement did the representatives of the Catholic Church play an important role. Here the pater of the Jesuites Delp ought to be mentioned before all others; he participated in the conspiracy that led to 20 July. Later on Delp was executed by the Gestapo. A particularly important part in the struggle of the

CONFIDENTIAL

resistance movement against Hitler played the lawyer Joseph Müller, who lives in Munich, Gedonstrasse 4. He had been the political representative of the Archdiocese Munich. At the beginning of the war, Joseph Müller became a captain in the CI-section under Admiral Canaris. In this function Joseph Müller was to influence the attitude of the dignitaries of the Catholic Church against Hitler and also to negotiate with the Vatican. The aim of these negotiations was to find out, through the Vatican, under what conditions a Germany liberated from Hitler could make peace. On the part of the Vatican, the negotiations were conducted by the personal secretary of Pope Pius XII, Padre Leiber. In the course of years, the negotiations were exceeded also to the diplomatic representatives at the Vatican, the powers at war with Germany. In this, the English representative, Osborn, played a major part. The negotiations were recorded in writing. The documents were finally assembled by Admiral Canaris. Later, a part of them was discovered by the Gestapo. The result was that Canaris and his collaborators were hanged. Joseph Müller escaped by luck. He is the only person who possesses detailed information on the complex of these questions. At the same time Joseph Müller had orders from the Catholic Church to negotiate with representatives of the Protestant Church in order to harmonize their measures in the struggle against Hitler.

3). Relationship of the Catholic Church with Hitler since 1933:

The Protestant Church in Germany does not have a hierarchic but a democratic constitution. Apart from that, it is constituted by 28 provincial churches. Therefore it did not have the congeniality and strictness of the Catholic Church. That is why the struggle of the Protestant Church against Hitler became much more difficult. If it was the clerics that

CONFIDENTIAL

bore the brunt of the struggle within the Catholic Church it was the congregation that became the nest of resistance within the Protestant Church. The man who was the first to see Hitler as what he was, and through whose example large sections of the Protestant Church were incited, is without doubt Pastor Martin Niemöller. Many Protestant ministers supported him in this struggle. Here are to be named: Pastor Asmussen, Pastor Gruber, General Superintendant Dibelius, Bishop Wurm. All these men had taken up the fight against Hitler in speeches and in writings. But the majority of them was silenced by being put into the concentration camp or by being prohibited to speak or write. That did not prevent their followers from continuing the struggle. Bishop Wurm, in a memorandum to Minister Frick, opposed the killing of the insane, ordered by Hitler. In spite of all prohibitions, the Protestant Church, under the leadership of Pastor Gruber in Berlin, created an organization that helped save the lives of thousands of Jews. Initial in this action was Assessor Perels Justiziar of the Confessional Church, who entered the political struggle more and more. In this, the following personalities played an important role: Pastor Dietrich Bonhoffer, Konsistorialrat Gerstenmeier, Pastor Schonfeld, Pastor Freudenberg, Pastor Bethge, Pastor Lilje, and others. While in the Catholic camp, Joseph Müller kept up the contact with politics; Dietrich Bonhoffer played the same role in the Protestant camp. They cooperated with Joseph Müller. This way, the struggles of the Catholic and of the Protestant churches were coordinated. Dietrich Bonhoffer also entered into the services of the CI-section under Admiral Canaris. Bonhoffer undertook many trips to Switzerland and to the Scandinavian countries. This way, he contacted the Protestant churches in Europe outside of Germany, informed them about the events in Germany, and so created a common bond between resistance movements

CONFIDENTIAL

in Germany and Hitler's enemies outside of Germany. By this Bonhoffer became an important figure in the preparations for the Coup d'Etat of 20 July 1944. He was later executed. Dr. George Bell, bishop of Chichester, possesses information on all the details of their work. First Lieutenant Steltzer worked in the same direction. He held contact with the Norwegian bishop Berggrave, who can certify as to the correctness of this statement.

4.) Conclusion:

The resistance movement of the Catholic and Protestant churches in Germany has covered the following:

A. The churches have furnished the political resistance movement with spiritual and religious weapons.

B. The churches have carried the idea of the resistance against Hitler into the large masses of the people. Many ministers of both churches have become martyrs because of their resistance.

C. The churches, through their connections with foreign countries, have informed the world of the events that took place in Germany and have constantly kept contact with non-German resistance groups.

v. Schlabrendorff

VS/jes

CONFIDENTIAL

HQ & HQ DETACHMENT
OFFICE OF STRATEGIC SERVICES
APO 413
U.S. ARMY

9th July 1945

TO   : Col. M. C. Bernhays, G.S.C.
          Executive, U.S. Chief of Counsel

FROM   : Lt. Walter Rothschild
          Chief, Documentary Research Unit

SUBJECT: German Monists Organization

1. Attached is a report published by PID of the foreign office in the PID/PW Series No. 15 dealing with the German Monists Organization.

2. This report might be useful in connection with the persecution of religious organizations by the Nazi government.

Enclosure:
as stated above

16 July

Comm Dr. Donovan –
Rec. file

TO   :   Maj. Wiliam Coogan
FROM :   Lt. (jg) Carl E. Schorake, USNR
Subject: R&A 3114.4, THE PERSECUTION OF THE
              CHRISTIAN CHURCHES

In the interest of rapid distribution to the staff of the War
Crimes prosecution in the field, the attached study is presented in unedited draft form. The document is still seriously
lacking in evidence of probative value and is consequently ill
suited to serve as a basis for any international discussion.

Care has been taken to cite primary sources (*Reichagasetablatt,
Juristische Wochenschrift,* etc.) whenever possible. Secondary
works are cited only where the authors of such works did not
cite original sources and where more solid evidence was
unavailable from other sources. German legislation as represented in the *Reichagasetablatt* has been fully covered. The correspondence of Bishop Wurm, referred to on pages fifty-two
and sixty-one, is in process of translation and will be forwarded as an appendix when completed.

Particular attention is called to the appended list of probable
witnesses. These should be contacted as quickly as possible. It
is suggested that the interrogators be briefed by a thorough
study of the attached document and that they be cognizant
not only of the weaknesses made explicit in the text but also
of other weaknesses suggested by critics in the field.

It will be noted in particular that much of the material on the
persecution of the Catholic Church has been obtained from
a secondary work entitled *The Persecution of the Catholic Church
in the Third Reich* (Burns Oates, London, 1940). This volume
contains many valuable materials but is poorly documented.
Its author is not identified. It would be most profitable if a
member of the staff in London could discover the author or
authors through Burns Oates, the publisher, and secure the
more solid documentary evidence, which must be in his, or
their, possession. *(Editor's note: Inquiry at Burnes Oates reveals no
surviving documents that might identify the author.)*

CONFIDENTIAL

APPROVED BY THE
PROSECUTION
REVIEW BOARD

OFFICE OF STRATEGIC SERVICES
Research and Analysis Branch

R & A No. 3114.4

THE NAZI MASTER PLAN

ANNEX 4: THE PERSECUTION OF THE CHRISTIAN
CHURCHES

Description

This study describes, with illustrative factual evidence, Nazi purposes, policies, and methods of persecuting the Christian churches in Germany and occupied Europe.

DRAFT FOR THE WAR CRIMES STAFF

6 July 1945

CONFIDENTIAL

TABLE OF CONTENTS

THE PERSECUTION OF
THE CHRISTIAN CHURCHES   <u>Page</u>

CONFIDENTIAL

CONFIDENTIAL

CONFIDENTIAL

CONFIDENTIAL

THE PERSECUTION OF THE
CHRISTIAN CHURCHES

I. THE NATURE OF THE PERSECUTION
Throughout the period of National Socialist rule, religious liberties in Germany and in the occupied areas were seriously impaired. The various Christian churches were systematically cut off from effective communication with the people. They were confined as far as possible to the performance of narrowly religious functions and, even within this narrow sphere, were subjected to as many hindrances as the Nazis dared to impose. Those results were accomplished partly by legal and partly by illegal and terroristic means.

II. THE PROBLEM OF ESTABLISHED CRIMINAL RESPONSIBILITY
To establish criminal responsibility in connection with this persecution, it is sufficient to show that measures taken against the Christian churches were an integral part of the National Socialist scheme of world conquest. In many cases it is also possible to show that the measures in question were criminal from the standpoint of German or of international law, depending on the region in which any given act was committed.

A. Acts Committed in Germany Proper
By Articles 135 (freedom of faith and conscience), 136 (right to the enjoyment of civil and political rights independent of religious creed), 137 (freedom of religious association and incorporation), 138 (computation of state contributions to religious bodies), 139 (legal recognition of Sundays and public holidays), 140 (right to carry out religious work in the army and public institutions), and 149 (maintenance of religious instruction in the German educational system) of the Weimar Constitution, which were never formally abrogated by the National Socialist regime, many

CONFIDENTIAL

basic rights were granted to religious organizations. Although Articles 114 (freedom of the person), 115 (freedom from searches and seizures), 117 (secrecy of communication), 118 (freedom of speech and of the press), 123 (freedom of assembly), 124 (freedom of association), and 153 (rights of property) were suspended on 28 February 1933[1], Articles 135-40 and 149 were left untouched and still remain theoretically in force. Respect for the principle of religious freedom was reiterated in various official pronouncements by Nazi leaders.[2] Specific religious liberties were also guaranteed in various enactments of the National Socialist state, particularly the Concordat of 20 July 1933.[3] To demonstrate the illegality of specific acts of persecution, it is sufficient to show that they were in violation of these legal provisions.

B. Acts Committed in Areas Incorporated into the Reich
The legal situation with regard to acts of persecution in these areas depends upon the attitude taken concerning the legal effect of incorporation. If it is assumed that incorporation actually took place, religious guarantees included in the Weimar Constitution, the Concordat, and other German enactments would presumably apply to the incorporated territories. In that case the problem of establishing the illegality of acts of persecution committed in these areas subsequent to incorporation[4] would be the same as in the case of acts committed in Germany proper. If it is assumed that the act of incorporation, as an incident of aggressive warfare, was invalid and without legal effect, the problem of establishing the illegality of acts of persecution committed in these areas would be the same as in the case of acts committed in other occupied areas considered below.

C. Acts Committed in Other Occupied Areas
The rights and duties of the Nazi authorities in these

CONFIDENTIAL

regions were governed by the provisions of international law, particularly Article 46 of the *Hague Regulations (1907) Respecting the Laws and Customs of War on Land,* which provides that "religious convictions and practice must be respected." To demonstrate the illegality of specific acts of persecution in these areas, it is sufficient to show that they constituted a violation of these provisions.

III. THE BASIC NATIONAL SOCIALIST ATTITUDE TOWARD CHRISTIAN CHURCHES

National Socialism by its very nature was hostile to Christianity and the Christian churches. The purpose of the National Socialist movement was to convert the German people into a homogeneous racial group united in all its energies for prosecution of aggressive warfare. Innumerable indications of this fact are to be found in the speeches and writings of Hitler and other responsible Nazi leaders. The following statements by Hitler may be taken as indicative:

"Every truly national idea is in the last resort social; i.e., he who is prepared so completely to adopt the cause of his people that he really knows no higher ideal than the prosperity of this—his own people, he who has so taken to heart the meaning of our great song 'Deutschland, Deutschland uber alles' that nothing in this world stands for him higher than this Germany, people and land, land and people, he is a Socialist!" (Speech given in Munich, 28 July 1922, translation from Adolf Hitler, *My New Order,* edited by Raoul de Roussy de Sales, Reynal and Hitchcock, New York, 1941, p. 39)

"Even today we are the least loved people on earth. A world of foes is ranged against us and the German must still today make up his mind whether he intends to be a free soldier or a white slave. The only possible conditions under which a German State can develop at all must therefore be: the unification of all Germans in Europe, education towards a national consciousness, and readiness to place the whole national strength without exception in the service of the nation." (Speech given in Munich, 10 April 1923, translation from Hitler, *Ibid.*, p. 28)

"If cowards cry out, 'But we have no arms!', that is neither here nor there! When the whole German people knows one will and one will only—to be free—in that hour we shall have the instrument with which to win our freedom. It matters not whether these weapons of ours are humane: if they gain us our freedom, they are justified before our conscience and before our God." (Speech given in Munich 1 August 1923, translation from Hitler, *Ibid.*, p. 65)

"The conception of pacifism translated into practice and applied to all spheres must gradually lead to the destruction of the competitive instinct, to the destruction of the ambition for outstanding achievement. I cannot say in politics we will be pacifists; we reject the idea of the necessity for life to safeguard itself through conflict—but in economics we want to remain keenly competitive. If I reject the idea of conflict as such, it is of no importance that for the time being that idea is still applied in some single spheres. In the last resort, political decisions are decisive and determine achievement in the single sphere." (Speech given before the Industry Club at Dusseldorf, 27 January 1932, translation from Hitler, *Ibid.*, p. 101)

"There can be no economic life unless behind this economic life there stands the determined political will of the nation ready to strike—and to strike hard." (Same speech, p. 111)

"We National Socialists once came from war, from the experience of war. Our world ideal developed in war; now, if necessary, it will prove itself." (Speech given at the Sportpalast, Berlin, on 10 October 10 1939, translation from Hitler, *Ibid.*, p. 759)

Although the principal Christian churches of Germany had long been associated with conservative ways of thought, which meant that they tended to agree with the National

CONFIDENTIAL

Socialists in their authoritarianism, in their attacks on Socialism and Communism, and in their campaign against the Versailles Treaty, their doctrinal commitments could not be reconciled with the principle of racism, with a foreign policy of unlimited aggressive warfare, or with a domestic policy involving the complete subservience of church to state. Since these are fundamental elements of the National Socialist program, conflict was inevitable.

Important leaders of the National Socialist party would have liked to meet this situation by a complete extirpation of Christianity and the substitution of a purely racial religion tailored to fit the needs of National Socialist policy. This radically anti-Christian position is most significantly presented in Alfred Rosenberg's *Myth of the Twentieth Century* (one of the great bestsellers of National Socialist Germany and generally regarded, after Hitler's *Mein Kampf*, as the most authoritative statement of National Socialist ideology) and in his *To the Obscurantists of Our Time (An die Dunkelmaenner Unserer Zeit).* Since Rosenberg was editor in chief of the chief party newspaper, the *Voelkischer Beobachter,* the Reich leader of ideological training and the possessor of other prominent positions under the National Socialist regime, his ideas were not without official significance. Thus in a declaration of 5 November 1934, Baldur von Schirach, German youth leader, declared in Berlin: "Rosenberg's way is the way of German youth."[5] So far as this sector of the National Socialist party is concerned, the destruction of Christianity was explicitly recognized as a purpose of the National Socialist movement.

Considerations of expediency made it impossible, however, for the National Socialist government to adopt this radical anti-Christian policy officially. Thus the policy actually adopted was to reduce the influence of the Christian churches as far as possible through the use of every available means, without provoking the difficulties of an open war of

CONFIDENTIAL

extermination. That this was an official policy can be deduced from the following record of measures actually taken for the systematic persecution of Christian churches in Germany and in German-occupied areas.

IV. POLICIES ADOPTED IN THE PERSECUTION OF THE CHRISTIAN CHURCHES

The nature of the influence exercised by the Christian churches varied considerably in the various regions under National Socialist control. Policies adopted in an attempt to counteract that influence were correspondingly varied.

A. Policies Adopted in Germany Proper

Persecution of the Christian churches in Germany proper gave rise to very special problems. Since Germany was destined to provide the central force for the coming wars of aggression, it was particularly necessary that the German people be withdrawn from all influence hostile to the National Socialist philosophy of aggression. This meant that the influence of the Christian churches would have to be minimized as thoroughly as possible. On the other hand, the predominantly conservative and patriotic influence exerted by the larger Christian churches was a factor of some positive value from the National Socialist standpoint and insured those churches a substantial measure of support from conservative groups destined to play an important part in the National Socialist plans for aggression. Persecution of the churches in this region had therefore to be effected in such a way as to minimize their effective influence without breaking the unity of the German people and without destroying the capacity of the churches to fulfill their historic mission of conservative social discipline. This could only be accomplished, at least in the case of the major Christian churches, by a slow and cautious policy of gradual encroachment.

CONFIDENTIAL

In accordance with this necessity, the Nazi plan was to show first that they were no foes of the church, that they were indeed interested in "Positive Christianity," were very good friends of the churches, and did not at all want to interfere in religious matters or with the internal affairs of the different denominations. Then, under the pretext that the churches themselves were interfering in political and state matters, they would deprive the churches, step by step, of all opportunity to affect German public life. The Nazis believed that the churches could be starved and strangled spiritually in a relatively short time when they were deprived of all means of communication with the faithful beyond the church building themselves and terrorized in such a manner that no churchman would dare to speak out openly against Nazi policies. This general plan had been established even before the rise of the Nazis to power. It apparently came out of discussions among an inner circle comprising Hitler himself, Rosenberg, Goring, Goebbels, Hess, Baldur von Schirach, Frick, Rust, Kerrl, and Schemm. Some Nazi leaders or sympathizers, and some later collaborationists who were faithful Catholics or Protestants, such as von Epp, Buttmann, and von Papen, may have been left in ignorance of the real aim of Nazi church policy.

The Problem of Proof. The best evidence now available as to the existence of an antichurch plan is to be found in the systematic nature of the persecution itself. Different steps in that persecution, such as the campaign for the suppression of denominational and youth organizations, the campaign against the denominational schools, the defamation campaign against the clergy, started on the same day in the whole area of the Reich or in large districts and were supported by the entire regimented press, by Nazi Party meetings, by traveling Party speakers. As to direct evidence, the directives of the Reich Propaganda Ministry, if they have not been

CONFIDENTIAL

destroyed, would be most authoritative. If they have been destroyed, questioning of Nazi newspapermen and local and regional propagandists might elicit the desired evidence. It is known that Hitler used to discuss the plans of his political action with those members of his inner circle who were especially concerned with the respective problems. Rosenberg, Goring, Goebbels, Frick, Rust, Baldur von Schirach, Kerrl, and Schemm are the leading Nazis who took a special interest in the relationship of state and church. (See Hermann Rauschning, in his chapter on Hitler's religious attitudes in *The Voice of Destruction,* and Kurt Ludeke, *I Knew Hitler.* Both witnesses, however, are to be used with caution.)

But even though the basic plan was uniform, the opportunities for carrying it into effect, and hence the specific policies actually adopted, differed substantially from church to church. The principal churches to be considered in this connection are the following:

1. The Catholic Church. National Socialist relations with the Catholic Church fall into three clearly marked periods:

a. The Period Prior to the Seizure of Power. During this period the relations between the Nazi Party and the Catholic Church were extremely bitter. As an opposition party, the National Socialists had always violently attacked "Political Catholicism" and the collaboration of the Center Party with the Social Democrats in the Reich and Prussian governments, declaring that they could find no difference among the so-called **System-parteien** (parties that collaborated in the system of constitutional government). On 8 March 1933, Goring, in a speech at Essen, summed up the Nazi attitude toward the Center as follows: "Each time the red robber was about to steal some of the German people's properties, his black accomplice stood thieves' watch."[6] On their part, the German bishops, stigmatizing the Nazi

CONFIDENTIAL

movement as anti-Christian, forbade the clergy to participate in any ceremonies, such as funerals, in which the Nazi
Party was officially represented, and refused the sacraments
to party officials. In several pastorals, they expressly warned
the faithful against the danger created to German
Catholicism by the party.[7]

**b. The Period from the Seizure of Power to the
Signing of the Concordat.** During this period, the main concern of the new regime was to liquidate the political opposition. Their strategy was to convince conservatives that the
efforts of the government were being directed primarily
against the Communists and other forces of the extreme left
and that their own interests would remain safe in Nazi hands
as long as they would consent to refrain from political activity. Immediately after their rise to power, therefore, the
Nazis made unmistakable overtures to the churches and
tried to convince the Catholic hierarchy in particular that
after the dissolution of the Center Party and some Catholic
organization of more or less political character, such as the
Friedensbund deutscher Katholiken, no obstacle could remain in
the way of complete reconciliation between the Catholic
church and the Nazi state. The German Catholic bishops,
influenced by the experiences of their Italian colleagues,
whose relations with the Fascists under the Lateran Treaty of
1929 had been fairly smooth, accepted the Nazi proposition.
Pour parlers from a Reich Concordat started immediately.

Meantime the Nazi government abrogated all laws and
regulations of the republic protecting nondenominational
groups of the population and abolished the right to pursue
antireligious and antichurch propaganda. The Prussian government closed the so-called secular *(weltliche)* schools in
which no religious instruction was given and reestablished
religious instruction in professional and vocational schools.[8]
All organizations of free thinkers were forbidden. When the

CONFIDENTIAL

Reichstag elected on 5 March 1922 convened, the government organized religious ceremonies for the Protestant and the Catholic members of Parliament.[9]

And in his speech before the Reichstag, to which he presented his government, Hitler declared:

> "While the regime is determined to carry through the political and moral purging of our public life, it is creating and ensuring the prerequisites for a really deep inner religiosity. Benefits of a personal nature, which might arise from compromises with atheistic organizations, could outweigh the results which become apparent through the destruction of general basic religious-ethical values. The national regime seeks in both Christian confessions the factors most important for the maintenance of our folkdom. It will respect agreements concluded between them and the states. Their rights will not be infringed upon. Conversely, however, it expects and hopes that the national and ethical uplifting of our people, which the regime has taken for its task, will enjoy a similar appreciation. The national regime will concede and safeguard to the Christian confessions the influence due them, in school and education. It is concerned with the sincere cooperation of church and state. The struggle against a materialistic philosophy and for the creation of a true folk community serves the interests of the German nation as well as our Christian belief."[10]

Under such circumstances, the conference of German bishops, meeting as usual in Fulda, decided on 28 March 1933 to lift all restrictions imposed on members of the church adhering to the Nazi movement.[11] This opened the door to mass adherence to the party of practicing Catholics. The rush started immediately. All those German Catholics who were inclined to adopt Nazi political views and had hesitated only because of the anti-Nazi attitude of the hierarchy hastened now to join the victorious party of the "national revolution." Former members of the Center Party's right

CONFIDENTIAL

wing, who had always advocated collaboration with the parties to the right of the Center and with the German nationalist movements established themselves now as so-called "bridge builders" trying to explain ideological affinities between the antiliberal character of Catholic politics and the Nazi system. They insisted especially on the fact that the church was guided like the Nazi movement by the leadership principle.[12] They were soon joined by turncoats from the left wing of the Center and the Catholic youth movement, persons who insisted that the "socialist" and anticapitalist character of the Nazi doctrine coincided marvelously with their own views on the necessity of social reform.

In order to remind the Catholics of the danger of not coming to an agreement with the Nazi state, a certain amount of pressure was at the same time maintained against them. A thorough job was done in purging Reich, state, and municipal administration of officials appointed for their adherence to the Center or Bavarian People's parties. Former leaders of those parties, including priests, joined Communist and Social Democrat leaders in the concentration camps, and the campaign of hatred against the "black" was resumed.[13] By April 1933 the bishops were making appeals for clemency toward former civil servants who, they pointed out, were not able to join the celebration of national awakening because they had been dismissed from position in which they had given their best to the community of the German people. And on 31 May 1933 a meeting of the Bavarian bishops adopted a solemn statement directed against the tendency of attributing to the state alone the right of educating, organizing, and leading ideologically the German youth.[14] A few weeks later, on 18 June 1933, the breaking up in Munich by Nazi hordes of a manifestation of the Catholic Journeymen Association *(Gesellenyereine)* became the starting point of a Nazi propaganda campaign against

CONFIDENTIAL

alleged efforts to keep "Political Catholicism" alive.

Tension was mounting again when news that a Concordat had been signed on 8 July 1933 in Rome between the Holy See and the German Reich seemed to alter the situation completely. For the first time since the Middle Ages, the Reich itself had entered into an agreement with the Roman Catholic Church. Moreover, the new treaty was apparently entirely to the advantage of the church. In return for the retreat of German Catholicism from the political scene, demonstrated by the self-dissolution of the Center Party[15] and the synchronization *(Gleichschaltung)* of the Catholic press,[16] an official guarantee was given the church in the form of an international treaty, of all the church rights that "Political Catholicism" had fought for: freedom for Catholic organizations, maintenance of denominational schools, and preservation of the general influence of the church on the education of the German youth.

Among the 33 articles of the Concordat, 21 treated exclusively rights and prerogatives accorded to the church; reciprocation consisted only in a pledge of loyalty by the clergy to the Reich government and in a promise that Catholic religious instruction would emphasize the patriotic duties of the Christian citizen and insist on a loyal attitude toward the Fatherland. Since it had always been the practice of the Catholic Church to abide by established governments and to promote patriotic convictions among the faithful, these stipulations of the Concordat were no more than legalizations of an existing custom.

The Concordat was hailed by church and state authorities as marking the end of a period of distrust and suspicion and the beginning of close and fruitful collaboration. Hitler himself advised the state and party officials to adopt a friendly attitude toward the Catholic Church and its institutions on German soil. He expressed the wish that Catholic

CONFIDENTIAL

organizations, now under the protection of a treaty of friendship between Nazi Germany and the Holy See, should no longer be regarded by his followers as symbols of an effort to remain outside the national community and to form a way of life apart from the official line of the totalitarian Third Reich.[17]

   c. The Period Following the Signature of the Concordat. During this period, relations between the Nazi state and the Catholic Church became progressively worse. Having gained the support of the Catholic hierarchy in the crucial early days of the regime by signing the Concordat, they took advantage of their subsequently increasing strength to violate every one of the Concordat's provisions, gradually stripping the church of all its more important rights. Specific instances of the various phases of this persecution are presented in section V below.

   By 1937 it had become clear that the Nazi state was not to be appeased by Catholic efforts to accommodate the church and the state in the form of a Concordat, and that Hitler's government had no intention to adhere to its part of the document. Convinced, therefore, that the church had been in error, in the face of the irreconcilability of its teachings with those of National Socialism, in abandoning its earlier opposition to the movement, the church resumed its controversy with Nazi doctrine, while continuing to suffer from Nazi practice.

   The new campaign may be considered to have been inaugurated by Pope Pius XI in his Encyclical of 14 March 1937, entitled *Mit brennender Sorge,*[18] which by underground means was spread by Catholic youth throughout Germany and was first published to the world in the original German text by a reading (21 March 1937) from all Roman Catholic pulpits in Germany. Pope Pius XI denounced the violation of the Concordat by the Nazi state. He described the actions

278 HITLER CAME FOR NIEMOELLER

of the Nazi government against the church as "intrigues which from the beginning had no other aim than a war of extermination. . . . In the furrow of peace in which we had labored to sow the seeds of true peace, others . . . sowed the tares of suspicion, discord, hatred, calumny, a secret and open fundamental hostility to Christ and his church, fed from a thousand different sources and making use of every available means."

The support of the Holy See encouraged some of the German bishops, either in courageous sermons, diocesan pastorals, or in their collective pastorals issued usually from Fulda, the seat of their annual conferences, to protest vigorously against both Nazi ideology and practice. Especially notable in this work were Cardinal Faulbaber of Munich, Bishop von Preysing of Berlin, and Bishop von Galen of Munster. Among the more notable protests were the pastoral issued form Fulda on 19 August 1938,[19] the Fulda pastoral of 1941, which was read from all pulpits on 6 July 1941, the Fulda pastoral of 22 March 1942 and the Fulda pastoral of 19 August 1943.[20] In spite of these protests, there is no evidence that the Nazis were in any way deterred from their campaign, in violation of the Concordat, to destroy the position and influence of the Catholic Church in Germany.

2. The Evangelical Church. Unlike the Catholic Church, the Evangelical churches of Germany were organizations whose supreme administrative organs were located within the borders of Germany. Among the Evangelical clergy and laity there was also a substantial group, the more extreme members of which were known as the German Christians, who were entirely in accord with the purposes of the National Socialist government. With regard to the Evangelical churches, therefore, the policy of the National Socialists was not simply, as in the case of the Catholic Church, to limit the activities and influence of the church organization but to capture and use the church organization for their own purposes. The attempt to accomplish this purpose falls into two main periods.

a. The Period of German Christian Predominance. The essential strategy of the first period of the National Socialist government was to impose highly centralized organs of administration upon the German Evangelical Church and to place the exercise of the powers thus created in the foliable Nazi hands of German Christians. In this way it was hoped to secure the elimination of Christian influences in the Evangelical Church by legal or by quasi-legal means.

The campaign began with a congress of German Christians, held at Berlin on 3 and 4 April 1933,[21] which declared itself in favor of a united Evangelical church organized according to the leadership principles and the tenets of the party (including anti-Semitism). One of its leaders was the army chaplain, Ludwig Müller, a friend of Hitler, who on 25 April was appointed the Führer's representative "with full powers to deal with the affairs of the Evangelical church" in its relations with the state.[22] Yielding to the clamor for unification, the Committee of the German Church Confederation on 23 April 1933 authorized its president, Dr. Kapler, to carry through a reorganization of the constitution of the church. After the constitution had been accepted by the Council of the Church Federation and representatives of the *Landeskirchen*, it was published on 14 July 1933 by the government of the Reich, together with a law recognizing the new German Evangelical Church as a corporation of public law.[23] The essential purpose of this legislation, while ostensibly leaving the *Landeskirchen* independent in matters of confession and worship, was to create a central administrative organ, headed according to the leadership principle by a Reich bishop, and vested with complete power to control administrative and legal activities of the church.

CONFIDENTIAL

To insure the use of this powerful new machinery for the accomplishment of Nazi purposes, it was necessary that it be placed in the hands of reliable German Christians. Typical Nazi pressures were therefore used to control the election of the first Reich bishop. Before the election, German Christian control of the Evangelical Church in Prussia was insured by the appointment by Dr. Rust, Prussian *Kultusminister*, of a State Commissioner for Church Affairs in Prussia. This official, Dr. Jäger, was a German Christian, and through his subcommissioners for the church provinces of Prussia, he took the administration of the church virtually out of its own hands.[24] In preparing the elections for the national synod, which was in turn to elect the Reich bishop, it is said that the clergy were not allowed to exercise their traditional right to limit the voters to active church members.

The night before the election, Hitler intervened with a radio address strongly supporting the German Christians.[25] The result was a victory for the German Christians. On 5 September their candidate, Müller, was elected to the entirely new office of Bishop of Prussia by a General Synod of the Protestant Church of Prussia in a session dominated by a German Christian majority,[26] and in which 75 members of the opposition who desired to protest were not allowed the floor and withdrew from the synod. On 27 September Müller was elected Reich bishop by the National Synod and proceeded to fill the central administration with other German Christians, such as Bishop Schöffel of Hamburg, and Pastor Hossenfelder of Elberfeld, leader of the German Christians and vice president of the Prussian Supreme Church Council.[27]

The new administration proceeded as rapidly as possible to use its powers for the accomplishment of the Nazi church program. Various measures were taken to impair the freedom of the clergy and to secure the dissolution of religious associations. (For specific details, see section V

CONFIDENTIAL

below.) In his attempt to integrate the various *Landeskirchen*, Müller was aided by Dr. Jäger, formerly state commissioner for church affairs in Prussia, who in April 1934 was taken into the Spiritual Council as legal member and head of the Church Chancery. On 9 August 1934 Müller summoned a National Synod packed with Nazis to Berlin. It transferred all its powers to Müller and prescribed a form of oath for all pastors and church officials.[28]

In spite of the formidable legal powers vested in the Reich bishop, the attempt to control the Evangelical Church by these means failed. The churches of Hannover, Württemberg, and Bavaria, under the leadership of their respective bishops, Marahrens, Wurm, and Meiser, refused to yield to pressure and were supported by a vast majority of their pastors. When Wurm and Meiser were placed under house arrest, public demonstrations occurred in their support.[29] On 28 October 1934 a civil court declared all of Jäger's acts in Bavaria to have been illegal.[30] Opposition finally crystallized in the so-called Confessional Church, made up of the churches of Bavaria and Württemberg and representatives of protesting Evangelical clergymen in other parts of Germany. On 29 through 31 May 1934 and 20 October 1934, the first and second Confessional Synods of the Evangelical Church of Germany were held at Barmen and at Dahlem respectively[31] and succeeded in uniting a large part of the German Evangelical Church in protest against the doctrines and church policies of the Reich bishop. Obviously the attempt to make the church a united agency for the accomplishment of Nazi purposes had failed. Thus Reich Bishop Müller, although never being forced officially to resign his position, was gradually superseded by other agencies of Nazi control and faded from the scene.

b. The Period of Direct Administration. Around the middle of 1935, a new attempt was made to establish unity within the German Evangelical Church, this time by the use of government authority rather than through the agency of the German Christians operating within the church government. To this end the powers of the government in church affairs were strengthened. On 26 June 1935 a *Law on the Settlement of Legal Questions Arising in the Evangelical Church*[32] deprived the Evangelical churches of their right to sue before the regular courts and set up a special administrative court *(Beschlussstelle)* with the power of final decision in such matters. This deprived the churches of the rights of self-administration and protection in the civil courts to which as corporations of public law they were entitled under Article 137 of the Weimar Constitution. On 16 July 1935 Hitler announced the creation of the post of a Reich minister for ecclesiastical affairs.[33] One of the first acts of the new minister, Dr. Hanns Kerrl, was to transfer the *Beschlussstelle* from the Ministry of Interior to his own jurisdiction. On 27 July 1935 he made himself president of this special court. On 24 September 1935 the organization of the ministry was further developed by a *Law for the Safeguarding of the German Evangelical Church*[34] by which "The Reich Minister for Ecclesiastical Affairs is impowered, for the restoration of orderly conditions in the German Evangelical Church and the Regional Evangelical Churches, to issue ordinances with binding legal force." On 20 March 1937 the minister for church affairs delegated the administration of the church to Dr. Werner, president of the Church Chancery of the German Evangelical Church.[35] On 10 December 1937 the appointment was made permanent, and he was authorized to promulgate ordinances on all church matters except questions of faith and worship.[36] Thus the exercise of control over the entire church administration was placed in the hands of government appointees. In this way, formal legal validity was given to all subsequent acts directed against the German Evangelical churches.

CONFIDENTIAL

The principal victims of the ensuing persecution were members of the Confessional Church. At first an attempt was made to conciliate them by the appointment on 14 October 1935 of church committees, on which friends of the Confessional Synod were represented, for the government and administration of the churches.[37] Although some of the protesting Landeskirchen were thereby reconciled, many of the Confessionals refused to accept the authority of these committees. This was met with a series of repressive measures against the Confessional Church. On 2 December 1935 the minister for ecclesiastical affairs declared their central organs (Provisional Church Government and the Council of Brethren of the Confessional Synod) illegal.[38] On 2 December 1935 the authority of the church ministry was expressly denied by Dr. Niemöller, leader of the Confessionals.

In May 1936 the leaders of the Confessional Church addressed a memorandum to Hitler denouncing the anti-Christian acts of the government.[39] When this was met with further acts of repression, the failure of the church committees to effect a reconciliation was admitted by Ecclesiastical Minister Kerrl, in a report to Hitler. From that time onward the official attitude was that the Confessional Church was illegal, and its activities were persecuted to the point where they became almost completely ineffective. For specific instances of this persecution, see the following section.

3. The Christian Sects. Certain of the smaller Christian sects, especially the Jehovah's Witnesses *(Ernste Bibelforscher)* and the Pentecostal Association *(Freie Christengemeinde)*, were particularly objectionable from the Nazi standpoint because of their advanced pacifist views. Since they were without important influence at home or abroad, it was possible to proceed against them more drastically than against the larger Christian churches. Both groups were therefore

CONFIDENTIAL

declared illegal[40] and there were times when almost no adherent of either group was outside a concentration camp.[41] For specific instances of this persecution, see below, pp. 287-88).

B. Policies Adopted in the Incorporated Areas

In areas like Alsace-Lorraine or western Poland, and to some extent in Austria, where the Nazis were attempting to incorporate a substantial non-German population into the body of the Reich, local church organizations were feared primarily as potential centers of national resistance to German domination. The policies adopted against the churches in these regions were therefore particularly severe, the most seriously afflicted being western Poland. A summary statement of the measures taken in these regions, together with a vigorous protest against them, is to be found in the memorial of 15 December 1942, addressed to the German minister for church affairs, the German minister for the interior, and the chief of the chancery, by the German Catholic bishops assembled at Fulda.[42] For specific details see section V below.

C. Policies Adopted in Other Occupied Areas

In other occupied areas, which were designed to support but not to take a leading part in the Nazi campaign of world conquest, the need to impose a unified Nazi philosophy was less great than in other regions. Thus there was no general motive for persecution in these areas. In regions like Slovakia, where the churches proved generally cooperative with the occupying authorities, they were officially favored. But in countries where the spirit of national resistance was widely supported by the local churches, the Nazis felt no compunction about persecuting them vigorously. The countries to suffer most in this respect were the general government of

CONFIDENTIAL

Poland and occupied Norway. For specific instances of persecution in these areas, see below, section V.

V. METHODS USED TO IMPLEMENT THE POLICY OF PERSECUTION

In order to implement their general policy of persecution, the National Socialists interfered at every possible stage in the activities of the Christian churches. Sometimes they accomplished their purposes by direct intervention of the Reich or land governments under their control or, in the case of Norway and other occupied but unincorporated areas, by intervention of a native puppet government. At other times they preferred to accomplish their purposes through the use of the SA, the Hitler Youth, and other party organizations. The principal forms of intervention were the following:

A. Interference with the Central Institutions of Church Government

The easiest way to achieve rapid results in the destruction of the Christian churches was to paralyze their central institutions, and thus deprive them of the advantages of central leadership. This was accomplished either by the direct seizure and exploitation of those institutions by Nazi or pro-Nazi personnel, or by interference with the effective operation of those institutions that could not be thus subjected to seizure and exploitation.

1. **The Direct Seizure of Central Institutions of Church Government.** This could be most easily accomplished in the case of Christian churches that had a long tradition of dependence upon state authority. This aspect of the persecution was generally carried out through the forms of law, without the necessity for any important admixture of illegal action. The most important cases of this sort were the following:

CONFIDENTIAL

a. The Seizure of the German Evangelical Church.
The steps whereby legal control over the central governing
institutions of the German Evangelical Church was established, first on behalf of German Christian supporters of the
Nazi government and later on behalf of the Nazi government itself, are outlined in section IV, "2. The Evangelical
Church" through "3. The Christian Sects."

THE PROBLEM OF PROOF. The major steps in
this process are a matter of legal record. The principal laws
and ordinances by which the seizure was accomplished are
cited above.

b. The Seizure of the Norwegian National Church.
The Evangelical Lutheran State Church, to which 98.6 percent of the population adhered, was a state church established by royal decree. Church affairs were handled by the
Department of Church and Education. When the Germans
invaded the country and set up a Reichskomissar for the
occupied Norwegian territories,[43] they gained control over
this central organization. Pro-Nazi Norwegians were placed
in charge of the Department of Church and Education, subsequently replaced by the Ministry for Culture and Enlight-
enment. These powers were exercised in such a way that the
entire Norwegian pastorate, with insignificant exceptions,
decided on Easter Sunday, 1942, to make joint resignation
of their public offices and salaries,[44] thus proclaiming their
conviction that the central institutions of the state church
were no longer available for the accomplishment of
Christian purposes.

THE PROBLEM OF PROOF. Although native
Norwegian collaborators played the principal role in the
persecution of the Norwegian church, it is a matter of legal
record that final control over and hence final responsibility
for their actions rests with the German Reichskommissariat
for Norway. All necessary evidence with regard to the course

of the church conflict in Norway can no doubt be obtained from Norwegian church authorities.

2. Interference with the Normal Operation of Central Institutions of Church Government. In the case of the Catholic and of some Protestant churches, the Nazis were unable to gain control of the central institutions of church government. In these cases they tried as far as possible to prevent those central institution from operating. The methods used were more or less drastic, depending on the circumstances.

a. Legal Abolition of Central Institutions of Church Government. In accord with the generally cautious policies adopted by the Nazis in their campaign for the persecution of the Christian churches, this device was sparingly used. The principal cases are the following:

i. Prohibition of Certain German Sects. Under the Nazi regime, the organization and activities of the *Ernste Bibelforscher* and *Freie Christengemeinde* were declared illegal. They were rigorously suppressed by the police.

THE PROBLEM OF PROOF. For general references, see above (p. 283). The dissolution of the Jehovah's Witnesses was declared in violation of Article 1937 of the Weimar Constitution in a case decided on 26 March 1934 by the Special Court of Darmstadt (*Juristische Wochenschrift* (hereinafter abbr. *J. W.*) 1934, p. 1747). Most courts, however, upheld the decision of the government. For cases illustrating some of the ways in which members of this sect were persecuted, the following court decisions should be consulted: (1) Refusal of a peddler's license. *Bayerischer Verwaltungsgorichtshof,* 8 May 1936 (Refer, Vol. 37, p. 553); (2) Refusal of a permit to practice as a midwife. *Sächsisches Oberverwaltungsgericht,* 4 December 1936 (J. W. 1937, p. 1368); (3) Dismissal of a postal clerk. *Reichsdienststrafhof, 11 February 1935* (Zeitschrift für Beamtenrscht 1936, p. 104);

CONFIDENTIAL

Refusal of the right to conduct family worship in the home. Reichsgericht, 17 February 1938 (J. W. 1938, p. 1018); Removal of children from the custody of their parents. Landgericht Hamburg, 6 May 1936 (*Jgdrecht u. Jgdwohlfahrt* 1936, p. 281).

ii. Prohibition of the Central Governing Organs of the German Confessionals. On 20 December 1935 the Provisional Church Government and the Council of Brethren of the Confessional Synod were specifically declared illegal by the minister for ecclesiastical affairs. Although the repressive measures actually taken were not sufficient to prevent these groups from acting, this ruling prevented them from enjoying the privileges of public law corporations, to which the Evangelical Church was entitled under existing German law.

THE PROBLEM OF PROOF. See above, pp. 282-83.

b. The Imposition of Financial Controls upon the Operation of Church Governments. The principal Christian churches of Germany had long derived their main financial support from state-collected church taxes. To maintain effective control over these organizations, it was therefore sufficient to deprive them of all other sources of revenue and to impose state restrictions upon the expenditure of state-collected funds. The Sammlungsgesetz of 5 November 1934,[45] which placed severe restrictions on the right of churches and other organizations to solicit contributions, was an important hindrance to the financial independence of all churches.

i. Financial Control of the German Evangelical Church. The establishment of machinery for financial control played a major part in the Nazi capture of the German Evangelical Church organization. Under earlier German law, local church authorities had exercised considerable authority in determining the rate of and allocating the revenues from church taxes. On 11 March 1935 the Prussian government deprived the Prussian church of this power by setting up state-controlled finance departments for the management of the finances of all Evangelical churches in Prussia. By ordinance of 25 June 1937,[46] state-controlled finance departments were set up for the German Evangelical Church and for each of the provincial churches, with the right to regulate the conditions of service of all officials of the general church administrations, of the pastors, and of the local parish officials and employees. By an ordinance of 9 June 1937 it was provided that all church collections had to be subject to the approval of the central church authorities.[47] Since the control of the central authorities of the German Evangelical Church was in Nazi hands, this meant that all Protestant congregations, including those Confessional congregations that had been maintained by voluntary contributions, could be deprived of all financial support at the discretion of the Nazi authorities.

THE PROBLEM OF PROOF. The legislation by which this control was exercised is a matter of record. For a specific instance of the way in which the resulting power was exercised, see below, Case 1.[48]

CASE 1. THE FINANCIAL COERCION OF THE DAHLEM PARISH. The Dahlem parish of the German Evangelical Church, being located in a fashionable part of Berlin, was comparatively prosperous. It enjoyed an income of around 400,000 marks, half of which exceeded its immediate needs. When its pastor, Dr. Niemöller, leader of the Confessionals, was dismissed from his pastorate by the Reich Bishop Müller on 1 March 1935, the congregational assembly refused to obey the order and asked him to continue to serve. They refused to transfer their income to the central church offices and devoted about half of it to the Confessional Church. The transfer was finally enforced,

CONFIDENTIAL

however, by a commissioner appointed by the finance department.

THE PROBLEM OF PROOF. Evidence should be obtainable from Dr. Niemöller and from other serving members of the parish.

c. Interruption of Official Communications within the Church Government. The effective operation of any large organization depends on the maintenance of free and confidential communication between officials. This right was guaranteed for the Catholic Church in Germany by Article IV of the Concordat, which reads: "In its relations and correspondence with the bishops, clergy and other members of the Catholic Church in Germany, the Holy See enjoys full freedom. The same applies to the bishops and other diocesan officials in their dealings with the faithful in all matters belonging to their pastoral office." Violations of this right played an important part in the total Nazi scheme for the persecution of the Christian churches. As early as 1935 the bishops were made to realize that their correspondence and telephone calls were subject to constant surveillance by the police.[49]

The following cases might repay investigation.

i. Cases in Germany Proper.

CASE 2. In February 1937 Dr. Zöllner, the chairman of the Reich Church Committee was prevented by the police from visiting nine Confessional pastors of Lübeck who had been arrested by the secret police. This interference with his attempted conciliation led to the resignation of Zöllner and his committee on 14 February 1937.

THE PROBLEM OF PROOF. Evidence should be obtainable from serving Confessional leaders.

CASE 3. When the bishop of Wuerzburg, Mgr. Ehrenfried, traveled to Rome in November 1938, he was held up on the German frontier and had to stand by while all his luggage and documents were searched. Photostats were made of everything written in Latin.

THE PROBLEM OF PROOF. Case 3 is reported in *The Persecution of the Catholic Church in the Third Reich,* page 42. Since Mgr. Ehrenfried is alive and still bishop of Wuerzburg, it would be easy to have himself as a witness.

CASE 4. In 1936 the offices of the diocesan administration of Freiburg in Breisgau were raided by the Gestapo.

THE PROBLEM OF PROOF. Case 4 is reported in *The Persecution of the Catholic Church in the Third Reich,* p. 41. Archbishop Groeber and every member of the Diocesan Administration of Freiburg who held his position prior to the reported incident might be witnesses.

CASE 5. In 1937 fifty officials of the Gestapo searched the offices of the Administration of the Archdiocese of Cologne.

THE PROBLEM OF PROOF. Case 5 is reported in *The Persecution of the Catholic Church in the Third Reich,* page 41. Every member of the diocesan administration who held his position prior to the reported incident is a potential witness.

CASE 6. In 1937 the offices of the vicar-general in Aachen were searched.

THE PROBLEM OF PROOF. Case 6 is reported in *The Persecution of the Catholic Church in the Third Reich,* page 42. Every member of the diocesan administration who held his position prior to the reported incident is a potential witness.

CASE 7. On 31 August 1938 Cardinal Faulhaber's offices in Munich were searched.

THE PROBLEM OF PROOF. Case 7 is reported in *The Persecution of the Catholic Church in the Third Reich,* page 42. Cardinal Faulhaber and every member of the diocesan administration who held his position prior to the reported incident might be a witness.

CASE 8. On 15 April 1939 the offices of the bishop

CONFIDENTIAL

of Limburg on the Lahn were searched. The archives of certain ecclesiastical foundations were confiscated and carried away, together with the money belonging to them.

THE PROBLEM OF PROOF. Case 8 is reported in *The Persecution of the Catholic Church in the Third Reich,* page 42. Mgr. Hilfrich, bishop of Limburg, and every member of the diocesan administration who held his position prior to the reported incident might be a witness.

CASE 9. In the diocesan administration buildings in Berlin, the German bishops had set up an Information Bureau under the direction of Mgr. Banasch. This office was raided in December 1935. All papers were examined, and Mgr. Banasch was arrested and held in jail until March 1936.

THE PROBLEM OF PROOF. Case 9 is reported in *The Persecution of the Catholic Church in the Third Reich.* Count v. Preysing, bishop of Berlin, Mgr. Banasch himself, and every member of the diocesan administration who held his position prior to the reported incident could be witnesses.

ii. Cases in the Incorporated Areas

CASE 10. In 1938 a search was carried out in the ordinariates of Vienna, Salzburg, and Seckau.

THE PROBLEM OF PROOF. Case 10 is reported in *The Persecution of the Catholic Church in the Third Reich,* page 42. Cardinal Innitzer, Bishop Pawlikowski, and every member of the three diocesan administrations who held his position prior to the reported incidents might be witnesses.

B. Interference with the Persons of the Clergy and of Lay Workers

Insofar as it was not possible or prudent to control the churches through their central administrative apparatus, it was possible to cripple their work by intimidating or eliminating those clergymen or lay workers who were attempting to carry out church policies. So far as the Catholic Church is

CONFIDENTIAL

concerned, the rights of the clergy to special protection were guaranteed in Article V of the Concordat, which read: "In the exercise of their spiritual activities the clergy shall enjoy the protection of the State in the same way as State officials. The state will take proceedings in accordance with the general provisions of State law against any outrage offered to the clergy personally or directed against their ecclesiastical character, or any interference with the duties of their office, and in case of need will provide official protection." In spite of this, interferences with the personal security of the clergy, both Protestant and Catholic, and of leading lay workers of the churches was very freely used as a means of hampering the activities of the Christian churches. This was accomplished by the following means:

1. The Murder of Church Leaders. In line with their generally cautious policies of church persecution, the Nazis were somewhat sparing in the use of these means. The official Nazi policy was expressed by Robert Wagner, Gauleiter of Baden, when he said: "The Catholic church need not imagine that we are going to create martyrs. We shall not give the church that satisfaction—she shall have, not martyrs, but criminals."[50] Even within the borders of Germany proper, however, there were some instances of the murder of church personalities, and in the incorporated areas, where the reactions of public opinion were less to be feared, the numbers of such cases were quite substantial.

a. Cases in Germany Proper. The cases in this category most worthy of investigation are the deaths of the Catholic leaders Klausener, Beck, and Probst. They are considered in detail on pages 8-10 of the report on "Criminal Responsibilities in Connection with the Purge of 1934," R&A No. 3113.1.

b. Cases in the Incorporated Areas. The murder of large numbers of Catholic priests is reported by the Polish

CONFIDENTIAL

Ministry of Information in London as having occurred in the incorporated regions of western Poland.[51] Since no sufficient details are given, it would be necessary to get in touch with the informed Polish authorities in order to prepare specific cases. The possibility that patriotic Polish priests may actually have been engaged in acts against the occupying authorities will somewhat complicate the problem of proving persecution in these instances.

    c. Cases in the Occupied Areas. The murder of numbers of Catholic priests is reported by the Polish Ministry of Information in London as having occurred in the incorporated regions of western Poland.[52] The problem of proof is the same as in section ii above.

    2. The Assaulting of Church Leaders. In order to hamper the church leaders in carrying out their work, they were frequently subjected to actual or threatened personal violence. The SA, the SS, the Hitler Youth, and other party organizations were most frequently used in carrying out this aspect of the persecution.

    a. Cases in Germany Proper.

    CASE 11. Bishop Dr. Sproll of Rottenburg, absent from his diocese because of the disturbances caused by his having failed to vote in the elections of 10 April 1938, returned to his residence on 15 July 1938 on instructions from the Holy See. The next day demonstrations started in which about 100 young people, members of the Hitler Youth, took part. Few of them were from Rottenburg itself. The demonstrators forced an entrance into the bishop's residence through the chancellery. A group of them came shouting and yelling into the bishop's private chapel, where he knelt before the exposed Blessed Sacrament. They hesitated and withdrew, making contemptuous remarks. So did another party when they saw the bishop in prayer. Finally, the editor of the *Flammenzeichen* of Stuttgart, with five other men, appeared and tried in vain to persuade the bishop to leave the town. Meanwhile, the rest of the intruders ransacked the offices and private belongings of the bishop. Finally the mob marched off, singing the Horst Wessel song and "Deutschland üeber Alles." Next day a representative of the Gestapo visited the bishop and told him to leave Rottenburg, threatening that otherwise the demonstration would be repeated. The bishop replied: "I have strict orders from the Holy See to return to my diocese. I am the bishop of Rottenburg, and I shall remain in Rottenburg, even if I lose my life in doing so."

On 18 July another demonstration occurred. This time the demonstrators numbered between 1,500 and 2,000, and again the majority are believed to have come from other places. The bishop's residence was stoned. In the bishop's study alone four large rocks were found.

A third demonstration occurred on 23 July. The demonstrators had been brought to Rottenburg in cars and buses from as much as 30 miles away. Again the crowd forced its way into the building. In the bishop's private chapel they found the archbishop of Freiburg, who had arrived in Rottenburg, the vicar-general, and some of the cathedral canons. They insulted the archbishop and showed their contempt for the exposed sacrament by smoking and keeping their hats on. The bishop was then expelled from his diocese by order of the Ministry of Interior of Rottenburg and left for Freiburg.

THE PROBLEM OF PROOF. Evidence as to the planned nature of these demonstrations is contained in a letter received by Bishop Sproll a few days after the incident and published subsequently in a Swiss paper.[53] This letter declares: "I was one of those present last Saturday—not indeed of my own free will, but by order. I have always been proud of my country, but last Saturday I was, for the first

CONFIDENTIAL

time, ashamed to call myself a German. And a number of the comrades of my section think the same way as I do. We were ashamed of ourselves for having—without our knowledge—allowed ourselves to be used for such a scandalous affair. . . . By staging this demonstration the Party had given us an involuntary proof that you acted rightly on 10 April. The mere fact that the SA had to attend in civilian dress indicated that the Party itself had the feeling that what was happening was not the proper thing for the 'dress of honor' of the SA."

Soon after the departure of the bishop, the Nazi area leader, Dr. Fritsch, declared before a thousand political leaders of the Freiburg district in the Festhalle that "the archbishop should be thankful that he was still able to reside in his house and had not already received the proper answer to his goings on. This ragamuffin was spreading lying statements in the foreign press, and that was high treason. Here, publicly, I call him a knave, a liar, and a traitor to his country."[54]

The "Sproll incidents" were described in an official ecclesiastical announcement that was read in several German dioceses on the last Sunday of July 1938. Concerning the last demonstration of 23 July, *Der Deutsche in Polen* (Katovice) printed on 14 August 1938 a copy of the authentic information sent by the diocesan authorities to the Reichminister for ecclesiastical affairs.

Bishop Sproll, Archbishop Groeber, the members of Bishop Sproll's household, and the members of his diocesan administration who held office prior to the reported incidents could be witnesses.

CASE 12. On 12 May 1935 the late Archbishop Klein of Paderborn paid a visit to Hamm. On his arrival he was mobbed by the Hitler Youth, members of which tried to overturn his car, spat at him, and attacked with their "daggers of

CONFIDENTIAL

honor" some Catholics who tried to protect him. The address of welcome to the bishop at the St. Agnes-Kirchplatz had to be abandoned. The Nazi manifestation had obviously been carefully prepared. Hitler Youth leaders from Dortmund and Hamm took part in it.

THE PROBLEM OF PROOF. The members of the Catholic clergy of Hamm who were residing in that community at the time of the reported incident could be witnesses. Case 12 is reported in *The Persecution of the Catholic Church in the Third Reich,* page 252.

CASE 13. On 26 May 1934 the bishop of Trier, Mgr. Bornewasser, was insulted by Hitler Youth at the end of the Confirmation service in Kreuznach.

THE PROBLEM OF PROOF. Case 13 is reported in *The Persecution of the Catholic Church in the Third Reich,* page 253. Bishop Bornewasser himself could be a witness.

CASE 14. At the beginning of 1935 the murder of Cardinal Faulhaber was demanded in public meetings in Munich. Examples: a meeting of 15 February of the German School Union, at which the Nazi City School Inspector Bauer spoke; a meeting on 17 May of the German Faith Movement; a meeting on 13 June 1935 at which a Dr. Engel of the Ludendorff movement was the speaker.

THE PROBLEM OF PROOF. Case 14 is reported in *The Persecution of the Catholic Church in the Third Reich,* page 252. Members of the diocesan administration of Munich could be witnesses.

CASE 15. In June 1937 the bishop of Trier, Mgr. Bornewasser, was attached bodily in the Hunsrueck area.

THE PROBLEM OF PROOF. See *The Persecution of the Catholic Church in the Third Reich,* page 253. Bishop Bornewasser himself could be a witness.

CASE 16. At the end of November 1938, after a speech by Gauleiter and State Minister Wagner in Munich,

CONFIDENTIAL

uniformed detachments in motorcars and on motorcycles arrived in front of the cardinal's residence. A hail of stones was directed against the windows, while the men shouted, "Take the rotten traitor to Dachau." Armed with crowbars, the demonstrators shattered the window frames and shutters.

THE PROBLEM OF PROOF. Eyewitness report published in *Der Deutsche in Polen* of 27 November 1938. Cardinal Faulhaber himself could be a witness.

CASE 17. On 21 September 1935 the walls of ecclesiastical buildings in Freiburg Breisgau were covered with inscriptions insulting the clergy.

THE PROBLEM OF PROOF. Official report of Vicar-General Rösch, 26 September 1935, No. 14091.

CASE 18. In May 1939 abusive demonstrations against Cardinal Faulhaber were renewed in several places in Bavaria, such a Gars, Wang, and Muehldorf on the Inn, where at seven or eight points around the town posters were displayed saying, "Away with Faulhaber, the friend of the Jews and the agent of Moscow."

THE PROBLEM OF PROOF. See *The Persecution of the Catholic Church in the Third Reich,* page 262, with facsimile of the Muehldorf poster on the opposite page. Cardinal Faulhaber himself could be a witness.

CASE 19. On 25 October 1936 members of the Hitler Youth hurled insults at Cardinal Faulhaber as he was entering his car in Giesing, a suburb of Munich.

THE PROBLEM OF PROOF. See *The Persecution of the Catholic Church in the Third Reich,* page 254. Cardinal Faulhaber himself could be a witness.

b. Cases in the Incorporated Areas

CASE 20. On 8 October 1938 at 8:15 P.M. demonstrations took place against the residence of Cardinal Archbishop Innitzer in Vienna. Stones were thrown, all windows were broken, and a heavy door was broken. A quarter of an hour later the mob broke in, destroying everything they could find in the antechambers. Reaching the episcopal chapel, they struck a secretary of the cardinal unconscious and destroyed the statue of a saint and other property. The purple pectoral cross and ring of the cardinal were stolen. The archbishop's master of ceremonies was hit on the head with a candelabra. One of the priests was dragged to the window and only just saved from being thrown out. On the rumor that the police were coming, they left, first demanding a signed statement from the inmates of the residence that they would never reveal these events. Not one of the intruders, who left singing "Deutschland über Alles," was in any way interfered with in going out. The only person arrested was a correspondent of *The Times*.

THE PROBLEM OF PROOF. These events were reported in the *Osservatore Romano* of 15 October 1938. Eight days later, Gauleiter Buerckel of Vienna held a mass meeting on the Heldenplatz, in which he announced that an attempt by the clergy had been made to work the people up to a putsch against the Nazi government, and that therefore some stern measures had had to be taken. This speech was reported in the Vienna newspapers. Cardinal Innitzer could name eyewitnesses of the Nazi demonstration.

CASE 21. On Friday, 7 October 1938, following a service for Catholic youth in St. Stephen's Cathedral in Vienna, at which Cardinal Archbishop Innitzer gave the sermon, Hitler Youth and SA gathered outside shouting, "Down with Innitzer. Our faith is Germany." Later bands of SA men gathered in front of the bishop's residence and staged demonstrations, shouting that the cardinal should be taken to Dachau.

THE PROBLEM OF PROOF. These facts were reported in the *Osservatore Romano* of 15 October 1938.

CASE 22. On 8 October 1938 a mob broke into a

house of the Cathedral Curia in Vienna and, after thoroughly wrecking it, threw a curate, Fr. Kravarnik, out of the window. His life was reported to be in danger.

THE PROBLEM OF PROOF. These events were reported in the *Osservatore Romano* of 15 October 1938. Diocesan officials in Vienna might serve as witnesses.

CASE 23. In June 1938 when Cardinal Innitzer journeyed through the northern parts of Lower Austria for visitation and confirmation he was subjected to such outrages and mobs that he decided to break off his journey. In one town the cardinal covered his dress with the parish priest's cape and left the church. He was recognized, however, by a teacher, who gave the signal for attack, and was bombarded with rotten eggs and potatoes and struck at with umbrellas.

THE PROBLEM OF PROOF. Case 23 is reported in *The Persecution of the Catholic Church in the Third Reich,* page 262. Cardinal Innitzer himself could be a witness.

3. Defamation of the Clergy. In order to reduce the influence of the clergy, systematic propaganda campaigns were carried out to depict them in an unfavorable light. The most vigorous of these campaigns were the press campaigns in connection with the "Currency Trials" and the "Clerical Immorality Trials" of 1935 and 1936, which tried to discredit the Catholic clergy as financial manipulators and moral degenerates. The Catholic Church was the principal victim of these tactics.

THE PROBLEM OF PROOF. Evidence here consists in the files of all German newspapers for the period. The extent and sensational coloring of the reports of these trials, quite apart from any case of the guilt or innocence of the particular defendants, is proof of the antichurch purpose of the campaign, which was underlined in violent outbursts of Hitler and Goebbels themselves made in official speeches. See especially the speech made by Goebbels in a mass meeting in the *Deutschlandhalle* (Berlin) on 28 May 1937.

CONFIDENTIAL

4. Arrest of the Clergy. The activities of the clergy were frequently interrupted by arrest and imprisonment. Catholics and Protestants were equally affected by this form of persecution.

a. Cases in Germany Proper

CASE 24. In 1933 Dr. Jäger, as head of the church chancery, had the Gestapo place Bishop Wurm of Wurttemberg and Bishop Meiser of Bavaria under house arrest. The latter act was held illegal by court decision.

THE PROBLEM OF PROOF. Evidence not available here. It could no doubt be furnished by the bishops in question.

CASE 25. A prominent Protestant clergyman of Stuttgart, Stadtpfarrez Lic. Lempp, prepared a written sermon to be read on Sunday, 12 September 1943, in churches where only lay readers were available to carry out the services. In this sermon, he criticized the government for its persecution of the Evangelical Church in the incorporated areas of western Poland. On 11 September 1943 he was arrested by the Gestapo on orders of the Reichssicherheitshauptant. He was released on 14 September but forced to pay a fine for "criminal incitement" *(verbrecherlicher Volksarhetzung)*.

THE PROBLEM OF PROOF. The facts of this case are set forth, and the position of Pastor Lempp defended, in a letter of 4 October 1943 addressed by Bishop Wurn of Württemberg to the Reich minister of the interior. A translation of this letter is given below in the appendix.

CASE 26. In January 1937 nine Confessional pastors of Lübeck, who had disagreed with their German Christian bishop, were arrested by the secret police.

THE PROBLEM OF PROOF. Evidence not available here. Could no doubt be obtained from confessional leaders in Germany.

CASE 27. On 1 July 1937 Martin Niemöller,

Confessional leader, was arrested and put in prison. On 7 February 1938 he was tried before a special court in Berlin. On 2 March he was sentenced to seven months imprisonment in a fortress (i.e., honorable imprisonment) for violation of the Pulpit Law. He was also fined 500 marks for a violation of the rules of the Emergency Decree of 28 February 1933 (originally directed against the Communists) and 1,500 marks for another violation of both laws. He was acquitted of the charge of "underhand attacks on State and Party." As he had been eight months in prison he was allowed to go free. On leaving the court he was arrested by the Gestapo and sent to a concentration camp where he remained until the end of the war.

THE PROBLEM OF PROOF. Newspaper reports of the Niemöller arrest and trial. Niemöller himself could be a witness.

CASE 28. In May 1935 the parish priest of Koblenz-Neuendorf was sentenced to six months imprisonment because he had "ridiculed" the Winter Relief Work and the National Socialist Welfare Work.

THE PROBLEM OF PROOF. Reported in *Germania* (Berlin) 12 May 1935.

CASE 29. In May 1936 a curate in Mannheim was sentenced to four months imprisonment because he had spoken critically of the Hitler Youth.

THE PROBLEM OF PROOF. Reported in *Kolnische Volkszeitung*, 18 May 1936.

CASE 30. On 16 April 1935 the special court in Schwerin sentenced to one and a half years imprisonment Mgr. Leffers, parish priest of Rostock, for remarks made in a discussion of Rosenberg's *Myth* with three students, supporters of Ludendorff's anti-Christian movement, who visited him under the pretext that they were seeking spiritual advice.

THE PROBLEM OF PROOF. Reported in *Frankfurter Zeitung*, 17 April 1935.

CONFIDENTIAL

CASE 31. On 22 July 1 937 Father Rupert Mayer S. J. was sentenced to six months imprisonment because he did not comply with the prohibition on his preaching imposed by the Gestapo.

THE PROBLEM OF PROOF. See *The Persecution of the Catholic Church in the Third Reich,* page 68 and Appendix III to that book, pages 538-543.

b. Cases in the Incorporated Areas

CASE 32. In 1938 at Seckau (Austria) Prince Bishop Dr. Pawlikowski was kept under guard for several days by 2 SS men.

THE PROBLEM OF PROOF. See *The Persecution of the Catholic Church in the Third Reich,* page 42. Bishop Pawlikowski himself could be a witness.

i. Cases in Western Poland. The imprisonment of large numbers of Catholic priests is reported by the Polish Ministry of Information in London as having occurred in the incorporated regions of western Poland.[55] Since no sufficient details are given, it would be necessary to get in touch with informed Polish authorities in order to prepare specific cases. The possibility that patriotic Polish priests may actually have been engaged in acts against the occupying authorities will somewhat complicate the problem of proving persecution in these cases.

c. Cases in the Occupied Areas

i. Cases in Norway. The imprisonment and detention in house arrest of large numbers of Norwegian clergymen took place during the Nazi regime. All necessary evidence with regard to these arrests can no doubt be obtained from Norwegian church authorities. The case of Bishop Eivand Berggrav was especially notable.

ii. Cases in the General Government of Poland. The imprisonment of large numbers of Catholic and Protestant clergymen is reported by the Polish Ministry of

Information in London as having occurred in the general government of Poland.[56]

5. Removing Clergymen from Office. Without being arrested, clergymen were occasionally removed from office by order of the Nazi authorities. In the case of churches whose central organs of administration were under Nazi control, this could be done by order from the higher church authorities. In other cases, alleged violations of state laws were sometimes punished in this fashion. The use of essentially ecclesiastical penalties for the violation of state law would seem to be of doubtful legality.

a. Cases Involving Protestant Clergymen

CASE 33. On 1 March 1935 Niemöller was dismissed by Reich bishop from his pastorate in Dahlem.

THE PROBLEM OF PROOF. Niemöller himself could be a witness.

CASE 34. During the Munich crisis of 1938, the Confessionals, through their provisional government of the Evangelical Church, issued an order of a Service of Prayer for Peace. On the grounds that this was a treasonable act, the Reich minister for ecclesiastical affairs ordered that the salaries of these Confessionals be stopped and that they be removed from their parishes.

THE PROBLEM OF PROOF. Evidence would have to be obtained from surviving Confessional leaders and the file of the Reichs Ministry for Ecclesiastical Affairs.

b. Cases Involving Catholic Clergymen

CASE 35. In the summer of 1938 Mgr. Dr. Sproll, bishop of Rottenburg, was expelled from his diocese. This measure was justified by the German News Agency (DNB) on the grounds that he "was the only citizen of his locality who failed to participate in the election of 10 April."

THE PROBLEM OF PROOF. Newspaper reports. Bishop Sproll himself could be a witness.

CONFIDENTIAL

CASE 36. On 27 June 1938 a priest named Vorwerk, the official representative of the bishop of Muenster for that part of his diocese which lay in the territory of Oldenburg, was expelled because he had protested the conversion of the denominational schools in Oldenburg into Nazi community schools at the order of the Nazi minister of public instruction of Oldenburg.

THE PROBLEM OF PROOF. Pastoral of the bishop of Muenster, Count von Galen, read from the pulpits on 31 July 1938.

CASE 37. In April 1937 the parish priest of the cathedral parish in Eichstaett was served with an order of expulsion. This order was not carried into effect only because the diocesan bishop, Mgr. Rackl, proclaimed from the cathedral pulpit that he had ordered him not to leave his parish.

THE PROBLEM OF PROOF. Mgr. Rackl himself could be a witness. See *The Persecution of the Catholic Church in the Third Reich,* page 44.

C. Interference with the Activities of the Clergy

When clergymen were not molested in their own person, they were frequently prevented from fulfilling the normal functions of their office. The following forms of intervention were particularly frequent:

1. Closing of Church Buildings. This most drastic form of interference with clerical activities was used primarily in the incorporated and occupied territories.

a. Cases in Incorporated Areas. The partial or complete closing of large numbers of churches in the incorporated territories of western Poland is reported by the Polish Ministry of Information, London.[57] This statement was confirmed in the memorial of 15 December 1942 addressed by the Catholic bishops of Germany to the German minister of ecclesiastical affairs, which said that with a very few exceptions all churches in the dioceses of Posen and Litzmannstadt had been withdrawn from use for worship and either sealed or used for warehouses or other profane purposes, in one case as a riding school.[58]

b. Cases in Occupied Areas. Although the closing of churches was less frequent in the general government of Poland than in the incorporated territories, several cases are mentioned by the Polish Ministry of Information, London.[59] The following notable case from Norway should also be mentioned.

CASE 38. On Sunday, 1 February 1942, the government authorities demanded the use of the Cathedral of Trondheim for a Quisling pastor during the morning hours. Dean Fjellbu therefore decided to postpone the regular worship service until the afternoon. When large crowds sought admission to the cathedral for this service, the police barricaded all entrances and refused them admission.

THE PROBLEM OF PROOF. Reported by the Norwegian Information Service, 3516 Massachusetts Avenue, Washington, D.C., on 26 January 1945. Although the agency directly responsible was the Norwegian puppet government rather than the German occupying authority, the relations between the two were such that the Germans might be found responsible. The problem of German responsibility for actions of puppet governments is treated in a separate study on Nazi occupation policies and methods.

2. Interference with Freedom of Speech and Writings. As organizations devoted to the teaching and propagation of Christianity, the Christian churches are peculiarly dependent upon freedom of speech and writing for the accomplishment of their normal mission. When constitutional guarantees of freedom of speech and writings were suspended by the *Law for the Protection of People and Reich*[60]

CONFIDENTIAL

official assurances were given that the position of the churches would not be affected. Actual measures of repression started almost immediately. In the fall of 1934 Dr. Frick, minister of education, prohibited all discussion of the church question in the press, in pamphlets, or in books. Early the next year Dr. Frick repeated this order, and Dr. Rust, the minister of education, ordered the professors of theology in the universities not to participate in the church dispute. On 28 October 1935 the Propaganda Ministry imposed censorship before publication on all church periodicals,[61] and on 30 November 1935 this was extended to all writings and picture material multigraphed for distribution. After 1937 the German Catholic bishops gave up all attempts to print their pastorals and had them merely read from the pulpits. They were confirmed in this attitude by a letter from the Reich minister for ecclesiastical affairs, who threatened any printing of pastorals "with confiscation by the Gestapo or complete prohibition, as well as further measures on the part of the Reich minister for popular education and propaganda."[62] After the war, the paper shortage was used as an excuse to enforce the cessation of virtually all church publications.[63] In the case of the Catholic Church, these orders and acts were in violation of Article IV of the Concordat, which read: "Instructions, ordinances, Pastoral letters, official diocesan gazettes and other enactments regarding the spiritual direction of the faithful issued by the ecclesiastical authorities within the framework of their competence (Art. 1, Sec. 2) may be published without hindrance and brought to the notice of the faithful in the form hitherto usual."

a. Cases Involving the Catholic Church

CASE 39. On Palm Sunday, 14 March 1937, in most of the parish churches of the Third Reich, the papal encyclical letter about the situation of the Catholic Church

CONFIDENTIAL

in Germany *(Mit brennender Sorge)* was read from the pulpits. Immediately the state proceeded with severe measures of retaliation. Twelve printing offices that had printed the encyclical were closed without compensation. Parish magazines and diocesan gazettes that had copied the text were banned for three months. All the copies that the policy could get hold of were seized. People who had transcribed or even circulated the text were arrested. In the village of Essen in Oldenburg seven Catholic girls who had distributed the encyclical were taken into custody and released only because of the threatening attitude of the inhabitants.

THE PROBLEM OF PROOF. See *The Persecution of the Catholic Church in the Third Reich,* page 59. Witnesses could be members of all German diocesan administrations holding office at that time.

CASE 40. The encyclical on the Christian education of youth of 31 December 1929 was reprinted in Huber's printing office in Munich. In March 1937 it was forbidden because of passages it contained about the denominational schools. A calendar for Catholic parents published in 1935 was seized because some parts of the same encyclical were quoted in it.

THE PROBLEM OF PROOF. Reported in *The Persecution of the Catholic Church in the Third Reich* (page 59). A member of the diocesan administration of Munich holding office in 1937 could be witness.

CASE 41. The Nazis gave orders that the reading in Catholic churches of the encyclical of October 1939 by Pius XII, *Summi Pontifioatus,* was to be noted by the Gestapo, that priests who had a share in it were to be reported, and that steps were to be taken by the police against reproduction and distribution of the text.

THE PROBLEM OF PROOF. See case 39.

CASE 42. On 5 May 1935 a pastoral letter of the

Prussian episcopate was issued for what is called "Educational Sunday," dealing with Catholic principles of education. It was forbidden, and such parish magazines as had printed it were confiscated on the grounds that it "contained in several passages intolerable criticism of the *Landjahr* organization."

THE PROBLEM OF PROOF. *Germania* (Berlin) 5 May 1935.

CASE 43. On 21 July 1935 a pastoral letter by Bishop Kaller of Ermland that dwelt on the great importance of Catholic organizations and their current hardships was confiscated before it could be read.

THE PROBLEM OF PROOF. Reported in *The Persecution of the Catholic Church in the Third Reich* (page 60). Bishop Kaller could be a witness.

CASE 44. Common pastoral letters of the bishops in March and May 1936, and a pastoral of the Bavarian bishops of June 1936, were forbidden and confiscated after having been read.

THE PROBLEM OF PROOF. *Voelkischer Beobachter* No. 120, 29 April 1936 and *The Persecution of the Catholic Church in the Third Reich*, pages 60-61.

CASE 45. On 1 September 1935, a pastoral letter of the Bishops Conference at Fulda was read publicly. It complained about the restrictions set on the freedom of the church. It was confiscated in the ordinariates, in the printing offices, in bookshops, and presbyteries. It was even removed from the credence tables of the churches by policemen. Catholics who had helped to circulate the letter were arrested, as in Munich.

THE PROBLEM OF PROOF. See *The Persecution of the Catholic Church in the Third Reich*, page 60.

CASE 46. A joint pastoral letter of the Bavarian bishops read on 13 December 1936 was not allowed to be published.

CONFIDENTIAL

THE PROBLEM OF PROOF. See *The Persecution of the Catholic Church in the Third Reich,* page 61.

CASE 47. A pastoral letter of the Bishops Conference expressing uneasiness about the future of the denominational schools, which was read on 20 September 1936, was not allowed to be published.

THE PROBLEM OF PROOF. See Case 46.

CASE 48. A pastoral letter of the archbishop of Freiburg in Breisgau, Mgr. Groeber, could not be printed because the Gestapo insisted, contrary to the Concordat, on censoring the diocesan gazette.

THE PROBLEM OF PROOF. See Case 46. Archbishop Groeber could be a witness.

CASE 49. A pastoral letter of 13 December 1936, by the archbishop of Freiburg, describing the struggle to preserve the crucifix in its old place in the schools in Oldenburg was forbidden and in large measure confiscated before being read.

THE PROBLEM OF PROOF. See Case 46. Archbishop Groeber could be a witness.

CASE 50. In February 1937 the Lenten pastoral of Mgr. Kaller, bishop of Ermland, was forbidden and in large measure confiscated before being read. In many churches the confiscation took place during Mass itself by the police snatching the letter out of the hands of priests as they were in the act of reading it.

THE PROBLEM OF PROOF. See Case 46. Bishop Kaller could be a witness.

CASE 51. The pastoral letter of the Bavarian bishops of 4 September 1938 was confiscated and forbidden to be read.

THE PROBLEM OF PROOF. See Case 46. Cardinal Faulhaber could be a witness.

CASE 52. The pastoral letter of the Bishops Conference of Fulda on 19 August 1938 was confiscated and forbidden to be read. In the diocese of Rottenburg any

CONFIDENTIAL

parish priest who had read it was fined 30 RM. Duplicating machines were seized from several ordinariates.

THE PROBLEM OF PROOF. See Case 46. Bishop Sproll could be a witness.

CASE 53. On 27 January 1937 the minister of public instruction of the state of Baden prohibited the sale of the book *Truths of Catholicism,* edited by the German Bishops Conference, with special reference to four questions judged "injurious to the state." One of these questions was question 34, which read: "Who alone has the ultimate right over our bodies and our health?" Answer: "God alone had the ultimate right over our bodies and our health."

THE PROBLEM OF PROOF. See Case 46. Archbishop Groeber could be a witness.

CASE 54. On 19 February 1936 the police of Munich confiscated the festival sermon in honor of the pope, preached by Cardinal Faulhaber.

THE PROBLEM OF PROOF. See Case 46. Cardinal Faulhaber could be a witness.

CASE 55. In 1936 the *Regensburg Catholic* Sunday paper was suspended because it printed Bishop Buchberger's sermon on "The Threat to Catholic Faith."

THE PROBLEM OF PROOF. See Case 46. Bishop Buchberger could be a witness.

CASE 56. Early in 1937 the second and third series of the "Sermons of the Cardinal of Munich" were confiscated and destroyed by the police.

THE PROBLEM OF PROOF. See Case 46. Cardinal Faulhaber could be a witness.

CASE 57. On 20 July 1935 the bishop of Muenster was forbidden to speak or give a blessing to a crowd of Catholics who shouted greetings to him in the streets of Hamm. The same thing happened to him on 8 November 1938 in Sterkrede.

CONFIDENTIAL

THE PROBLEM OF PROOF. See *The Persecution of the Catholic Church in the Third Reich* (pages 253 and 261). Bishop Count Galen could be a witness.

b. Cases Involving the German Evangelical Church

CASE 58. In January 1935, Niemöller's memorandum "The State Church Is Here" was confiscated by the secret police before it could be distributed. **THE PROBLEM OF PROOF.** Niemöller himself could be a witness.

CASE 59. On 4 December 1935, Dr. Niemöller, Confessional leader, was forbidden to speak anywhere in the Reich. **THE PROBLEM OF PROOF.** Niemöller himself could be a witness.

CASE 60. On Reformation Day, 31 October 1937, Bishop Marshrens, representing the leaders of the "intact" Landeskirchen; Pastor Müller of Dahlem, representing the Council of Brethren of the Confessional Church; and Dr. Breit of Munich, representing the Council of the Lutheran Churches of Germany, issued a declaration in which they protested against Rosenberg's demand that the German nation give up the Christian faith and inquired whether the leadership of the Nazi Party intended to permit the churches to continue as places of worship, where the gospel of Christ could be preached without exposing preachers and hearers to the danger of being suspected as traitors and enemies of the state. Printed copies of this declaration were confiscated by the police. Parsonages all over Germany were searched. The printing shop of Köhler, in Elberfeld, where the declaration had been printed, was closed. **THE PROBLEM OF PROOF.** Bishop Marshrens could be a witness.

CASE 61. On 21 February the Provisional Church Government (Confessional) issued a manifesto against the

New Paganism of Alfred Rosenberg. When the Confessional pastors read this manifesto from their pulpits, some 700 of them were arrested, 500 to be put in prison and 200 under house arrest. When the ministers continued nevertheless to read the manifesto, fanatical Nazi governors made use of the concentration camp.

THE PROBLEM OF PROOF. The members of the Provisional Church Government (Confessional) could be witnesses.

3. Interferences with the Educational Functions of the Clergy. Clerical participation in the processes of education had been a traditionally important means for the spreading of Christian doctrines and for the maintenance of church influence. The National Socialists were interested in securing a monopoly on education for the propagation of their own aggressive philosophy. The campaign to eliminate the clergy from the educational field was therefore a major element in the persecution of the Christian churches. The following were the principal elements of that campaign:

a. The Closing of Theological Seminaries. As educational facilities for the teaching of the clergy itself, the seminaries are particularly important for the continuing influence and vitality of the Christian churches. So far as the Catholic Church is concerned, this interest was recognized in the first sentence of Article 19 of the Concordat, which read: "Catholic theological faculties in State universities were to be maintained." In spite of this, the Nazis were eager to weaken and eliminate them as far as possible. Direct evidence of the Nazi attitude toward Catholic seminaries is provided in a recently captured Gestapo document (Top-secret Survey of the Fulda Bishops Synod, circulated by Heydrich in January 1941, as published by the Supreme Headquarters, Psychological Warfare Division, Intelligence Section, Reference: DE 384/DIS 202), which gives the

CONFIDENTIAL

reduction of the educational level of the Catholic priesthood as a deliberate Nazi objective. The Nazi attitude can also be inferred from the following cases of suppression directed against Catholic and Protestant theological seminaries in all parts of Nazi controlled Europe.

i. Cases in Germany Proper

CASE 62. At the third meeting of the Confessional Synod at Augsburg (4 June 1935), it was decided to avoid the contamination of Nazi theology by setting up independent theological seminaries for the training of the Confessional ministry. Establishments of this sort were set up at Elberfelde, Bielefeld, Naumberg, Findenwalde, and Bloestau. From December 1936 onward these institutions were persistently searched and otherwise harried by the Gestapo, in an attempt to force them to close down.

THE PROBLEM OF PROOF. The leading members of the Provisional Church Government (Confessional) could be witnesses. At that time they were Niemöller, Dibelius, Jacobi, and Asmusson, all Berlin pastors.

CASE 63. In May 1939 the theological faculty of the University of Munich was closed. The Reich minister for public instruction, Dr. Rust, appointed two professors who were decisively rejected by Cardinal Faulhaber. When Rust maintained his appointments, Faulhaber forbade the students to attend their lectures. Rust and Reich Minister for Church Affairs Kerrl replied by closing the university.

THE PROBLEM OF PROOF. See *The Persecution of the Catholic Church in the Third Reich*, page 51. Cardinal Faulhaber could be a witness.

CASE 64. Early in 1939 the theological faculty in the University of Graz was closed. The lesser seminaries, in which those who aspire to the priesthood study the humanities before proceeding to the higher studies in philosophy and theology, were without exception closed down throughout the whole of Austria. The same fate befell the lesser seminary in Mariaschein in the Sudeten district.

THE PROBLEM OF PROOF. See Case 63. Witness could be Bishop Pawlowski.

ii. Cases in the Incorporated Areas

CASE 65. In 1938, by order of the minister of the interior in Vienna, the theological faculty at the University of Innsbruck was closed down. At the same time the Canisiamm, the seminary connected with this faculty, was shut.

THE PROBLEM OF PROOF. *The Universe* of 6 January 1939 published an eyewitness report of an American student given out by the NCWC News Service.

CASE 66. In 1938 the theological faculty in Salzburg was closed down.

THE PROBLEM OF PROOF. See Case 63. Witness could be Archbishop Rohracher.

iii. Cases in the Occupied Areas

CASE 67. Early in March 1944, the last remaining independent theological school in Norway, the congregational faculty in Oslo, was ordered closed by the Department of Church and Education. Simultaneously, this department intensified its campaign to enlist students for a new course in theology designed to produce pro-Nazi clergymen in record time.

THE PROBLEM OF PROOF. Reported by the Norwegian Information Service, 3516 Massachusetts Avenue, Washington, D.C., on 17 March 1944. Although the agency directly responsible was the Norwegian puppet government rather than the German occupying authority, the relations between the two were such that both can properly be held responsible. See separate study on Nazi occupation policies and methods.

b. The Closing of Denominational Schools. Private

CONFIDENTIAL

and public denominational schools under the supervision of the churches were permitted and played a substantial part in elementary education under the Weimar Republic. So far as the Catholic Church is concerned, the right to maintain such schools was guaranteed by Article 23 ("The retention of Catholic denominational Schools and the establishment of new ones is guaranteed."), Article 24 ("In all Catholic elementary schools only such teachers are to be employed as are members of the Catholic Church and who guarantee to fulfill the special requirements of a Catholic school."), and Article 25 ("Religious orders and congregations are entitled to establish and conduct private schools, subject to the general laws and ordinances governing education.") of the Concordat.

Summing up the meaning of all these articles, the Nazi minister for public instruction, Rust, declared in July 1933 at a party-district congress in Guben: "We have conceded the denominational school in a Concordat. What we have promised that we shall observe."[64]

Two years later the same minister declared (June 1937): "The exercise of denominational influences in the education of the young is from now on, and for all times, impossible. From that it follows as a consequence that denominational distinctions between German school should be brought to an end as soon as possible."[65]

This purpose was implemented by a systematic and protracted campaign, combining legal and illegal pressures.

Early in 1935 a sort of trial attack on the Catholic schools was staged in Munich with the result that at the beginning of school on 13 February only 65 percent of the children (as against 84 percent in 1934) were entered for denominational schools. Meetings of Catholic parents were forbidden.[66] Violent propaganda was immediately launched throughout the Reich. In some districts, such as the dioceses

CONFIDENTIAL

of Hildesheim and Paderborn, the authorities even dared to convert denominational schools into National Community Schools by decree and without consulting the parents.

The main assault, however, started in 1936. Attacks were concentrated against the many schools that were directed by religious orders, especially in the field of secondary education. The Catholic orders and congregations had altogether 12 secondary schools for boys and 188 for girls.[67]

Sixty-four percent of the Catholic girls attending secondary schools were studying at private Catholic institutions. Gradually, these schools were eliminated. Nazi authorities exerted strong pressure on the Reich, state, and municipal officials to send their children only to public schools.[68]

The main base from which pupils for the private schools were recruited was thus removed. It was further decided that the so-called preparatory classes would be suppressed.[69] Most private schools had derived the majority of their pupils from the preparatory classes of Catholic convent schools. Finally, the lower classes of the Catholic secondary schools were suppressed, a death sentence for the schools themselves.[70] In 1939 the Bavarian Ministry of Public Instruction forbade the clergy to exercise any function or activity in secondary schools.[71] In the official *Gazette of the Reich Ministry of Education,* early in 1937, a notice was published stating: "In about 400 public elementary schools for girls the instruction of the pupils was confined to Catholic religious orders or congregations of women. The dispersal of such teachers is provided for in the bylaw of 16 November 1936 to the school Provision Law. Of about 1,600 teaching posts occupied by members of religious orders at the beginning of this year, 300 already have been made over to lay teachers. The remaining posts are to be vacated in the course of this year, so that the entire elimination of teachers belonging to religious orders is in prospect."[72]

CONFIDENTIAL

On 19 July 1938 the Ministry of Interior in Vienna deprived all the private schools in Austria of public recognition and rights.[73] The final closing of these schools followed almost immediately. Such famous institutions as the *Schottengymnasium* in Vienna, directed since the thirteenth century by members of the Benedictine Order, and *Stella Matutina*, the Jesuit College in Feldkirch, were among those eliminated. By a decree issued in the summer of 1939 by the minister of education, all Catholic private schools, including mission schools, had to be closed down by April 1, 1940.

Meanwhile, the actual conversion of the denominational primary schools was carried out, either by means of the so-called "parents' vote" or by means of official ordinances. Controlling the parents' elections, the Nazis converted most of the denominational schools in Bavaria, Württemberg, and the districts of Brier and the Saar territory into National Community schools. Although they succeeded by propaganda and pressure in collecting vast majorities, they usually met with determined minorities among the parents and finally with private polls conducted among the faithful by church authorities, which brought large majorities in favor of the maintenance of denominational schools.[74]

Therefore in 1938 and 1939, the Nazi fell back on the decree as a means of converting denominational schools into National Community schools. They started in the smaller states like Oldenburg and in rural communities and finally extended over the whole of greater Germany. At the time of the outbreak of the war, the abolition of the Catholic denominational schools was complete.[75]

c. Elimination of Religious Instruction from Other Schools. A certain amount of religious instruction was provided, for those who wished it, in the public schools of Germany under the Weimar Republic. The continuance of this system was guaranteed, so far as the Catholic Church is concerned, by Article 21 ("Catholic religious instruction in elementary, senior, secondary, and vocational schools constitutes a regular portion of the curriculum, and is to be taught in accordance with the principles of the Catholic Church.") and Article 22 ("With regard to the appointment of Catholic religious instructors, agreement will be arrived at as a result of mutual consultation on the part of the bishop and the government of the State concerned.") of the Concordat. In spite of this guarantee, steps were taken to eliminate instruction of this sort as rapidly as possible. The purpose of the Nazis was indicated in 14 June 1939 in a statement by Bauer, Munich city school inspector, who declared: "Religious instruction must disappear from the schools. We make our demand: Instruction in the German faith by German teachers in German schools. The man who is tied to the dogmas of the Churches need look for nothing from us in the future."[76]

Implementation of this objective started with the curtailment of religious instruction in the primary and secondary schools, with the squeezing of the religious periods into inconvenient hours, with Nazi propaganda among the teachers in order to induce them to refuse the teaching of religion, with vetoing of Catholic religious textbooks, and finally with substituting Nazi *Weltanschauung* and "German faith" for Christian religious denominational instruction.[77] The name "religious instruction" was maintained, but its aims were completely altered. At the time of the outbreak of the war denominational religious instruction had practically disappeared from Germany's primary schools.

D. Interference with Christian Organizations
Much of the work of the Christian churches has been done through organizations existing along the regular

ecclesiastical hierarchy. Dissolution of the political organizations favored by the churches, such as the Catholic-dominated Center and Bavarian People's parties, was demanded from the outset by the Nazi regime as part of its general policy of eliminating all political organizations other than the Nazi party.[78] The right of other church organizations to exist and operate was guaranteed, however, so far as the Catholic Church is concerned, by Article 31 of the Concordat, which read: "Those Catholic organization and societies which pursue exclusively charitable, cultural and religious ends, and as such are placed under the ecclesiastical authorities, will be protected in their institutions and activities. Those Catholic organizations which to their religious, cultural and charitable pursuits add others, such as social or professional interests, even though they may be brought into national organizations, are to enjoy the protection of Article 31 Section I, provided they guarantee to develop their activities outside all political parties." The significance of this enactment was underlined on 7 July 1933 in a statement by Adolf Hitler himself: "The conclusion of the Concordat between the Holy See and the German Government appears to me to give sufficient guarantee that the Roman Catholic citizens of the Reich will from now on put themselves wholeheartedly at the service of the new National Socialist State. I therefore decree: (1) The dissolution, carried out without directions from the Central Government, of such Catholic organizations as are recognized by the present treaty, is to be cancelled immediately. (2) All measures taken against clerical and other leaders of these Catholic organizations are to be annulled. Any repetition of such measures will in future be unlawful and will be punished through the normal legal procedure."[79] In spite of these assurances, attempts to cripple or suppress the activities of church organizations, both Catholic and Protestant, was quickly begun. Thus after the

CONFIDENTIAL

occupation of Austria, all Catholic associations there were dissolved.[80] In Germany proper, similar results were produced, though more gradually. The organizations particularly affected were the following:

1. Religious Orders. The position of religious orders was specifically guaranteed by Article 15, Section 1 of the Concordat, which read: "Religious orders and congregations are not subject to any special restrictions on the part of the state, either as regards their foundation, the erection of their various establishment, their number, the selection of members . . . pastoral activity, education, care of the sick and charitable work, or as regards their affairs and the administration of their property." They were also protected by Article 13, which read: "Catholic parishes, parish and diocesan societies, episcopal sees, bishoprics and chapters, religious orders and congregations, as well as institutions, foundations, and property which are under the administration of ecclesiastical authority, shall retain or acquire respectively legal competence in the civil domain according to the general prescriptions of civil law. They shall remain publicly recognized corporations insofar as they have been such hitherto. Similar rights may be granted to the remainder in accordance with those provisions of the law which apply to all." There are many cases in which these guarantees were violated.

a. Interference with Religious Orders in Germany Proper

CASE 68. On April 1935 the Bavarian Political Police published a "strictly confidential" circular to all police headquarters in Bavaria concerning "Security measures against the Jesuits." In this ordinance supervision of all lectures given by members of the Company of Jesus in Bavaria is requested; public meetings held by Jesuits are to be prevented by all means, private ones to be watched. "The Jesuits are instigating systematic and far-reaching activities in

Bavaria to undermine the Reich and bring contempt even on the Führer himself. In various semi-scientific lectures the philosophic principles of National Socialism are submitted to an acrimonious criticism which is nothing more or less than disguised incitement against the Reich. These lectures, moreover, are so ambiguously and cunningly composed that a judicial punishment of the lecturer is possible in only very few cases." The political police ordered, therefore, that statements injurious to the state be ruthlessly punished by "protective custody" (i.e., the concentration camp).

THE PROBLEM OF PROOF. Document published in the *Elsässischer Kurier* of 17 May 1935, reprinted in *The Persecution of the Catholic Church in the Third Reich,* p. 64.

CASE 70. The Franciscan Friary of Kolheim in the Rhineland was closed in 1939 because thirty bottles of wine or cordial were found on the premises, as well as butter and fat, given to the friars by the Catholic population of the district, and some sixty packets of cigars and cigarettes.

THE PROBLEM OF PROOF. Press reports quoted in *The Persecution of the Catholic Church in the Third Reich,* p. 45.

CASE 71. The Franciscan Friary of Hadamar in the Westorwald mountains were closed, following Gestapo allegations that the conditions there showed "shocking immorality."

THE PROBLEM OF PROOF. See Case 70.

b. Interference with Religious Orders in the Incorporated Areas

CASE 72. In 1939 the Missions Institute of St. Ruprecht in Kreuzberg (Salzburg) was dissolved by the Nazi authorities and the three houses of the Society of Christ the King in former Austrian territory were closed and its property confiscated. In the same year the old Austrian abbeys of Goettweig, Admont, and Engelzell were finally appropriated, and all the leased property of the foundation of

CONFIDENTIAL

Klosterneuburg near Vienna was taken over by the government. The Feldkirchner Hof, a hostel of the Sisters of the Holy Cross in Feldkirchen near Klagenfurt, was also confiscated by the Gestapo.

THE PROBLEM OF THE PROOF. See Case 70.

CASE 73. In Austria, in the course of 1938, by order of the Reich Commissar Buerckel, the property of various religious orders was seized. Among the groups affected were the German Order of Knights, whose property was taken over by the state; the nuns of Eggenberg, near Graz; the teaching nuns at Mariazel, who lost their school buildings and also their rest home, the Marienheim; the Benedictine foundation of St. Lamprecht; the Franciscan friars in Salzburg, who were driven out of a government building placed at their disposal; and the Cistercians of Mehrerau in Voralberg, whose buildings were taken for a state youth home.

THE PROBLEM OF PROOF. See Case 70.

2. The Youth Movement. One of the principal means whereby the various Christian churches exerted influence over the youth of Germany was through the activities of the various Christian youth organizations. As rivals to the Hitler Jugend, they were particularly obnoxious to the National Socialist authorities, who sought to abolish them completely. On 17 December 1933 this was effectively accomplished, so far as the Protestant Church was concerned, by the order of Reich Bishop Müller, who placed the entire Evangelical Youth Movement, with more than 700,000 members, under the leadership of Baldur von Schirach, leader of the Hitler Youth.[81] Although the Catholic Youth movement was protected by Article 31 of the Concordat, the campaign for its destruction was rapidly begun. As early as January 1934, the staff leader of the Hitler Youth, Lauterbacher, declared in Koblenz: "The Hitler Youth will not compromise but will go

CONFIDENTIAL

on its own way, which must necessarily lead to the destruction of all other youth organizations."[82] On 27 March 1934 the Reich youth leader, Baldur von Schirach, declared: "The incorporation of the Protestant Youth associations will some time or other be followed, and necessarily followed, by that of the Catholic Youth. At a time when all are abandoning their private interests, Catholic Youth no longer has any right to lead a separate existence."[83]

These declarations heralded a difficult period for the Catholic Youth associations, which tried with all means of diplomacy and endurance to retain their rights as guaranteed by the Concordat, confirmed in the decree of Hitler, and now curtailed almost daily through new restrictions and persecutions. A decree of Schirach forbade, on 30 July 1933, simultaneous membership in the Hitler Youth and in denominational youth organizations.[84] Two years later all activity that was not of purely ecclesiastical or religious nature was forbidden to denominational youth associations. Every method of propaganda and coercion was employed in order to bring all German youngsters into the Hitler Youth and to prevent them from joining denominational organizations. Finally the Catholic Youth associations were simply forbidden in entire districts of the Reich.[85] Physical terrorization did the rest. The number of incidents increased rapidly, and the police and courts were always on the side of the Hitler Youth.[86] By 1938, in almost all districts of the Reich, the Catholic Youth associations had been dissolved.

3. Other Church Organizations. Like the youth organizations, those of a professional character for adults, such as the Catholic Workers associations and the Catholic Journeymen associations, were the first to be put under almost unbearable pressure. Dr. Ley, head of the German Labor Front, forbade simultaneous membership in the Labor Front and in denominational professional organizations, which was tantamount to

CONFIDENTIAL

the loss of one's job.[87] After some years of desperate struggle, these Catholic organizations too were forbidden, district by district. Numerous other Catholic organizations ended by self-dissolution (e.g., the Catholic Teachers organizations, the Catholic student fraternities, and the organizations of their alumni). Others shared the fate of the youth and workers' organizations. Among these were the Association of Catholic Women Teachers, the Catholic Civil Servants Union, the Albertus Magnus Union for the Support of Catholic Students, and the Christian Union of German Railwaymen.

VI. ORGANIZATIONS BEARING PARTICULAR RESPONSIBILITY IN CONNECTION WITH THE PERSECUTIONS

As a necessary step in preparation for the National Socialist scheme of world conquest, the persecution of the Christian churches becomes part of the responsibility of all those who participated in that scheme. Responsibility for specific criminal acts can be assigned to certain individuals and groups in connection with the specific acts of persecution described in the preceding section. There are also certain groups, which, because of their central position in the planning and execution of Nazi church policies, may be ascribed a more general responsibility for the persecution as a whole. The more important of these groups are the following:

A. The Reich Bishop and Spiritual Council of the German Evangelical Church

Prior to the creation of the Reich Ministry for Ecclesiastical Affairs on 19 July 1935, the Reich bishop, Ludwig Müller, and his chosen collaborators on the Spiritual Council (Forsthoff of Koblenz, Engelke of Hamburg, and Otto Weber of Göttingen), played the principal part in the persecution of German Protestantism. The sweeping nature of their powers and responsibilities is set forth in the legislation cited above (pp. 278-82). The illegality of measures taken by their authority in Bavaria was attested by a civil court decision of 28 October 1934.

B. The Reich Ministry for Ecclesiastical Affairs

From the time of its creation of 19 July 1935, this ministry was the principal agency for the persecution of the German Evangelical Church. From 1935 to 1941, the position of Reichsminister was held by Hanns Kerrl. Thereafter Wuhs headed the ministry as acting minister. The sweeping nature of its powers and responsibilities is set forth in the legislation cited above (pp. 282-83). Through the Beschlussstelle, transferred to it from the Reich Ministry of the Interior on 27 July 1935, it exercised supreme judicial power over the churches, and thus prevented any test of the legality of its actions being taken before the ordinary courts.[88] Although relatively little concerned with the management of Catholic affairs, the Ministry for Ecclesiastical Affairs was officially associated with a number of acts in violation of the Concordat. Its responsibility for persecution in the annexed areas was the subject of a memorial of protest addressed to it, and other authorities, by the Catholic bishops at Fulda on 27 July 1935.

C. The Church Chancery of the German Evangelical Church

As chief legal and administrative department of the German Evangelical Church, the Church Chancery played a leading part both in the earlier and in the later phases of the persecution of the German Evangelical Church. In 1934 Dr. Jäger, as head of the Church Chancery, was a principal collaborator of Reich Bishop Müller and gave the orders for the acts of persecution in Bavaria subsequently declared illegal. On 20 March 1937 the Ministry of Ecclesiastical Affairs delegated its powers of administration over the Evangelical Church to Dr. Werner, president of the Church Chancery.[89]

CONFIDENTIAL

This delegation was made permanent on 10 December 1937.[90] On 8 March 1938 all the provincial churches were forbidden by Werner to make any regulations except in matters of faith or worship without his consent.[91] Clearly this was one of the principal agencies of National Socialist control over the German Evangelical Church.

D. Finance Department of the German Evangelical Church

By ordinance of 10 and 29 June 1937, state-controlled finance departments were set up for the German Evangelical Church and for each of the Provincial churches, with full power to make regulations with force of law concerning the condition of service of all officials of the general church administrations, pastors and other church officials. These departments were responsible to the Ministry of Church Affairs and were its principal agency in the maintenance of financial controls over the German Evangelical Church. (See above, pp. 288-90). The chairmanship of the financial department of the chancery of the German Evangelical Church was held first by Dr. Werner, later by Dr. Coelle.

E. Reich Education Ministry

Principal agency for measures against the Protestant and Catholic churches in the field of education.

F. Reich Propaganda Ministry

As chief agency for the control of Nazi propaganda, it bears chief responsibility for the systematic campaign of defamation waged against the German clergy. (See above p. 300). It was also the direct agency for the issuance of certain orders for the censorship of church publications. (See above pp. 306-8). Sections or persons particularly responsible for carrying out this phase of the work of the ministry cannot be determined here.

CONFIDENTIAL

G. Reich Ministry of the Interior

Prior to the creation of the Ministry for Ecclesiastical Affairs, the Ministry of the Interior was the principal agency for direct government action in church affairs. Certain orders curtailing freedom of discussion were directly issued by it during this period. From 26 June to 27 July 1935 the Beschlussstelle was located in this ministry. Since the Ministry for Ecclesiastical Affairs had no executive agents of its own, its orders were carried out primarily through the police forces controlled by the Reich Ministry of the Interior, or by its dependent organs, the ministries of the interior of the several Länder. Among the ministries most compromised in this connection were those of Bavaria, Württemberg, and, in the period following the Anschluss, of Austria. Sections or persons particularly responsible for carrying out this phase of the work of the several ministries cannot be determined here.

H. The Gestapo

Among the police forces at the disposal of the various ministries of the interior for the carrying out of acts of persecution, the political police were, naturally, in view of the political nature of the issue, the favorite agents. Evidence of their use is to be found throughout the specific instances of persecution presented in section V above. Sections or persons particularly responsible for this phase of Gestapo activities cannot be determined here.

J. The German Christians

The important part played by this group, particularly in the earlier phases of the persecution of the German Evangelical Church, is set forth above. (pp. 278-82). The head of the association "German Christians" to 1938 was Dr. Rehm. Since 1938 the name has been changed to "Luther

CONFIDENTIAL

Christians," and the headship was assumed by Dr. Petersmann.

K. The SS, the SA, and the Hitler Youth

Acts of intimidation and violence taken against the clergy and laity, insofar as they were not entrusted to the police itself, were largely left in the hands of these organizations. Instances in which the planned nature of these demonstrations can best be shown are presented above (pp. 294-310). The Hitler Youth was also particularly active in the breaking up of the church youth movements and in the work of antichurch indoctrination of German young people. (See above pp. 323-25.) Sections or persons particularly responsible for this phase of their activities cannot be determined here.

L. The German Occupation Authorities in Norway and Poland

Evidence presented above in section V shows that these were the occupied regions in which the persecution of the Christian churches was most severe. Sections or persons of the occupation regimes that were particularly responsible for this phase of their work cannot be determined here.

VII. LIST OF CHIEF WITNESSES IN THE CASES CONCERNING PERSECUTION OF THE CHRISTIAN CHURCHES IN GERMANY AND OCCUPIED TERRITORIES

(Starred names indicate key witnesses.)
Among the members of the German episcopate:

Michael Cardinal von Faulhaber, Archbishop of Munich and Freising

Konrad Count Preysing, Bishop of Berlin

Galen, Clemens Angust, Bishop of Muenster in Westphalia

CONFIDENTIAL

Gröber, Konrad, Archbishop of Freiburg in Breisgan
*Sproll, Johannes Baptista, Bishop of Rottenburg

Other members of the Catholic clergy:
*Mgr. Banasch, with the diocesan administration in Berlin, secretary of the information service set up by the German bishops
P. Gundlach S. J.) Members of the editorial staff of the
P. Overmanns S. J.) *Stimmen der Zeit,* the monthly of the
P. Prsyvars S. J.) German Jesuits and special advisers to
P. Noppel S. J.) the Holy See on German affairs. (Now
P. Friedrich Muckermann S. J.) living in Switzerland.)

Catholic laymen:
Konrad Adenaner, Mayor of Cologne (dismissed by the Nazis, reappointed by AMG)
*Elfes, former Catholic labor leader, former police-president in Krefeld, now appointed by AMG as mayor of Muenchen-Gladbach.
Joos, Joseph, former member of the German Reichstag, former chief editor of the *Westdeutsche Arbeiterzeitung,* freed from concentration camp by AMG
Spiecker, Karl, former Ministerialdirektor, former chief of the Reich press service, author of the book *Hitler gegen Christus,* Paris, 1937 (Miles Ecclesiae), probable author of the book *The Persecution of the Catholic Church in the Third Reich,* London, 1940, former director of the weekly press bulletin *Kulturkampf,* published in Paris 1935 to 1939; now residing in London, scheduled to go to Germany by the British authorities

Protestant witnesses:
Reinhold von Thadden, lay member of the Bruderrat der Bekennenden Kirche.

CONFIDENTIAL

*Wurm, Lutheran Landesbischof of Wuerttemberg, Stuttgart.

*Professor Ludwig Bergstraesser, former professor of history at the University of Frankfurt (Main), later living in Darmstadt (after his dismissal by the Nazis), former member of the German Reichstag, worked underground during Nazi rule, now appointed member of the administration organized by AMG in the Palatinate, North-Baden, Hessen district under the direction of the former mayor of Mannheim, Heimerich

*Pastor Freudenberg, representative of the Federal Churches of Christ of America in Geneva (Switzerland)

CONFIDENTIAL

NOTES

Appendix B

1. By the *Decree of the President of the Reich for the Protection of the People and the State, RGBI,* I (1933) p. 83.

2. See below p. 12-13.

3. *HGBI. II (1933) p. 679. For an English translation see* The Persecution of the Catholic Church in the Third Reich (London, Burne Oates, 1940) p. 516-22.

4. Austria was incorporated 13 March 1938. Western Poland was incorporated 26 October 1939. See special memorandum *The Incorporation and Annexation of Territories by Nazi Germany.*

5. Cited in *The Persecution of the Catholic Church in the Third Reich,* (London, Burnes Oates, 1940), p. 83.

6. *Essener Nationalzeitung* and other German newspapers for 9 March 1933.

7. See declaration of the German bishops on the Reichstag elections of July and November 1932, quoted in the German press, especially in such Catholic papers as *Germania, Koelnisohe Volkszeitung,* and *Rhein— Mainische Volkszeitung.*

8. See Cuno Horkenbach, *das Deutsche Reich von 1918 bis heute* (Berlin 1935, Presse- und Wirtschaftsverlag GmbH) p. 66.

9. Ibid., p. 124.

10. Ibid., p. 133.

11. Ibid., p. 146.

12. See the program of the Arbeitsgemeinschaft Katholischer Deutcher, Ibid., p. 436 and 504. See also the declaration of Archbishop Groeber, Ibid., p. 463.

13. See Ibid., p. 186, 263, 268.

14. See *Persecution of the Catholic Church in the Third Reich* p. 516. See also Horkenbach, Ibid., p. 170.

15. See Horkenbach *op cit.* p. 275.

16. See the *Law Concerning Editors* of 4 October 1933 (*RGBI.*, I 1933 p. 713).

17. Statement of 8 July 193. Quoted in Nathaniel Nicklem, *National Socialish and the Roman Catholic Church* (Oxford University Press, 1939) p. 69.

18. English translation in *The Persecution of the Catholic Church in the Third Reich*, p. 523.

19. Substantial excerpts in English are to be found Ibid., p. 30-34.

20. All these pastorals are certainly available in the offices of every German diocese.

21. Horkenbach, Ibid., p. 157.

22. Ibid., p. 185.

23. *RGBI.*, I (1933) p. 471.

24. Ibid., p. 262-63.

25. For the German text, see Ibid., p. 300. For an English translation, see Hitler, Ibid., p. 185-88.

26. Horkenbach, Ibid., p. 370.

27. Ibid., p. 418.

28. Gerd Ruhle, *Das Dritte Reich* (1934) Hummerlverlag, Berlin, p. 383.

29. Reported in the foreign press. Evidence should now be available from the bishops themselves, or from members of their dioceses.

30. Citation unavailable here.

31. Reports of these events were kept out of the press. Details should now be available from Niemoeller and other Confessional leaders.

32. *RGBI.*, I (1935) p. 774.

33. Ruhle, *Das Dritte Reich* (1935) p. 301.

34. *RGBI,* I (1935) p. 1178.

35. Ibid., I (1937) p. 333.

36. Ibid., p. 1346.

37. Ruhle, *Das Dritte Reich* (1935) p. 304. Authority for the appointment of these committees was given in the ordinance of 3 October 1935 (*RGBI, I, p. 1221.*)

38. Ibid., p. 306. Authority for this action was given in an ordinance of the same date (*RGBI.*, I (1935) p. 1370).

39. Not reported in the current German press. Evidence should be obtainable from Niemöeller and other Confessional leaders.

40. This was done not on a national but on a local basis. Thus the dissolution in Hesse was accomplished by an ordinance of 18 October 1933 issued by the Hesseschen Staatsministeriums and published in the official *Darmstadter Zeitung.* (See J. W. (1934) p. 1747).

41. See Micklem, *op. cit.*, p. 51, and Franz Zuercher, *Kreuzzug gegen das Christentum* (Zurich, 1938, Europa-Verlag).
42. Not available here. Should be obtainable in the offices of German dioceses.
43. *Deutsche Verordnungsblatt für Norwegen*, 20 April-6 May, p. 2.
44. *Neue Zuricher Zeitung* 4/7/42.
45. *RGBI.*, I, (1934) p. 1086
46. Ibid., I, (1937) p. 697.
47. Citation unavailable here.
48. Citation unavailable here.
49. *The Persecution of the Catholic Church in the Third Reich*, p. 42.
50. In a speech delivered to Lœrrelch (Baden) in the fall of 1935, as quoted in *The Persecution of the Catholic Church in the Third Reich.*
51. See: *The Nazi Kultur in Poland*, London, 1945, p. 9-11.
52. See: Polish Information Service, *The Nazi Kultur in Poland*, London, 1945, p. 19-20.
53. *Ostschweiz*, 13 October 1938.
54. Printed in the *Schaffhausener Zietung, Schaffhausen*, Switzerland, 13 September 1938.
55. See *The Nazi Kultur in Poland*, London, 1945, p. 10-11.
56. Ibid., p. 19-32.
57. Ibid., p. 14.
58. This memorial is not available here.
59. See *The Nazi Kultur in Poland*, London, 1945, p. 22-24.
60. *RGBI*, I (1933) p. 83.
61. See *The Persecution of the Catholic Church in the Third Reich*, p. 76-77.
62. Quoted in a pastoral of the bishop of Muenster of 21 December 1936. Not available here but should be obtainable in the diocesan offices at Muenster.
63. See the letter of protest addressed on 1 April 1942 by Bishop Wurm of the *Württembergesche Evangelische Landeskirche* to Reichminister Dr. Goebbels, an English translation of which is given below in the appendix, p. __.
64. *Germanis* (Berlin) No. 154, 3 June 1935
65. See *The Persecution of the Catholic Church in the Third Reich* (page 118)
66. Ibid., p. 119.
67. Ibid., p. 130.
68. Ordinance of the Reichministry of the Interior, September 1937. Quoted in *The Persecution of the Catholic Church*, p. 131. Direct citation not available here.

69. Decree of the minister of education, 4 April 1936. Citation not available here.

70. See *The Persecution of the Catholic Church in the Third Reich*, pages 130-31.

71. Ibid., p. 132.

72. Ibid., p. 135.

73. Ibid., p. 135.

74. Ibid., p. 156.

75. *Nationalsozialistisches Bildungswesen* No. 10, 1938 further evidence given in *The Persecution of the Catholic Church in the Third Reich*, pp. 158-59.

76. *Osservatoro Romano,* 8 July 1939.

77. Given in *The Persecution of the Catholic Church in the Third Reich,* pp. 163-86.

78. See Horkenbach, pp. 265, 268, 274.

79. Ibid., p. 278.

80. *Diocesan Gazette Linz* No. 5, 1938.

81. See Horkenbach, pp. 693-94.

82. *Koelnische Volkszeitung,* 14 January 1934.

83. *Schlesische Volkszeitung,* 29 March 1934.

84. *The Persecution of the Catholic Church in the Third Reich,* p. 84.

85. Ibid., p. 108.

86. Ibid., pp. 91-108.

87. Ibid., pp. 187-99.

88. As of 1943, the personnel of the Beschlussstelle was as follows:

Chairman:	Muhs
Legal members:	Dr. Weber (Berlin)
	Dr. Dahm (Kiehl)

Members representing the ministry:

Dr. Stahn, Ministerialdiregent

Dr. Ruppel, Ministerialrat

Haugg, Landgerichtsrat

89. *RGBI* I (1937) p. 333.

90. Ibid., p. 1346.

91. Citation unavailable here.